Thames and Hudson

Charles Kightly   photographs by Peter Chèze-Brown

strongholds of the realm

Defenses in Britain from prehistory
to the twentieth century

with 193 illustrations, 20 in color

Acknowledgments

For their kindness and courtesy in giving me access to some of the subjects in this book I am indebted to the following: Department of the Environment; The Scottish Office; The Welsh Office; The National Trust for Scotland; National Museum of Antiquities of Scotland, Edinburgh; Southampton City Museums; The Corporation of London, Tower Bridge; The National Trust; The Rev. R. F. S. Eke, St Lawrence Church, Alton; Mr Christopher C. Harley, Brampton Bryan; Dr P. R. Hill, Caister Castle; Col. R. I. G. Taylor, Chipchase Castle; Mr Jonathan Appleyard, Comlongon Castle; Major F. Blackett, Halton Tower; Mr Kenneth Bell, Thornbury Castle; Mr S. T. Critchlow, Wingfield Manor; Mr Graham Flakingham, Wressle; and Mr J. G. Altham, Yanwath Hall. May I take this opportunity to pay tribute to those who maintain their historic houses as part of the national heritage, and also to the professional and voluntary workers upon whose dedication the survival of the historic fabric of Great Britain depends.

Finally, I should like to thank the following who have given me advice and help from the outset: Dr R. Allen Brown, Mr Peter Clayton, Mr Ronald Gregory, Mr Maurice S. Marks of the Midland Bank, and my friends Betty and Jesmond Woolf.

P.C.-B.

I should like to thank the following for help and advice during the writing of this book: Professor G. E. Aylmer, Mr Dennis Filtness of the National Westminster Bank, Mrs Elizabeth Hartley, Mr Brian McGarrigle, Mrs Sue Medd, Anne and Philip Thomas, Mr Alan Turton and, especially, Mr Christopher Wilson.

C.K.

For illustrations other than those by Peter Chèze-Brown, the authors and publishers would like to acknowledge the following sources: Anthony Barton 5, 6, 8, 12, 13, 16, 47, 94, 95, 108, 113, 116, 154, 166; Cambridge University Collection: copyright reserved 14, 30, 43, 74, 153, 157, 161; The National Museum of Wales, Cardiff (reconstruction by Alan Sorrell) 22; Archives Department, Cumbria County Council, Carlisle, by kind permission of the Clerk and Chief Executive 91; Crown Copyright: reproduced by permission of the Controller of Her Majesty's Stationery Office 57, 141, 164, 168; John Dewar 143; Imperial War Museum, London 170, 171; Martin Weaver 75. Other line illustrations are based on these sources, which we gratefully acknowledge: Department of the Environment (Crown Copyright) 28 (from S. Johnson, *Roman Fortifications of the 'Saxon Shore'*, 1977), 79 (drawn by L. Monroe), 146; G. Jackson, *Bolton Castle* (Dalesman Books, Clapham, W. Yorks., 1974) 121; S. Toy, *Castles of Great Britain* (Heinemann, London, 1954) 83. The Bayeux Tapestry (48, 49) is housed in the Episcopal Museum, Bayeux; the originals of ills. 152, 155 and 156 are in the British Museum, London; and *The Siege of Oxford* (159) is on loan to the Oxford City Museum (photo Vernon Brooke).

1 (half-title page) The sixteenth-century 'yett', a hinged grating made of interlaced iron bars, guarding the entrance to Blackness Castle, Central. It formed a second line of defence behind a reinforced oak outer door, whose hinges are seen on the right of the archway (p. 120).

2 (title page) Hadrian's Wall, looking east towards the fort at Housesteads, Northumberland.

Library of Congress Catalog Card Number 78-55190

Text and monochrome illustrations printed in Great Britain by BAS Printers Limited, Over Wallop, Hants Colour illustrations printed in Great Britain by Balding & Mansell Limited, Wisbech, Cambs. Bound in Great Britain

Contents

3 The multiple glacis ramparts on the southern side of Maiden Castle, Dorset, looking east (see pp. 10–11 and ill. 14).

1 'For the warres in owld times': British fortresses from the earliest times until 55 BC

Fortification – the art of building defences – is an activity almost as old as the human race itself, traceable from the day when the first man raised a stockade to protect himself from wild beasts or dangerous neighbours. The date when the first 'fortresses' appeared in Britain is quite unknown, and the manner of their early development is, like most other aspects of prehistory, still very much a subject for speculation. Rapid advances in archaeological science – notably the dating of objects by analysis of their radio-carbon content – are, admittedly, making the picture somewhat clearer, but the very speed with which new interpretations of the pre-Roman period are emerging is in itself confusing, and for the non-specialist the study of the earliest British defences remains fraught with almost as many pitfalls as the defences themselves.

There is little doubt that the oldest British fortifications now recognizable on the ground are the structures known as hill-forts. Technically defined, they are fortified enclosures defended by one or more continuous banks and ditches, and usually sited on high ground. They vary greatly in size, the largest enclosing an area of nearly 200 acres (some 78 hectares) and the smallest only a fraction of an acre: the majority cover from 1 to 30 acres (0.5 to 12 hectares). A small fort, in other words, might have an internal diameter of 200 feet (60 metres) or so, while Maiden Castle, by no means the largest, has an internal length of nearly 2,000 feet (600 metres) and a maximum breadth of 900 feet (275 metres). The strength of defences also varies, ranging from insignificant banks now only a few feet high to massive ramparts still towering 40 feet (12 metres) above the bottom of the ditch set in front of them.

Some forts, eroded by centuries of ploughing or grazing, are today difficult to find even with the aid of an Ordnance Survey map, but many more, like Old Oswestry in Salop, an isolated hill girded by seven banks and six ditches, remain vastly impressive. Round such awe-inspiring works clustered legends aimed at explaining their silent presence, and with their original names long forgotten they came to be known as 'Devil's Dykes' or 'Giant's Towns'. Our less superstitious ancestors fathered hill-forts on Caesar or the Vikings or, like the guide who showed a tourist round Maiden Castle in 1635, declared simply that they had 'served for the warres in owld times'.

We can now be somewhat more exact, and current expert opinion is that hill-forts, known in Europe from about 1000 BC, were being raised in Britain by 850 BC. Their origins, then, belong to the latter part of the Bronze Age, the period when this alloy of copper and tin was replacing stone in the manufacture of some tools and weapons. Their heyday, however, was the subsequent Iron Age, when Britain was being colonized by successive migrations of iron-using peoples from the Continent: held to have begun here by 500 BC, this period ended (at least in England) with the Roman invasion of AD 43. Thereafter hill-fort building ceased abruptly as the Romans extended their sway. Many forts were then voluntarily or forcibly depopulated, and only in the parts of Scotland where the legions never penetrated did their importance continue uninterrupted. Subsequent chapters will show, however, that a number of forts were re-occupied after the Romans left, while others became the sites of Norman castles and some were used as temporary strongholds at still later dates.

The popularity of hill-fort sites for later strongholds pays tribute to the prehistoric planner's eye for a commanding position, and the most striking characteristic of hill-forts is the way in which they use and reinforce natural defences. The commonest type, the 'contour fort', was constructed by digging a bank and ditch along the contour line surrounding a knoll of high ground. In forts like Old Oswestry such ramparts enclose an entire hill, but in other cases they encircle only the summit, block a narrow ridge, or cut off a spur, the strongest defences being always dug on the sides which are easiest to attack.

Natural defences are still more efficiently used in the 'promontory fort', where a spit of high ground is protected on three sides by unscaleable cliffs, leaving only one approach to be defended by a bank and ditch across the narrowest neck of the peninsula. Alternatively, where no proper headlands were available, straighter lines of cliff-edge could be protected by L- or V-shaped ramparts. Rocky coastlines provided ideal sites, and the majority of promontory forts occur on Britain's western seaboard, like Maen Castle in Cornwall, though a number can also be found on the heights above inland river valleys. Uncomplicated to build and defensible by small numbers of warriors, these 'cliff-castles' did have one major demerit: it must have been im-

possible to escape from them if an enemy did manage to break in.

Dependent as they are on the natural lie of the land, not all forts will fit snugly into one of the categories mentioned. Some, for reasons not clearly understood, were built half-way down hill slopes, while others again are situated on flat plains or plateaux.

Taking all types of site together, there are almost 3,000 hill-forts still to be seen in Britain. Of these about half are south of Hadrian's Wall, but English and Welsh forts are by no means evenly distributed: the great majority of them lie south-west of a line drawn from Liverpool to London, and the greatest concentration is in the extreme west, with 294 forts in Devon and Cornwall and 282 in the Welsh county of Dyfed. In those areas they are the commonest of all remaining fortifications. Most of these forts in the extreme west are small and simple, contrasting with the massive and complicated strongholds of the 'Wessex tradition' found in Hampshire (where 50 occur), Wiltshire (49) and Dorset (31, including Maiden Castle and Hod Hill), and with similar large and spectacular forts in the Welsh border counties of Powys (105) Gloucestershire (60), Salop (43, including Old Oswestry) and Herefordshire (28). In the

extreme east of England hill-forts are rare: the large county of Lincolnshire has only three, Suffolk only one, and Huntingdonshire none at all.

There are a further 1,500 hill-forts north of Hadrian's Wall, the majority of them situated in southern Scotland between the Forth–Clyde line and the Borders. At present far less is known of them than of their English and Welsh counterparts: a large proportion seem to belong to the simple far Western tradition, though some large forts do occur in south-east Scotland, most notably Traprain Law, Lothian, and Eildon Hill, Borders.

All these hill-forts, it must be emphasized, were not occupied simultaneously. Detailed studies of individual sites often reveal intermittent periods of disuse, and at any one time only a fraction of the total number may have actually been in commission.

Having considered siting and distribution, it is now time to investigate how hill-forts were built, beginning with their ramparts. Whether these were basically of earth or stone depended largely on the geological nature of the surrounding land, and methods of construction were also influenced by the materials available. At Maen Castle, for instance, large blocks of granite fallen from the cliffs were set in soil to form a barrier across the promontory. In

14
8

1

4

9

5 Artist's reconstruction of hill-fort ramparts: (a) 'dump' or 'glacis' type, with palisade; (b) 'revetted' earth rampart piled behind palisade; (c) 'timber-laced' rampart.

rocky areas where such large blocks do not occur naturally, stone rubble of the sort now used for dry-stone walls was employed, and the strength of such defences is attested at Tre'r Ceiri, Gwynedd, whose dry-stone ramparts still stand up to 12 feet (3.5 metres) high in places. There, too, the parapet and rampart walk for defenders survive, as do the ramps by which they were reached. In order to resist both frost and enemy action, such unsupported and unmortared walls needed to be almost as thick as they were high. Alternatively, less massive ramparts could be strengthened by wooden palisades at front and rear, preferably with the uprights held together by horizontal cross-ties passing through the wall, and 'timber-laced' forts of this kind are not uncommon in northern Scotland.

Most hill-forts are built mainly of earth rather than stone, the simplest method of construction being to dig a ditch and cast the excavated soil inwards to form a 'dump' or 'glacis' rampart. Often reinforced by a wall or palisade along the bank-top, such defences were nevertheless vulnerable to determined attackers using the momentum of a charge to carry them up the slope, and rows of stakes or sharp stones were sometimes fixed on the far side of the ditch to discourage this tactic. Alternatively, as at Maiden Castle, the ditch might – with a great deal of labour – be dug very deep, and the bank made consequently high and steep. If the material of the bank, moreover, was piled behind a wooden palisade, the rampart could be given a steep vertical face which was impossible to overrun, and stronger defences still could be achieved if the bank were fully reinforced in the manner of a 'timber-laced' fort. In some cases the spaces between the uprights of the outer palisade were filled in with horizontal logs, and elsewhere the gaps were faced with dry-stone walling, giving an impressive appearance to the fort as well as adding to its strength. Though time has now reduced these complex ramparts to shape-less grassy mounds, archaeology has revealed that they were once relatively numerous. Beneath the apparently simple banks of the Caburn in Sussex, for instance, excavation uncovered the post-holes of front and rear palisades, while horizontal cavities containing a dark powder marked the places where earth and chalk had formed like a mould around long-decayed cross-ties.

Excavation has also established that, by and large, the earliest hill-forts had only one line of ramparts. However these were constructed, they were basi-cally designed to prevent the enemy from storming the fort, and if possible to trap him in the ditch, where he would be at the mercy of the defenders' stones and javelins. Little attempt was made to keep the attacker at a distance, for warfare at this time was conducted hand-to-hand and without efficient long-range weapons. No contemporary account of one British Iron Age tribe attacking another's fort is known, but Julius Caesar recorded how their Gaulish relations went about it: 'They begin by surrounding the whole circuit of the wall with a large number of men, and showering stones at it from all sides: when they have cleared it of defenders, they lock their shields over their heads, advance close up, and undermine it.' Where ramparts were reinforced with wood attempts may have been made to destroy them by fire: this is what seems to have happened at several Scottish forts where the stone walls have been fused together or 'vitrified' by the heat of their burning framework. Plain earthen 'dump' ramparts were, of course, invulnerable to fire and very difficult to undermine, and this may be one reason why some forts with timber-laced defences were later rebuilt in the simpler style.

By the second or third century BC there seems to have been a radical development in hill-fort de-fences, perhaps attributable to the appearance in Britain of a new weapon. This was the sling, which could propel a rounded stone weighing up to 2 ounces (60 grammes) – half the size of a billiard ball – for 200 yards (180 metres). Slings are also remarkably accurate: David killed Goliath with one, and the Israelite tribe of Benjamin could 'sling stones at an hair's breadth, and not miss', while Fijian slingers early in this century could rely on hitting a thin stick at 150 yards (almost 140 metres). Sling-armed attackers could thus clear the ramparts of a fort while themselves remaining out of reach of swords or flung spears, and in dry weather the Gauls, if not the British, would also sling red-hot clay pellets to fire the thatched houses within the defences.

6 *Different types of hill-fort entrances: (a) overlapping ramparts (Hod Hill, Dorset); (b) staggered entrances (Hammer Wood, Sussex); (c) entrance guarded by an outwork (Yarnbury, Wiltshire); (d) inturned ramparts (the Wrekin, Salop); (e) multiple defences (west gate, Maiden Castle, Dorset: see ill. 14).*

The new method of warfare made it important to keep an enemy out of slingshot range, and this could best be achieved by raising one or more extra lines of banks and ditches beyond the main rampart. About one-third of British forts (many of them originally constructed with a single bank and ditch) are equipped with such multiple ramparts. According to Sir Mortimer Wheeler, these were intended to give defending slingers a slight height advantage over their enemies beyond the outermost ditch. Defenders would therefore outrange attackers, who would have to fight their way through the outer defences before they could make effective use of their slings. The ideal system of multiple ramparts needed to be wide enough to render the inner bank relatively safe from enemy fire, but narrow enough to bring the attackers just within the greater killing-range of the defenders. Again according to Wheeler, the defences of both Maiden Castle and Hod Hill in 3 Dorset exactly meet these requirements, and his 14 theories concerning their purpose were borne out by 8 finds of sling-stones there. At Maiden Castle a pile of over twenty thousand beach pebbles came to light near the entrance, and at Hod Hill many of the houses within the fort had smaller hoards of ammunition just outside their doorways. It must be pointed out, however, that the design of many multiple-ramparted forts does not fit in with the 'sling theory', and a simpler explanation for their development is that two or three lines of defence must always be better than one.

Even the strongest forts needed to have entrances, 6 and these gaps in the ramparts would naturally be weak points, especially vulnerable to rush attacks. It was important, therefore, to prevent an enemy from getting a clear run at them, forcing him instead to adopt a zig-zag course exposed to the fire of the defenders on the rampart tops. This could be achieved by overlapping the ends of single ramparts (a), by placing the gaps in multiple defences at differing points (b), or by constructing an outwork to cover the gateway from the front (c). In other forts there was (perhaps for the convenience of everyday traffic in times of peace) a more or less direct path to the gateway. Here, however, the rampart-ends could be turned inwards (d), as at Old Oswestry, or outwards, as at the Caburn, so that an attack on the gate would have to pass through a long narrow passage overlooked by the defenders and commanded by their fire. Finally, several of the devices mentioned might be used in conjunction for added strength, resulting in the extremely complex entrances at Maiden Castle and elsewhere (e). 14

11

7 *Remains of stone huts at Tre'r Ceiri, the 'Giant's Town' on the summit of Yr Eifl, Gwynedd, with the ramparts in the middle distance and Caernarfon Bay on the horizon.*

The entrance gaps themselves were not, of course, left open in time of war: at the very least they would be blocked by tree-trunks or thorn-bush barricades, but excavation has shown that important forts had much more sophisticated arrangements. Wooden gates (now long since rotted) were pivoted on massive uprights of the same material, and sometimes hung in a framework supporting an overhead catwalk for guards and lookouts. Some gateways, especially on the Welsh borders, also had 'guardrooms', shelters set into the thickness of the rampart-end where sentries could sleep at night or, when the gates were open, keep a check on incoming traffic.

Entrances were also the obvious place for displays of the power and prestige of the owners of the fort, and in at least two cases there is evidence for some form of 'triumphal arch' just inside the fort. At Bredon Hill in Worcestershire, a row of six severed heads decorated the top of the gate as a salutory warning to intruders. Not long after they were placed there, however, the fort was taken and the victors (perhaps the friends and relations of the dead men) massacred the defenders and hacked them to pieces, leaving sixty-four mutilated bodies to be found by the excavators. The gate itself was then burned, an action which seems to have been fairly usual when a hill-fort fell: it was both symbolic and practical, for a gateless entrance was virtually indefensible. By the same token, it was vital for the defenders to keep the gate in good condition, and the recent excavation at Croft Ambrey, Herefordshire, has found that the entrance there was five times redesigned during the occupation of the fort.

It is interesting to consider how these defences were constructed. Calculations based on a modern experimental earthwork at Overton Down, Wiltshire, have shown that one man can build about 12 cubic feet ($\frac{1}{3}$ cubic metre) of simple bank and ditch defences per day in a chalk area, using deer antler picks to break up the soil, shoulderblades of oxen to shovel it out, and wicker baskets to carry it to the bank. More complex ramparts would naturally take longer, and at the unfinished hill-fort at Ladle Hill, Hampshire, the ditch material was graded so that larger lumps of chalk could be placed at the core of the bank for added strength. In some cases, at least, magical protection was sought by burying the bodies of human sacrifices under the foundations. Defences were apparently built in sections by gangs, and the length of time taken would obviously depend on how many labourers were involved. As a very rough guide, it has been estimated that 150 men could fortify an enclosure of about 8 acres (3.25 hectares) with a single bank and ditch in about four months.

Having built the defences of the fort, how did the builders then make use of it? We shall find the answers, if anywhere, inside the ramparts. At first sight, the interior of most forts has little to offer save a few bumps and irregularities in the ground, so that research and excavation have until recently been concentrated on ramparts and gateways. This situation is partly responsible for the belief that forts were rarely inhabited permanently, serving rather as a temporary refuge in times of war or trouble. Supporting this theory is the fact that most forts are, by their nature, placed in exposed and inaccessible positions, lacking a water supply in the form of springs or streams: the builders, one would assume, would have preferred to spend their everyday lives in more sheltered and convenient lowland villages.

It is rapidly becoming clear, nevertheless, that many hill-forts were undoubtedly used as permanent settlements. One of the first to be recognized 7 as such was Tre'r Ceiri, where the foundations of about 150 stone huts can still be clearly seen, giving a possible population of up to 600 people. Despite the fact that its situation 2,000 feet (600 metres) above sea level must have made it, at times, a very uncomfortable place to live in, and that the only water supply was outside the walls, it was certainly occupied continuously for several hundred years. Other strongholds, less immediately obvious as settlements, have proved to be so when their interiors were investigated. The small fort at Castle

Dore, near Fowey in Cornwall, was found to contain 36 five huts and a granary, no doubt the remains of a small defended farm, and many of the smaller sites in the west of Britain may be of this type. Recent work on such large forts as Traprain Law, Eildon Hill and Hod Hill indicates that these were probably 8 tribal capitals, with a population comparable (in Iron Age terms) to a large modern town. Over 2,000 people, for instance, could be accommodated in the 500 or so huts at Eildon.

At Hod Hill, one of the chief towns of the Durotriges (the pre-Roman rulers of Somerset and Dorset), the houses were arranged in winding streets. Most were simple round huts, but some had walled courtyards attached and one, probably belonging to a chieftain, stood within its own small enclosure. The walled courtyards had been used for stabling horses (as was shown by their impacted dung) and also, perhaps, for parking chariots, for whose use in war the Britons were famous. These chariots – which did not, incidentally, have scythes on their wheels – were, according to Caesar, so well handled that they could manœuvre at full gallop even on a steep slope, and it is not impossible that hill-forts may at times have been used as bases for chariot warfare.

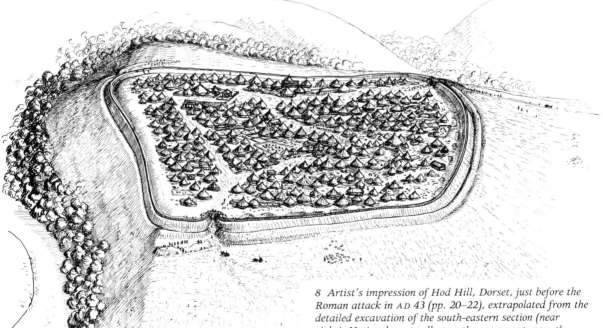

8 *Artist's impression of Hod Hill, Dorset, just before the Roman attack in AD 43 (pp. 20–22), extrapolated from the detailed excavation of the south-eastern section (near right). Notice the catwalk over the nearer gateway, the corrals for horses and chariots, and the chieftain's hut with courtyard (centre right, larger than the others) subsequently bombarded by ballistas.*

13

9 *The Borgue of Castlehaven, Dumfries and Galloway – the remains of a D-shaped, galleried dun overlooking an anchorage off Wigtown Bay.*

Another important recent dig, at Croft Ambrey near Leominster in Herefordshire, has shown that there the hill-fort was certainly no temporary refuge, being continuously inhabited from its construction in about 550 BC until AD 48. By the standards of present knowledge this is an unusually long period of occupation, but future excavations may well show that it is not exceptional. Here rectangular houses were set closely together in a carefully planned grid pattern, suggesting that the settlement was a more or less military one, perhaps used for the training of young warriors.

There is growing evidence, then, that a number of hill-forts were defended farms, villages, towns, or military camps, and that they contained permanent buildings including temples, granaries, stables and houses. Nor were these houses merely primitive shacks: their foundations show that most were competently built, and Dr A. H. A. Hogg has recently pointed out that the average Iron Age 'hut' was equal in floor area to a modern two-bedroom bungalow. Some forts (particularly large enclosures near upland pastures) may have been used to protect cattle from raiders, and others near the coast were probably fortified ports or trading stations. Still others were built for some specific local purpose, such as protecting a valuable mine or an especially sacred temple. Many forts, finally, will have been

used at some stage in their long active life for several of the purposes mentioned.

Though far and away the most numerous and widespread of pre-Roman fortifications in Britain, hill-forts are not the only prehistoric strongholds still to be seen. Three other distinctive types also exist, all belonging to the end of the Iron Age and each pertaining to a specific part of the country.

Duns and brochs, both stone structures, are found only in Scotland, duns in the west and south-west and brochs principally in the far north, the Orkneys and the Shetlands: in these areas, between them, they virtually replace conventional hill-forts. Duns are, however, really a specialized type of hill-fort adapted to provide protection for one family or small group. They are small, with an internal diameter of not more than 60 feet (18 metres) and a narrow doorway angled through dry-stone walls up to 15 feet (4.5 metres) thick. Usually circular or D-shaped, they were frequently built on coastal headlands, or even on the flat tops of rocky stacks rising out of the sea. Duns differ from hill-forts mainly in their complex internal accommodation. The Borgue of Castlehaven, in Dumfries and Galloway, for instance, had two-storey wooden structures built against the inside of its wall and a hollow gallery in the thickness of the wall itself, while more sophisticated duns had two-storey galleries and three-storey

9
12

14

10, 11 The broch of Dun Telve: exterior, showing the height of the wall and the narrow entrance, and interior, showing the entrance (at left) and the chambers and galleries within the thickness of the ruined wall.

internal buildings. An account of life in such forts, incidentally, can be found in the early Irish legends of Cuchulainn and the Red Branch heroes.

This tendency to build upwards rather than outwards probably reflected a need for fortifications with a short perimeter that could be defended by fewer people than a hill-fort rampart. Brochs, which probably developed from galleried duns, carried this process a stage further. The most impressive of all British Iron Age stone defences, brochs are best described as hollow towers, with internal courtyards roughly equal in diameter to the height of their walls. These walls, which in some cases originally stood up to 50 feet (15 metres) high, are thicker at the base than the top. They are often solid at ground level, while further up they divide into inner and outer walls, the space between being taken up with small rooms, staircases and galleries. These internal galleries can clearly be seen at Dun Telve, one of two neighbouring brochs near Glenelg, in the Highland Region. Here the walls still stand 33½ feet high and 13½ feet thick at their base (10.15 by 4.10 metres): they would thus have been, in their prime, almost impossible to climb and too thick to batter down. The small doorway is easily defensible, and the height of the tower would make it difficult for an attacker to throw burning material onto the wooden buildings within.

13
12

10
11

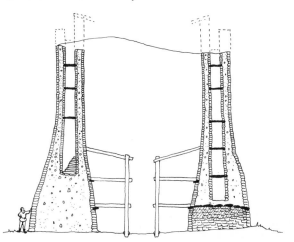

12 Cross-section of one wall of a typical galleried dun, showing wooden lean-to structures against the inner side.
13 Composite cross-section of a broch, showing chambers and galleries within the thickness of the wall and wooden lean-tos in the central courtyard.

15

14   If hill-forts are the castles and walled towns of the Iron Age, brochs and duns can best be compared to heavily fortified houses. Unlike hill-forts, they had a fairly short active life: their construction began in 200–100 BC, apparently as a defence against raids by the Caledonians of central and eastern Scotland, and had tailed off by AD 100, when the Caledonians were fully occupied with the Roman threat.

The final type of pre-Roman fortification that needs to be considered, the tribal 'oppidum' of southern England, differs greatly from the domestic defences of the far north, though it also belongs to the very late Iron Age. The word *oppidum* (from the Latin for a stronghold) is used by Caesar to describe a fortress in thick woods, protected by marshes and other natural defences as well as man-made banks and ditches. Such oppida are found on low-lying ground, often in river valleys, and were big enough to shelter a whole tribe with their flocks and herds. The largest of them, Grim's Ditch, near Woodstock in Oxfordshire, enclosed an area of 22 square miles (57 square kilometres), and the remains of another, at
2   Wheathampstead in Hertfordshire, include a ditch a quarter of a mile long, 40 feet deep and 120 feet wide (400 by 12 by 37 metres). It is plain that such lengthy defences could only be held by vast numbers of warriors, and it seems, as Caesar himself was to discover when he attacked Wheathampstead (p. 18), that oppida were in practice defended by a form of hit-and-run guerrilla warfare.

The question of who built these oppida brings us, for the first time, into the period of recorded British history. When Julius Caesar marched into Gaul (roughly speaking, modern France) in 58 BC, he found the area north of the rivers Seine and Marne occupied by a federation of warlike tribes called the Belgae, who a few centuries earlier had crossed the Rhine from Germany. Caesar noted that these same Belgae had also invaded England, coming first as raiders and later on as permanent settlers. One of their kings, a certain Diviciacus, had (apparently in about 70 BC) held sway on both sides of the Channel: he is thus the first British ruler whose identity is certainly known.

How far into Britain the Belgae had penetrated by Caesar's time is not clear, but their rule, or at least their influence, probably extended over much of south-eastern England. It is in this area that oppida occur, notably at Wheathampstead and St Albans in Hertfordshire, at Colchester in Essex, at Bagendon in Gloucestershire, at Silchester in Hampshire and near Chichester in Sussex. Since similar earthworks apparently existed in the Belgic homelands on the Rhine, there seems little doubt that this type of fortification was introduced into Britain by the invaders: the details, like so many other things concerning prehistoric fortresses, remain obscure. With Caesar's first landing in 55 BC, however, we move into a period where the history of Britain and its defences appears in a very much clearer light.

14 *The vast Iron Age hill-fort of Maiden Castle, Dorset, fell to the Romans in AD 44 after a furious fight around the eastern gate, at the right, the simpler of its two entrances (p. 20).*

15 The best-preserved stretch of Roman road in Britain, on Wheeldale Moor near Goathland, North Yorkshire, part of the route from Whitby to Malton and York. Its boulder foundation would originally have been covered by a layer of gravel or small stones.

2 The Roman conquest of Britain, 55 BC–AD 83

At about midnight on 26 August in 55 BC a Roman invasion fleet, carrying 10,000 legionaries under the command of Julius Caesar, put out of Boulogne and set course for the Kentish coast: France had already been overrun, and now the growing power of Rome was to be extended beyond the mysterious ocean that encircled the known world. It was this very ocean, always the most effective of Britain's defences, that played the largest part in frustrating Caesar's first expedition. Though his infantry fought its way ashore against stout resistance, his cavalry was blown back to France by the same storms that severely damaged his beached transports, and after only a few days in Britain the Romans had to withdraw. They had, however, met the British in battle, and been impressed by their formidable war-chariots. Caesar tells us that

In chariot fighting the Britons begin by driving all over the field hurling javelins, and generally the terror inspired by the horses and the noise of the wheels are sufficient to throw their opponents' ranks into disorder. Then . . . they jump down from the chariots and engage on foot. In the meantime their charioteers retire a short distance from the battle and place the chariots in such a position that their masters, if hard pressed by numbers, have an easy means of retreat. . . . Thus they combine the mobility of cavalry with the staying-power of infantry. . . . They can run along the chariot pole, stand on the yoke, and get back into the chariot as quick as lightning.

The hit-and-run tactics used by these light two-man vehicles could, however, never seriously endanger Caesar's disciplined and heavily armoured legionary infantry.

Far from being discouraged, Caesar launched a second expedition less than a year later, in July 54 BC. This time he brought five legions – about 25,000 infantry – and 2,000 cavalry, and landed unopposed near Sandwich in Kent. Marching swiftly inland, he easily forced the passage of the Stour at modern Canterbury, whereupon the Britons retired to a nearby stronghold 'previously prepared, no doubt, for some war amongst themselves'. This was probably Bigbury, a large but poorly defended hill-fort in the woods above Harbledown: clearly it had been hurriedly garrisoned, for the entrances were defended by felled trees rather than gates. Despite nuisance raids from the surrounding woods, the place soon fell to the men of the Seventh Legion. Locking their large rectangular shields over their heads to form a *testudo* (tortoise), they filled in part of the ditch to make a causeway which they then charged over in column.

The Roman advance was now delayed for ten days while repairs were made to their ships, damaged in yet another Channel gale. Meanwhile the British tribes had chosen as their leader Cassivellaunus, king of the powerful Belgic Catuvellauni, who raised a large confederate army and attacked the Romans in their camp. After some initial successes, the British chariots were driven off by legions and cavalry acting together, and Caesar was able to march northwards towards the Catuvellaunian lands in Hertfordshire. No other hill-forts lay in his path, but on reaching the Thames at London he found the only ford barred by sharpened stakes fixed in the riverbed to impale the unwary. Nevertheless the Romans stormed across, the infantry up to their necks in water, and routed the defenders on the northern bank.

Cassivellaunus now turned to guerrilla warfare, harassing Caesar's column with a force of 4,000 chariots and cutting off or ambushing scouts and foragers who ranged too far afield. These tactics, combined with the practice of hiding cattle in the woods to deny food to the enemy, might well have worn the Romans down, had not Cassivellaunus' local enemies revealed the whereabouts of his base, an oppidum amongst the forests and marshes round Wheathampstead. Braving the natural and earth-work defences, the legions stormed the oppidum in two places and captured the herds of cattle kept within it, though the British forces retired and once again melted away.

It was at this stage, according to Caesar, that Cassivellaunus sued for terms, but it may in fact have been the Romans who made the first approach, for it was obvious that Britain could not be easily conquered, and disturbing news of risings had come from Gaul. After exacting a promise of tribute from the Catuvellauni, therefore, Caesar's army re-crossed the Channel in early September, two months after their arrival in Kent. Caesar naturally claimed a victory, but later Roman historians wrote that he had revealed Britain without conquering it, while Cassivellaunus' grandchildren boasted of their descent from the man who had beaten Rome. British fortifications, however, insofar as they had played any part in the campaign, had proved quite inadequate to the onslaught of the most advanced and efficient military power of the ancient world.

During the century following Caesar's withdrawal Britain remained outside the Roman Empire, preserved from further invasion first by civil wars in Rome and later by imperial policy. In this period the Catuvellauni and their allies, led by Cassivellaunus' descendants, overran the whole of south-east England, moving their capital from Wheathampstead to an even larger and stronger oppidum at Camulodunum, the modern Colchester in Essex. Few developments in fortification are traceable to this century, though some hill-forts south of the Thames, including the Caburn in Sussex and Oldbury in Kent, were given very wide flat-bottomed ditches, broad enough to keep attackers at a distance and too large to be easily filled in. Similar ditches occur in northern France, where a fort so equipped had once repelled Caesar's forces. It is possible, therefore, that these defences were dug, in the area most vulnerable to invasion, with the Romans specifically in mind.

When the Roman attack came, in the summer of AD 43, it was in immense strength. An army of 40,000 men under the command of Aulus Plautius, including four legions and auxiliary cavalry (see p. 22), sailed from Boulogne and landed at a carefully chosen site, Richborough in north-east Kent, where their ships could shelter from the weather in a landlocked roadstead. The beachhead was at once fortified with a great double ditch: part of this, the earliest Roman fortification in Britain, is still to be seen. The landing, however, had been unopposed, for the British forces had dispersed, deceived by exaggerated rumours of a Roman mutiny in France. Even when the truth was known, the Britons appeared only in small numbers, following the familiar guerrilla tactics of Cassivellaunus. Their leaders, indeed, were the latter's descendants Togodumnus and Caractacus, joint kings of the Catuvellauni. No major battles were fought until the Romans reached the Medway, probably near the site of the modern M2 motorway bridge above Rochester. Here the British were defeated in a bitter two-day struggle, amongst those who distinguished themselves being Vespasian, commander of the Second Legion.

Next the Romans forced the passage of the Thames, though not without the loss of some over-enthusiastic units who pursued the enemy too far. Togodumnus was killed, and the way to the Catuvellaunian oppidum at Colchester lay open. Here, however, Aulus Plautius halted, sending to Rome for the Emperor Claudius, whose desire to mark his reign with a striking military victory had been one reason for the invasion. In mid-August the Emperor arrived, accompanied by a splendid entourage and by ceremonial elephants, to enter the enemy capital in triumph.

Whether he met with any serious resistance is doubtful. The Britons of the south-east had so far placed no reliance on their fortresses, and with the lesson of Caesar's capture of Wheathampstead in mind it is unlikely that Caractacus (now sole ruler of the Catuvellauni) would have staked all on the fate of a single oppidum. It was at about this time, indeed, that he retired to Wales to plot further resistance.

Claudius remained in Britain only sixteen days, during which time he ceremonially received the surrender of chieftains who had been defeated and the fealty of others who were already Roman allies (like Cogidubnus of Sussex) or who wanted to join the winning side (like Queen Cartimandua of the northern Brigantes). But Aulus Plautius was a long way from subduing even the southern part of England, and this was to be his next task. Establishing one legion (the Twentieth) at Colchester as a reserve, he now split the remainder of his army into task forces. The Ninth Legion was sent northwards, along the line of the old Great North Road, to subdue the east Midlands and build forts at Longthorpe, near Peterborough, and at Newton-on-Trent, near Lincoln. The Fourteenth marched north-westward to occupy Leicester and establish bases at Wall and Kinvaston, Staffordshire: the road they built, Watling Street (the modern A5), still follows their tracks.

The Second Legion, ordered to clear south-west England, may well have faced the hardest task of all. Vespasian, its commander, later became emperor, and his biographer records that the column under his command fought thirty battles, subduing two powerful tribes and storming more than twenty strongholds. They marched first to friendly Sussex, where they established a base at Chichester, and then moved westward along the coast, probably supported and supplied by a fleet. Having taken the Isle of Wight, Vespasian set up a forward post at Poole for his assault on the Durotriges, the warlike inhabitants of Somerset and Dorset.

Here the Second ran into tough opposition, for they had not only to defeat the Durotrigean field armies but also to reduce their hill-forts, the most formidable native strongholds in Britain. The apparent strength of their defences, however, betrayed the Britons into placing too much reliance

16 *A bolt-firing Roman spring-gun or 'cheiroballista', with its carrying cart, reconstructed from an example excavated at Ampurias in Spain and from carvings on Trajan's Column in Rome. The ballista, powered by twisted sinews contained in metal drums and tensioned by levers, is being operated by legionaries in full equipment, watched (right) by a centurion carrying his vine-staff of rank and by an auxiliary spearman (p. 22).*

on them, so that their forces, divided into garrisons, were easily defeated piecemeal: effective as the Durotrigean hill-forts may have been in tribal warfare, they were no match for Vespasian, provided as he was with armoured and disciplined infantry and with siege weapons. The most numerous of the latter were the spring-guns called 16 *cheiroballistae*, of which the Second probably had about sixty, carried on mule-carts and firing a bolt 12 inches (30 centimetres) long with an iron head. The contempt which Vespasian felt for British forts is demonstrated by the fact that (ignoring normal Roman practice) he did not trouble to build counter-works against them, relying on taking them by a single assault.

14 Maiden Castle, near the coast, may have been one of the first forts to fall. Its strongest defences were at its western end, and Vespasian probably skirted these, for the decisive attack was on the weaker eastern entrance. First the ramparts were cleared by ballista fire, a novel and terrifying experience for the defenders. One at least of the Britons was struck by a bolt, which penetrated his body below the heart and stuck fast in his spine: his remains, recovered by archaeologists, can be seen in Dorchester Museum. With the defences cleared, the legionaries advanced (perhaps under cover of a continuing barrage) through the complex earthworks of the entrance, burning some huts just outside the main gate. Then, obscured by the smoke, they stormed and took the gate itself. Something like a massacre ensued, for the skeletons of thirty-eight men and women were

found buried in the entrance. Several had deep head wounds, probably caused in battle by the short Roman sword, but others had been mutilated after death; one skull, that of a young man with exceptional muscular development (doubtless a noted warrior), had been splintered by nine sword cuts. When the killing stopped, the gates were smashed and part of the rampart demolished, so that the legion should not have to retake the place. The remaining inhabitants, however, were left in occupation, and allowed to bury their dead with the usual offerings (in one case a massive tankard) for use in the after-life.

Even greater slaughter took place at Spettisbury Rings, a hill-fort near Blandford, though here the details are less clear. In 1857 seventy or eighty skeletons, many bearing sword wounds, were found thrown into the fortress ditch, with the earth of the demolished rampart pushed down on top of them. Roman military equipment found nearby probably indicates that here was another of Vespasian's twenty conquered strongholds.

Perhaps because of a growing reputation of invincibility, the Second Legion had less trouble in taking a third Dorset hill-fort, Hod Hill, near 8 Stourpaine. This may actually have been the Duro-trigean capital, and frantic efforts were being made to strengthen the fortifications when Vespasian appeared before it. Placing their spring-guns on a prefabricated tower 600 yards (540 metres) away, the Romans concentrated their fire on a large hut, probably that of a chief, within the ramparts. Eleven

20

17 A Roman cavalryman of c.140 AD rides down stylized Caledonians. From the Bridgeness Stone, which once marked the eastern end of the Antonine Wall and is now in the National Museum of Antiquities, Edinburgh.

bolts were found in the area, eight within the foundations of the hut itself. This devastatingly accurate barrage seems to have persuaded the defenders to surrender, for there is no sign of a fight for the gates, though these were subsequently demolished. Here Vespasian took the precaution, unknown elsewhere in Britain, of building a small fort actually within the Durotrigean defences. It was garrisoned by mixed cavalry and infantry, and equipped with spring-guns mounted on platforms and aimed over a system of ditches designed to trap an attacker within their field of fire: doubtless they served as a reminder of defeat as well as a deterrent to further resistance.

Other forts further west which show evidence of capture by the Second are Worlebury, near Weston-super-Mare in Somerset, and Hembury in Devon, the latter in the territory of the Dumnonii, probably the second of Vespasian's subdued tribes. Vespasian himself was back in Rome by AD 44, when he took part in Claudius' triumph, his chief of staff being granted a 'mural crown', the decoration awarded for capturing fortresses.

Meanwhile the legions pushed on westwards and northwards, until by AD 47 a frontier had been established from Devon in the south-west to the Humber in the north. Along this line a strip of country up to 30 miles (46 kilometres) deep was occupied by garrisoned forts, and a communicating road, the Fosse Way, was built from Exeter to Lincoln via Cirencester and Leicester.

The Roman army which carried out this rapid conquest of the British lowlands was made up of two separate types of soldiers, the legionaries and the auxiliaries. Legionaries were recruited from Roman citizens from all over the Empire: in Claudius' time about half came from Italy, but a century later most were drawn from North Africa or the Balkans. Their equipment was remarkably uniform, consisting of a linen undergarment, a cuirass made from metal strips, a bronze helmet with an iron liner, and iron-studded sandals; they were armed with two throwing spears, a short stabbing sword and a dagger, and carried a large rectangular shield made of wood covered with leather and strengthened with metal. A legion, commanded by a legate, consisted of about 5,000 men, divided into 59 centuries usually of 80 men each; the latter were commanded by a centurion, and consisted of 10 units of 8 men each, called *contubernia* from the fact that they shared a tent. In Claudius' time the Roman forces consisted of about 29 legions, which like modern regiments had nicknames: the four involved in the conquest were the Second 'Augusta' (raised by Augustus), the Ninth 'Hispana' (from service in Spain), the Fourteenth 'Gemina' (the Twins, one legion made from two) and the Twentieth 'Valeria Victrix' (from victories under Valerius). Other legions were nicknamed 'Iron-sides' and 'Lightning-thrower'.

Auxiliaries, originally barbaric tribes allied to Rome, were drawn from frontier areas and were not citizens, though they became so on discharge. Amongst those that accompanied Aulus Plautius were units from Germany, Holland and Bulgaria, and later on Syrians and Yugoslavs formed part of the British garrison; these 'foreign' units were also recruited in the area where they were stationed, and probably included Britons in their ranks. The auxiliaries' equipment was much more varied than that of the legions, for units tended to retain elements of the dress and weapons of their country of origin (like the Gurkha regiments in the modern British army). They provided the Roman army with both light infantry and most of its cavalry, the infantry being formed into cohorts and the cavalry into *alae* (wings) of 500 or occasionally 1,000 men. There were also part-mounted cohorts, consisting of three-quarters infantry and a quarter cavalry. A Roman cavalryman of about AD 140 is represented 17 on the Bridgeness Stone, from the Antonine Wall in southern Scotland.

During most of the Roman occupation there were at least as many auxiliaries as legionaries in Britain, and towards the end there were considerably more. They were expected to man outposts and frontiers, the legions being kept in reserve for major expeditions or serious rebellions. Legionaries were also used as engineers, and it was they who were for the most part responsible for building the roads and fortifications on which Roman rule depended.

The Roman army, as one contemporary remarked, 'carried a walled town in their packs'. An expedition into unknown or hostile territory would, at the end of every day's march, construct a 'marching camp' to defend them overnight. Surveyors, sent on ahead, selected a dry piece of land free from undergrowth, and the troops themselves would raise an earth rampart 4–5 feet (about 1.5 metres) high, crowned with a palisade of pointed stakes tied together: each soldier carried two such stakes with him. Outside (unless the ground was too rocky) a ditch about 3 feet (1 metre) deep and wide was dug, and entrances were protected either by a separate section of bank and ditch outside them or by overlapping the rampart so that an enemy would have to enter at an angle. Inside the defences the soldiers pitched their

18 The Roman fort at Hardknott, Cumbria (centre right), built under Hadrian to guard Hardknott Pass and Eskdale and originally garrisoned by an auxiliary cohort from Yugoslavia.

eight-man leather tents (carried rolled up on mules) in ordered rows of ten, with the centurion's large tent at one end. The commander's marquee would be in the centre of the area, and latrines, cooking ovens and rubbish pits were placed at convenient points.

Marching camps were not meant to be defended against major attacks, but were designed as a protection against surprise raids and wild animals, as well as a safeguard against soldiers wandering off. A large number survive in Britain, the best preserved being in Wales, Scotland and northern England: their shape, usually rectangular, depends on the lie of the land and their size on the numbers in the expedition. Rey Cross, on the Yorkshire–Cumbria border, one of the most impressive of all, has a rampart 6 feet high and 20 feet wide (1.8 by 6 metres), but no ditch. It housed a whole legion, the Ninth, during their conquest of Brigantia.

After the enemy had been conquered, his territory would be controlled by means of more permanent fortifications. Unlike hill-forts, these were offensive in purpose, designed to be used as bases from which

the Roman garrison could march to attack opposing forces in the open. Their sites, therefore, were not chosen for natural defensibility, but rather for control of major routes, passes and river valleys. Thus Bainbridge fort in Wensleydale, Yorkshire, is placed at the junction of two river valleys, commanding them both, while Hardknott in Cumbria overlooks a pass through the Lakeland fells. 18

Again unlike prehistoric defences, Roman forts (especially on frontiers) were generally part of a mutually supporting system of defences, linked by the famous Roman roads. Many of these straight highways, for example Watling and Ermine Streets, are still in use and overlaid with modern metalling, but occasionally they can be seen in near original condition. One such stretch is at Wheeldale Moor in 15 North Yorkshire, on the route from Whitby to Malton and York. For the sake of drainage, roads were frequently laid on a raised embankment, sometimes with ditches at either side: foundations were of large stones, or occasionally of paving, topped with a layer of gravel which is now generally

23

lost. Essentially military in character, Roman roads were often built by legionaries, who not surprisingly hated the job.

The forts themselves usually had two or three lines of V-shaped defensive ditches. Sometimes, as at Hod Hill, the outermost ditch had a vertical outer face but an easy slope on the inside. Attackers could, therefore, easily drop down into it, only to find themselves met with a hail of fire from the ramparts and unable to climb back out again. Other hazards sometimes included entanglements in the shape of thorn hedges in the ditch bottom and, even more unpleasant, pits containing pointed stakes or spears. These 'lilies', as they were euphemistically called, were carefully concealed with brushwood so that attackers would suddenly fall into them and impale themselves: examples were found at Rough Castle on the Antonine Wall, in the Central Region.

Fort ramparts, at least in the conquest period, were often made of turf, stacked in uniform 'bricks' to form a vertical wall 10–18 feet (3–5.5 metres) thick and invulnerable to both fire and battering ram. Foundations were often made from a layer of logs, and timber was also used to strengthen ramparts at the front and to build battlements and fighting platforms on top of them. Gates, flanked by towers for small ballistas, were also made of wood as, indeed, were complete forts. By the time of Hadrian (AD 117–38) some wood and turf forts were being rebuilt in stone, and new stone forts like Hardknott were also constructed.

The interiors of forts contained, in some form or other, a headquarters building, commander's lodging, storehouses and, if the garrison were cavalry, stables; almost invariably there was also a bath-house, sometimes outside the walls. Barrack-blocks were clearly derived from the tent lines of a marching camp, consisting of a long narrow hut for each century: this contained a bedroom and a store-room for every eight men, with a block of roomier accommodation for the centurion and his assistants at one end. This plan can be plainly seen in the foundations of the barracks at Caerleon, the fortress [21] of the Second Legion in Wales. There, as in many [22] other places, the huts, originally of wood, were rebuilt in stone.

Forts varied tremendously in size, but were nearly always rectangular. The smallest examples might house a single century, while rather larger forts like Hardknott and Bainbridge were garrisoned by a [18] whole cohort of auxiliaries, in these cases units originating in Yugoslavia and the Frisian Islands. Hod Hill, built to consolidate Vespasian's conquests,

was designed for about 480 legionaries with 230 auxiliary cavalry. It was occupied for only eight years, but others were garrisoned for centuries. Legionary fortresses – Chester, York, Caerleon, [21] Exeter, Lincoln and the short-lived Inchtuthil – [22] were the largest of all, covering up to 60 acres (24 hectares) and housing over 5,000 men. They contained the permanent headquarters, an imposing house for the legate, a hospital, and a bath-house with exercise hall. Outside was the amphitheatre, used more often for assembly and weapon training than for gladiatorial displays.

Since fortification was so important to the Roman soldier, it is not surprising that it formed part of his training. 'Practice camps', consisting mainly of the difficult corners and entrances rather than the easy straight sections, are found on Llandrindod Wells Common in Powys and elsewhere, while at Cawthorn, near Pickering in South Yorkshire, the garrison of Malton practised building permanent forts. Troops also needed to be trained in siegecraft, and at Burnswark in Dumfries the army staged a [19] mock attack on a long-disused hill-fort, building earthwork camps and firing ballistas mounted on platforms raised outside them. These latter were the small spring-guns used at Hod Hill. It is doubtful whether any native fortress in Britain held out long enough to require the use of the Roman 'heavy artillery', the great engines that threw stones weighing up to a hundredweight (50 kilograms), but these 'onagers' – so called because when fired they kicked like an onager or wild ass – were mounted on some forts on Hadrian's Wall and the 'Saxon Shore'. This, however, is to anticipate.

The Roman Fosse Way frontier of AD 47 was doubtless intended to be permanent, but it did not last long, for the unconquered tribes outside it were restless. Most troublesome of all were the fierce Silures of south Wales, who under the leadership of the fugitive Catuvellaunian chief Caractacus launched a series of destructive raids on the border areas, perhaps using as a base the hill-fort of Amberley Camp near Stroud in Gloucestershire. Caractacus was finally defeated in AD 51, having unwisely penned his whole army into a strong hilltop position, fronted by a river and defended by makeshift ramparts of piled boulders. Where it was situated is uncertain, but it may have been near Dolforwyn in northern Powys or else close to one of the two hill-forts in Salop called Caer Caradoc, one near Church Stretton and the other near Clun. Neither the position nor Caractacus' army was a match for the Fourteenth and Twentieth Legions, who, Tacitus relates, 'locked

19 *The southernmost of two Roman practice siege camps outside the disused hillfort of Burnswark, in Dumfries and Galloway: note the ballista platforms guarding the camp entrances (centre left).*

shields to form a "tortoise", hurled down the rudely-built rampart, and brought about a hand-to-hand battle on equal terms. . . . It was a famous victory.'

Though Caractacus was later captured, the Silures were by no means cowed. Instead of trusting to the fortifications which had so far proved easy meat for the Romans, they turned to hit-and-run tactics, cutting up a Roman force sent to build a fort within their territory (perhaps at Clyro, near Hay-on-Wye), surprising and nearly overwhelming a large foraging party, and even defeating the Twentieth Legion in the field. For a time the southern end of the Fosse frontier was in chaos, with the Romans pinned in their forts and the Silurian guerrillas (who 'crept through the glens and swamps like bandits') ranging far and wide.

Even when the Silures had been thrown back the frontier was far from quiet, for now there was unrest at its northern end, amongst the powerful Brigantes. At one stage, in about AD 54–56, the Emperor Nero is even said to have contemplated a complete withdrawal from Britain, as being too costly and troublesome a province to hold. By AD 58 the opposite course had been decided upon: the Fosse frontier was to be abandoned, and Roman power to be extended to the north and into Wales.

The implementation of this policy had to wait another thirteen years. First, in AD 60, a serious revolt in the 'conquered' area, led by Queen Boudicca (or Boadicea), ravaged the whole south-east, killing 70,000 people, defeating the Ninth Legion and destroying the unwalled towns of Colchester, London and St Albans. When lowland Britain was again put in order, political upheavals and civil war in Rome itself supervened, until in AD 69 Vespasian, the old British campaigner, emerged from the chaos as emperor. During the next sixteen years he and his sons Titus (who had also served in Britain) and Domitian encouraged the extension of Roman control over virtually the whole island. With their special knowledge of British affairs, it is probable that they had come to the conclusion – shared by many later rulers of this island – that the only way to preserve the peace of the prosperous lowland south and east was to exercise control over the barbaric

25

20 Part of the ramparts, curving away into the distance, of the great Brigantian oppidum at Stanwick St John, North Yorkshire.

highland north and west. The highlands could be completely conquered, or they could be isolated behind a defensive barrier so strong that no hostile forces could penetrate it. With these alternatives in mind, Vespasian chose conquest.

First to be attacked were the Brigantes, who held most of the lands between Trent and Tyne. During the upheavals preceding Vespasian's accession, they had taken advantage of Roman disorganization to expel their pro-Roman Queen, Cartimandua, setting up instead her husband Venutius, the greatest British warrior of his day. This Venutius, an enemy of Rome, constructed for himself a fortress of unusual type at Stanwick St John, near Richmond in North Yorkshire, which is perhaps the most highly developed and certainly one of the latest 'pre-Roman' defences in Britain. It originated as an unexceptional hill-fort defending a low knoll, but this was soon supplemented by a much larger work with ramparts 2 miles (over 3 kilometres) long, enclosing a stream as a water supply for the defenders. Such a long defence line could not be

permanently manned even by a numerous tribe like the Brigantes, and it is clear that (like the oppida at Wheathampstead and Colchester) it was meant to be defended by a mobile force reinforcing threatened points. The entire rampart, in fact, was carefully designed to be within view of a command-post at the summit of the hill-fort, from which Venutius could coordinate overall defence operations. Not long afterwards the fortress was extended yet again, so that its ramparts were now over 5 miles (8 kilometres) long and included an area of 850 acres (345 hectares). Presumably the intention was either to make room for a very large army of allies or, more probably, to accommodate a whole tribe with its flocks and herds. These latest defences could not, of course, be either permanently manned or controlled from a central point. They look very like a desperate measure, though one for which a vast amount of labour would have been needed, for they measure up to 22 feet (6.7 metres) from rampart top to rock-cut ditch bottom, quite apart from their immense length.

20

21, 22 The legionary fortress of Caerleon, Gwent, from c. 75 AD headquarters of the Second Legion Augusta. Right: a reconstruction of the fort in its prime. Barrack-blocks surround the edge; two streets, the long Via Principalis and shorter Via Praetoria, meet at the headquarters or praetorium. Outside the walls is the amphitheatre. Below: the western corner.

Like all other British attempts to use fortifications against the Romans, Stanwick was a failure. In AD 71 the Ninth Legion, under the governor Quintus Petillius Cerialis, crossed the Humber and established a fort (soon afterwards a legionary headquarters) at York. After a series of battles, 'some not uncostly to the Romans', the Yorkshire Brigantes were defeated and Stanwick was overrun. Cerialis then pressed on over the high pass of Stainmore into Cumbria, leaving as evidence of his progress a fine series of legionary marching camps like Rey Cross.

By AD 74 the Brigantes were overcome, but before their lands could be brought under full control Roman attention was diverted by fresh trouble in Wales, and during the next four years Cerialis' successor Julius Frontinus was occupied in the conquest of that country, beginning with the Silures in the south. Large numbers of forts attest his success, the most impressive being the legionary fortresses he established at Caerleon and Chester. Some idea of their sheer size can be obtained from the photograph of Caerleon, where the church in the distance marks not the perimeter but the centre of the fortress. In the immediate foreground is a stone cook-house built against the perimeter rampart, and behind it is one of the sixty-four barrack-blocks which Caerleon sheltered.

The five years that followed the conquest of Wales, AD 79–84, saw the most spectacular expansion of Roman power during the whole occupation period. It was the work of Julius Agricola, whose campaigns were recorded by his son-in-law Tacitus. First, in AD 79, he established firm Roman control over the Brigantian lands as far north as the Tyne and Solway, and in the following years he marched north along Dere Street (the modern A68) into southern Scotland, storming the tribal stronghold of Eildon Hill near Melrose and establishing a fort nearby. The end of AD 80 saw Agricola's army on the line of the Forth and Clyde, with his scouts ranging north to the fringes of the Highlands. A year was spent in consolidation, fortifying the Forth–Clyde line and building roads, but in 82 the Romans overran south-west Scotland and reached the Irish Sea. Agricola even meditated an invasion of Ireland, but better counsels prevailed.

Instead, in 83 he pushed on up the eastern plains of Scotland as far as Aberdeen. Too wise a general to enter the Highlands, he secured his lengthening lines of communication by establishing a fort at the lowland end of every major glen. Highland raiders could thus be held off from the road home, and

warnings of large-scale flank attacks would reach the main army via chains of signal stations. To provide himself with a firm base, Agricola also founded a full-scale legionary fortress, meant as the headquarters of the Twentieth Legion, at Inchtuthil near Dunkeld in Tayside. The logistics of building such a major work so far from centres of supply are truly staggering, especially if we consider that 7 miles (some 11 kilometres) of timber and over a million nails would be needed for the barrack-blocks alone. Not content with this, in the following year the Romans marched on again, supported by a fleet which ventured as far as the Orkneys. The land forces crowned their year's campaign with a sweeping victory over the combined Caledonian forces at 'Mons Graupius', somewhere in northern Aberdeenshire, the modern Grampian Region.

The advance got no further, for during the winter that followed Agricola was recalled to Rome, some said because of the jealousy of the Emperor Domitian. During his northern campaigns he had built 60 forts and 1,300 miles (over 2,000 kilometres) of road, and come close to bringing the whole of Britain under Roman control. 'Perdomita Britannia', his biographer remarked bitterly, 'et statim missa' – all Britain was conquered, and then let slip. After Agricola's recall his brilliant work was undone, and the Romans withdrew from northern Scotland demolishing the fortress of Inchtuthil as they went. The legion that should have held it was sent to Chester to replace another ordered to eastern Europe. Never again would the opportunity arise to conquer all Britain and unify it as one Roman province. Had Agricola's work been finished, it is possible that there would have been no Hadrian's Wall, perhaps even no eventual distinction between England and Scotland.

But all this is speculation, and the fact is that the conquest of the far north was abandoned. Agricola's campaigns must have stretched Roman manpower to the limit, and to garrison his conquests would have required reinforcements which could ill be spared from the hard-pressed eastern frontiers of the Empire. By this time, in any case, the impetus was going out of the Roman drive for world domination, to be replaced by a policy of retrenchment and consolidation of the lands already held. For the next three hundred years the Romans in Britain were to be concerned with the defence of their province against increasing numbers of enemies, coming first from the north, then from the east, and finally from all sides at once.

21
22

23 Sentry's eye-view of the craggy central sector of Hadrian's Wall, looking eastwards towards the important fort at Housesteads, Northumberland (behind the distant clump of trees).

3   The Wall and the Saxon Shore

Verily I have seene the tract of it over the high pitches and steepe descents, wonderfully rising and falling.

WILLIAM CAMDEN, describing Hadrian's Wall in *Britannia*, 1610

Agricola's campaigns in the far north were the high tide of Roman expansionism in Britain, and at first the ebb was slow. The forty years after his recall saw a gradual withdrawal from Scotland, while, following the new policy of consolidation, the three legionary fortresses at York, Chester and Caerleon were given stone walls, and new forts like Hardknott were built in the Pennines. The northern frontier of the Roman province remained indefinite, and in a more or less permanent state of unrest.

It was perhaps fortunate, therefore, that Hadrian, who came to the throne in AD 117 and visited Britain four years later, was something of an expert on frontiers. He had served in the imperial borderlands of Syria and the Balkans, and early in his reign had reorganized the defences along the Rhine. Hadrian would have seen the British frontier not only as a shield for the province itself, but also as part of the defences of the Empire, stretching from the Rhine mouth to the Black Sea, from thence to Arabia, and right across north Africa to Morocco. The British sector was a vital one, for if this island fell to the barbarians then France and Belgium, occupied by closely related peoples, might well follow. Even so, the solution that the Emperor decided upon was a breathtaking one, unparalleled in its grandeur anywhere else in the Empire. By AD 123 detachments from the British legions were laying the foundations of a wall that was to run across north Britain from sea to sea, covering the 76-mile (122-kilometre) distance from Newcastle-on-Tyne in the east to Bowness on the Solway in the west.

As originally conceived, rather more than half of Hadrian's Wall was to be built in stone, 20 feet (6 metres) high and 8–10 feet (2.5–3 metres) thick, while the western sector, where no limestone for mortar was available, was to be constructed in turf. Within a few decades, however, the turf wall was rebuilt in stone. On the northern side ran a ditch, up to 40 feet (12 metres) wide and 10 feet (3 metres) deep. Every Roman mile along it stood a fortlet or 'milecastle', while between each pair of milecastles were two signal turrets, equipped with beacons for passing messages.

The milecastle shown in the photograph, near Cawfield in Northumberland, was built by the Second Augusta. It contained accommodation for thirty or so men and (more significantly) had an entrance at the front, towards the enemy, as well as

to the rear. These frontal entrances show that Hadrian's Wall was, like Roman forts, an 'active' rather than a 'passive' fortification. It was not intended to be used as a defensive fighting platform (like a castle or town wall) but rather as a barrier controlling enemy movement, patrolled by a garrison housed in milecastles and linked by signal towers. In the event of trouble this garrison was not merely to sit behind the rampart, but rather to issue out of its milecastles and engage the enemy in the field. Serious raids might call for aid (summoned by beacon) from neighbouring milecastles, which could take the enemy in the flank and pin him against the front of the wall itself. Full-scale attacks, on the other hand, might necessitate reinforcements from the strategic reserve, originally housed in forts several miles behind the wall.

The building of the wall gave rise to so much unrest, however, amongst both the warlike Brigantes to the south of it and their equally belligerent allies to the north, that some changes had soon to be made. The strategic reserve was brought forward into a series of forts built on the wall itself, which, like milecastles, had their principal gates facing towards the enemy, and a demarcation line, called the *vallum*, was constructed to the south. This last was a belt of land 120 feet (36 metres) wide, with a ditch in the middle, a patrol track, and earth banks at either side. The only causeways across it were at forts, where they could be easily controlled. Civilians crossing the vallum elsewhere would be intercepted by patrols as trespassers in the military zone of the wall, and in this way spies or suspicious characters could be prevented from slipping across the border to join the tribes in the north.

This, then, was the northern frontier of Britain and the north-west frontier of the Roman Empire – a borderline which dominated Roman military thinking in Britain just as another north-west frontier, the Khyber Pass, was later to dominate British military policy in India. At full strength, the garrison of Hadrian's Wall probably numbered about 12,000 men, of whom about a tenth formed the patrolling force while the remainder were the 'fighting garrison', or strategic reserve. Both forces were, virtually without exception, made up of auxiliaries rather than legionaries, and both cavalry and infantry were employed, the former placed in forts for use as fast-moving reinforcements or task forces.

*24, 25 Hadrian's Wall: milecastle 42 at Cawfields,
Northumberland, looking eastwards towards Thorny Doors
crag (above), and the causeway (with footings of gate-piers)
crossing the vallum at Benwell fort, two miles west of
Newcastle-on-Tyne.*

The crack Ala Petriana, the largest cavalry regiment
in Britain, was stationed near the dangerous western
end of the border, and amongst the infantry there
was a specialist regiment of Syrian archers as well as
units of *exploratores* or frontier scouts.

The wall probably took ten years to build; it was
finished in about 133, during Hadrian's lifetime.
Within a matter of a few years, however, the new
Emperor Antoninus Pius, for reasons that are not
certainly known, ordered a new advance into
southern Scotland. There, in about AD 142, the
governor Lollius Urbicus established a new frontier,
the Antonine Wall, which stretched for 37 miles (60
kilometres) from the river Forth in the east to the
Clyde in the west. Unlike Hadrian's Wall (which was
now only partially garrisoned) the Antonine fortification was made of turf throughout, and it lacked
a system of milecastles and turrets, being defended
instead by eighteen or nineteen forts at 2-mile (3.2-
kilometre) intervals and a system of outposts strung
out to the north.

17
26

31

26 Remains of the Antonine turf wall and ditch, looking westwards towards Rough Castle fort, near Bonnybridge, Central.

26   Though its turf has not survived as well as Hadrian's stone, the Antonine Wall is still impressively visible in many places, one of them the fort at Rough Castle, near Bonnybridge in the Central Region: in addition to the Antonine ditch (deeper than that of Hadrian's Wall), its defences included 'lilies', sharp stakes in concealed pits. It was a small post, garrisoned by German auxiliaries under a legionary centurion. Among their duties was probably the care of four nearby signal towers, which received messages from the road leading to the outpost forts north of the wall.

The fifty years after the establishment of the new wall were a period of almost continual upheaval on the northern border: twice, or perhaps three times, the Antonine defences were overrun and the Romans fell back to Hadrian's frontier, only to advance again. The occupation of the Antonine Wall, it appears, resulted in rebellions in the rear, amongst the Brigantes of northern England, while the retirement to Hadrian's line allowed the tribes of southern Scotland to take the warpath. For a time both walls seem to have been occupied simultaneously, though this must have been a heavy drain on manpower.

The pressure from the north culminated, in AD 197, in a total collapse of the frontier defences. Clodius Albinus, then governor, had stripped Britain of troops for an invasion of Europe in an attempt to make himself emperor. During his absence Hadrian's Wall was overrun, forts were burnt, and milecastles systematically demolished: in Yorkshire the ever-turbulent Brigantes set upon their local garrisons, destroying isolated posts like Bainbridge, and the Welsh tribes also raised the standard of rebellion.

Nearly ten years of campaigning, it seems, were necessary to restore Roman supremacy and to reconstruct Hadrian's Wall, in places from the very foundations up. Then came revenge, and between AD 208 and 211 large Roman armies (under the personal leadership of the emperors Severus and Caracalla) struck deep into Scotland, following in the footsteps of Agricola and utterly defeating the northern tribes. So thoroughly was this operation carried out that the northern frontier enjoyed unwonted peace for over eighty years afterwards.

Indeed, the whole of Roman Britain seems to have enjoyed a period of peace and prosperity during the first half of the third century AD. The unfortified towns of the province, many of which had been hurriedly defended by an earthwork bank and ditch when Clodius Albinus removed his troops in AD 197, now began to be protected by stone or masonry walls. One such wall surrounded Verulamium (St Albans, Hertfordshire): it was constructed of flint and mortar, and originally faced with smooth coursed stone now long since stolen and incorporated in later buildings. Built in about AD 240 it was, like other town walls of the period, backed and strengthened with an earthen bank. Some towns near the south coast, like Canterbury and Dorchester, remained without stone walls until the last decades of the third century, when a new threat to Britain gave a fresh incentive to fortification.

The new danger came not from the tribes beyond Hadrian's Wall, but from shipborne pirates raiding across the north-eastern seas and descending without warning on Britain's long and exposed coastlines. The raiders, Franks and Saxons, were seafaring peoples from northern Europe outside the imperial frontiers. Prevented from landward expansion by the Roman defences on the Rhine, they took to their boats – extremely small and flimsy by modern standards – and braved the fearsome North Sea crossing to plunder the rich provinces of Gaul and Britain. Striking at coastal settlements, or creeping up rivers and estuaries to beach further inland, their raids were impossible to predict, and no undefended site near the sea could be regarded as safe from them.

Britain, however, was not entirely unprotected. Profoundly un-maritime though the Romans were – their navy was a very inferior service under army control – they did maintain a Channel fleet, known as the *Classis Britannica*. During the period of conquest this fleet had been used to support the expeditions of Vespasian, Agricola and others, and by the second century it had headquarters bases at Dover (discovered as recently as 1971) and Boulogne. At both these places, too, stood lighthouses, one of which survives at Dover on the cliff-top near the medieval castle. Originally 80 feet (24 metres) high, it was topped by a beacon which sent out a column of smoke by day and of fire by night as a guide to shipping. Part of the task of this Channel fleet was to keep a watch on the south-east coast of Britain.

Pirate activity increased towards the end of the second century, and around AD 200 there seems to have been a damaging series of raids on the eastern coastline (traceable from burnt buildings and hoards of valuables hurriedly buried by owners who did not survive to recover them). Probably in response to this, the Romans began to build forts near a few

27

27 The second-century Roman pharos or lighthouse at Dover, with the castle keep in the background. The present top storey is medieval, but the original pharos probably stood higher still.

28 The Saxon Shore fortress system in Britain and Gaul.

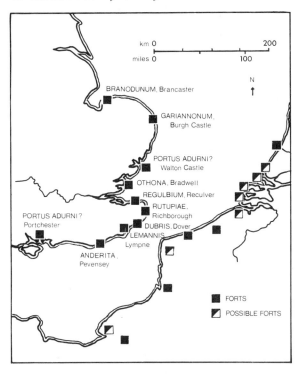

eastern harbours, both to provide safe anchorages for the defending fleet and to deter raiders, who always gave a wide berth to such fortifications. Amongst these were Brancaster, near Hunstanton in Norfolk, and Reculver, near Herne Bay on the north coast of Kent. The latter had been one of the Claudian invasion bases, and guarded one end of the sheltered channel (now silted up) between the Isle of Thanet and the mainland, the other end being covered by Richborough, which was also fortified at this time (about AD 230) with earthwork banks and ditches. At Reculver the square fort was defended by a plain stone wall; much of this has now fallen into the encroaching sea, but part is still to be seen. Ironically enough, the site is now dominated by the towers of the seventh-century church founded by Egbert, ruler of the Saxon kingdom of Kent.

A further and much greater crisis (attested by many finds of concealed coins) occurred in AD 276, when barbarian tribes from beyond the Rhine flooded into Gaul by land, accompanied by swarms of sea-rovers who established virtual control over the seas around Britain. Opinions are still divided, but it was probably around this time that a great chain of Roman forts was built on both sides of the Channel to guard those coasts of England and France later known collectively as the *Litus Saxonici* or Saxon Shore.

Taking the English forts in order from north to south, Brancaster in Norfolk was still in use, and further south Burgh, guarding the Waveney estuary near Yarmouth, had turrets added (though not fully attached) to its previously plain stone walls. Walton Castle, watching over three river mouths near Felixstowe, has now disappeared, and only fragments remain of the stone turreted fort at Bradwell, on the Blackwater river in Essex. In Kent, Reculver was incorporated into the chain, and at Richborough the earthworks were replaced by a magnificent stone fort with turreted walls over 10 feet (3 metres) thick and 25 feet (7.5 metres) high, surrounded by a deep double ditch. This, guarding one of the principal ports of Roman Britain, may well have been the nerve-centre of the whole system. Not far away a new fort was built to protect Dover harbour – apparently in a great hurry, for the walls cut through the house of a prosperous citizen – while another overlooked the fleet base at nearby Lympne. Much further west, on the edge of Portsmouth harbour in Hampshire, stands the most impressive of all the forts, Portchester, the only Roman fortress in northern Europe whose walls stand to their full original height of nearly 20 feet (6 metres). They also retain fourteen of their twenty semi-circular towers, though the elaborate gates were remodelled by the Normans who adapted the fort as a castle.

29–31 Saxon Shore forts:

29 The great double ditch and massive walls of the fort at Richborough, Kent, perhaps the headquarters of the whole Roman coastal defence system, seen from the south-west.

30 Portchester, Hampshire. The complete perimeter of Roman walls shelters Henry I's castle (p. 82), in the far corner, and the remains of an Augustinian abbey.

31 Burgh Castle, Norfolk. A change of plan added artillery turrets to the plain walls halfway through building operations, and they are therefore bonded in only to the upper portion of the structure (see also p. 42).

32 The Multangular Tower at York, showing the contrast between the Roman masonry of small, even stones, and the medieval work above, where the tower narrows and is pierced with arrow-slits.

33 The restored north gate of the Roman fort at Cardiff Castle. Built as a defence against Irish sea-raiders, perhaps c. 300, it was reconstructed during the 1860s, and affords some idea of how a Saxon Shore type fortress may have appeared in its prime.

This scheme of fortification, ambitious even by modern standards, was designed to combat the Saxon menace in a number of ways. First, it provided secure anchorage for the Roman fleet, of which it is possible that each fort had its own attached squadron. Certainly each had its own garrison: far-separated Burgh and Brancaster were manned by Yugoslavian cavalry regiments, which could strike quickly at raiders landing some distance from the fort, while the closely-set Kentish posts with a smaller area to protect were garrisoned by infantry. The forts themselves were eminently defensible, their external turrets (a novel feature in Roman fortification and specially added at Burgh) being designed for mounting artillery engines. Most probably carried bolt-firing spring-guns, aimed through U-shaped windows, one of which survived at Pevensey until 1940 when (appropriately enough) it was destroyed by the construction of a machine-gun post. At Burgh the turrets may have held much larger stone-throwing 'onagers'. Such engines, with a range of a quarter of a mile (400 metres), could be used not only to keep besiegers at a distance, but also to repel Saxon war-boats that ventured too close. In any case, the forts placed near estuaries would effectively prevent raiders from slipping inland unnoticed.

It has recently been suggested that the Saxon Shore forts in Britain and Gaul formed a unified system designed to prevent or discourage landings north of the Straits of Dover. Raiders coming from the north-east (as they must, the east and south being held by Rome) would therefore be funnelled into the narrowest part of the Channel, where they could be most easily intercepted by the Classis Britannica based on Dover, Richborough or Boulogne. Certainly this seems to have been the policy adopted by Carausius, a low-born Belgian sailor who rose to command the Channel Fleet in A D 285. He may have been responsible, too, for the novel device of camouflaging the hulls, sails and masts of Roman patrol ships in sea-green, the better to creep unnoticed on the pirates. At any rate, with the help of the fort system Carausius quickly defeated the Saxons and cleared the British seas, becoming so popular that in 286 he declared himself the first independent ruler of all Britain and the Channel coast of Gaul. He ruled for seven years, easily defeating a Roman fleet sent against him, until in 293 he lost his Gaulish possessions and was assassinated by Allectus, his finance minister. Allectus himself was overthrown in 296, when a Roman force under Constantius Chlorus (avoiding the Saxon Shore

system by invading from Gaul) slipped past the
British fleet and landed on the south coast to regain
Britain for the Empire.

The reigns of Constantius and his son Constantine,
the first Christian emperor, saw a further strengthening of defences against the barbarians who threatened Britain. Hadrian's Wall, overrun during the
unheavals of Allectus' brief rule, was again rebuilt,
and many fortresses in northern Britain, decayed
during the long peace, were recommissioned.
Command of the northern garrisons was given to an
official called the *Dux Britanniarum* – Duke (or
Commander) of the provinces of Britain – whose
headquarters were the legionary fortress of York:
40 this was given a magnificent new section of wall,
studded with projecting polygonal bastions, in
about AD 300. One of these, the western corner

tower or 'Multangular Tower', still stands to its full 32
height of 19 feet (5.8 metres), though it lost its Roman
crenellations and roof and was again heightened in
medieval times. The contrast between Roman and
later masonry can be clearly seen, the Roman section
being decorated with an ornamental course of tiles
and thickened at the base to ensure against undermining. Inside, about two-thirds of the way up, is
the Roman parapet walk.

At this time, too, defences were built on the west
coast of Britain against sea-borne invaders from a
new direction – the Ireland of the semi-legendary
heroes Cormac MacArt and Finn MacCool. These
works included a Saxon Shore type fort at Cardiff 33
(now largely rebuilt) and fortifications at Caernarfon
and Lancaster. In southern England the Saxon
Shore system was kept in full operation, and behind

all these fortifications Britain enjoyed another period of prosperity during the first part of the fourth century.

By about 340, however, barbarian raids had again become serious enough to warrant the building of a new fort at Pevensey in Sussex, on the long stretch of unguarded coastline between Lympne and Portchester. The whole system was now under the command of a general called the Count of the Saxon Shore. Pevensey, unlike earlier forts, was oval in plan rather than rectangular, but like them it protected a harbour and estuary. Its walls, 12 feet (3.6 metres) thick, are decorated with bands of tiles and ironstone and equipped with artillery towers. The fortress has had a long active life, being used successively for a Norman and medieval castle, an Elizabethan gun-emplacement, and a disguise for Second World War pillboxes.

Until now the enemies of Roman Britain had been more or less haphazard in the timing of their raids, but in 367 a 'barbarian conspiracy' – apparently sealed by the High King of Ireland's marriage to a Saxon princess – resulted in a devastating attack from many directions at once. The picts from northern Scotland overran Hadrian's Wall and invaded England, accompanied by the fierce and cannibalistic Attacotti, and while the Irish descended on the western coasts the Franks and Saxons struck at the east and south. The result was disaster, with the Dux Britanniarum captured, the Count of Saxon Shore killed, bands of plunderers roaming the countryside and mutiny and desertion rife among the Roman forces. Had the barbarians been settlers rather than plunderers, this might indeed have been the end of Roman Britain. As it was, Count Theodosius, sent from France with a relieving army, took nearly two years to reconquer the province.

This done, Theodosius set about yet another reconstitution of British defences: once again the wall was repaired, and treaties were made with the friendly tribes of southern Scotland who formed buffer states between the province and the Picts. Town walls were given projecting bastions to mount artillery, and new defences were built on the coasts, including a series of fortified signal towers, 90–100 feet (27–30 metres) high, along the Yorkshire clifftops. These would keep watch for Saxon or Pictish raiders, and could signal warnings either to inland garrisons or to intercepting squadrons stationed in the Tyne and Humber estuaries. One such tower stood at Scarborough, near the medieval castle; it was surrounded by a stone defending wall and an earthwork bank and ditch. Within twenty or thirty years of their erection, however, these signal towers had been destroyed by those they were built to warn against. At one of them, Goldsborough near Whitby, excavators found two unburied skeletons: one had been stabbed in the back, and the other had fallen onto the body of a powerful dog, perhaps one of the war-hounds for which Britain was famous.

For, despite the far-reaching Theodosian reorganization and the temporary lull in raiding that followed, the days of Roman control over Britain were numbered. Troops were withdrawn, never to return, by Magnus Maximus, a Dux Britanniarum who in 383 crossed to Europe and attempted to make himself emperor. More, including units raised in Britain, were ordered to Italy in about A D 400, when Rome itself was threatened by the Goths, part of the inexorable tide of barbarians engulfing the whole western Empire. At this time Hadrian's Wall was finally abandoned. Some of the departing troops, ironically, seem to have sailed from Richborough, the spot where Claudius' legions had landed three hundred and fifty years earlier.

Threatened by a renewal of Saxon attacks in A D 410, and now virtually stripped of regular troops, the British cities sent for aid to the Emperor Honorius in beleaguered Rome. They received in reply only the instruction to undertake their own defence – which, apparently, they did with some success. Whatever the circumstances, and these are far from clear, the control of the tottering Roman Empire was never re-established. In the dark years to come the defence of Britain would be up to the Britons themselves.

35 Offa's Dyke marching southwards up Llanfair Hill, in the central borderlands near Newcastle-on-Clun, Salop (see pp. 46–47). The ditch lies towards Wales.

4   The heroic age, *c*. 410–800

The dykes remain. He who dug them
Is no more . . .

From the elegy on Cynddylan of Shropshire, the last
British prince to rule part of lowland England,
killed by the Anglo-Saxons *c*.656.

The four centuries which followed the severance of Britain from the Roman Empire are perhaps the most crucial period in the history of the island. During this time the old Roman province, cast into the melting pot of continual war and invasion, dissolved into small warring states which eventually coalesced into something approaching modern England and Wales. North of Hadrian's Wall, meanwhile, equally far-reaching changes converted a tribal society into the kingdom of Albany, recognizably the ancestor of medieval Scotland.

Not for nothing, however, is this period sometimes called the Dark Ages, for its history is obscure in the extreme, and its records at times little better than legends of half-remembered heroes and villains – hence its more appropriate name of 'the heroic age'. In our brief survey we shall meet Old King Cole and King Arthur, Maelgwyn the Dragon of Britain and Aethelric the Firebrand of Northumbria. Only very recently have historians and archaeologists (drawing on sources as diffuse as a Welsh family tree and a brooch from a Saxon grave in Kent) begun the arduous task of constructing a comprehensible framework for these shadowy centuries of change and new birth.

Unlike the fortifications of the Roman period, which made an indelible mark on the British countryside, the defences of the heroic age have left little visible trace. In terms of fortifications, indeed, the era was one of regression: Roman defences, where they continued in use, were repaired rather than reconstructed, and long-abandoned hill-forts were in places re-occupied. Such new fortresses as were built were puny and primitive by the standards of Saxon Shore forts or the defences of Hadrian's Wall, reflecting a reversion to a type of warfare more reminiscent of the tribal disputes of the Iron Age than the sophisticated strategies of the Romans.

The collapse of the Roman province was at first gradual, and some form of the old way of life persisted for at least a generation after the removal of imperial control. What was immediately apparent was a vacuum of power, and in the absence of an obvious national ruler Britain fell under the sway of a diversity of local potentates. Though often giving themselves Roman titles, these men were in reality petty warlords or, as the British priest Gildas called them, *tyranni* – tyrants. Amongst them was a certain Coel the Old, probably an army officer, who for a

time ruled northern England: in later centuries he was honoured as the founder of several Welsh princely families, before finally being immortalized as the Old King Cole of the nursery rhymes.

In southern Britain, the heartland of the Roman province, the little kings had by about 425 come under the domination of one man, known to us only by his nickname of Vortigern or 'Overking'. He apparently came from the Welsh borders, and may have been a descendant of Magnus Maximus, declared 'Emperor of Britain' during the last period of Roman occupation. Vortigern found the western coast of his kingdom threatened by Irish invasion, while the north and east suffered continual raiding by seaborne Picts. Lacking a field army, he fell back on a policy of employing semi-barbarous tribesmen under their own leaders, who settled in the lands they regained from the enemy. Thus the Irish colonists in Wales were contained by King Cunedda with a force of borderers from north of Hadrian's Wall, while in the east Vortigern countered the Picts by settling a small force of Saxons, under an adventurer named Hengest, in the Isle of Thanet. Not long afterwards, more Saxons were established all along the eastern seaboard from Kent to Northumberland.

To Gildas, writing a hundred years later, Vortigern's actions in deliberately introducing within his gates 'the vile unspeakable Saxons, hated of God and man alike' seemed foolish, if not criminal. At the time, however, it appeared a relatively sensible course, for Germanic mercenaries and auxiliaries had long served in Britain with the Romans, and Hengest's followers proved effective in defending the province from what then seemed the greater menace of Pictish invasion, as well as in protecting Vortigern from his Romano-British rivals. But the time soon came when the Saxon mercenaries could be neither paid nor induced to leave. In about 442 Hengest, seeing the weakness and division of his employers and himself reinforced from across the North Sea, led his followers in a devastating attack on the old province, 'wasting town and country' in the east and raiding as far as the western sea. Despairingly the British appealed to Aetius, the Roman general in France, with a letter named 'The Groans of the Britons': 'the barbarians push us to the sea, the sea pushes us to the barbarians: between the two kinds of death we are either slain or drowned.'

Aetius, fully engaged with the hordes of Attila the Hun, could send no help, but the British counter-attacked alone, and for the next fifty years they fought more or less continuously against the Saxons and their allies the Angles and Jutes, the struggle flowing first this way and then that. In about 452 Vortimer, son of Vortigern, forced Hengest back to Thanet after a victory near the old Saxon Shore fort of Richborough, but then massive reinforcements from Germany turned the scales, and the Saxons pushed into the British heartlands. By the 460s the British forces were again achieving victories under the command of Ambrosius Aurelianus, a descendant of Roman officials chosen by the petty kings as their war-leader.

Ambrosius' successor was the famous Arthur, about whom so much has been written but so little can be firmly established. It seems probable that he too began as a war-leader, though one early source calls him 'amheradwyr' (the British form of *imperator* or emperor), and he may well have achieved rule of the whole of southern Britain by means of his victories. These are said to have numbered twelve, amongst them one in southern Scotland, probably against Picts, one in Caerleon or Chester, perhaps against the Irish, and several against the Anglo-Saxons near the east coast. Arthur's forces thus ranged wide, giving credence to the theory that he pitted fast-moving cavalry against the spear-armed barbarian infantry. His last and greatest victory, fought in about 495, was at Mount Badon, probably near Bath, where he routed the combined armies of the southern Saxons. There followed nearly half a century of relative peace, during which the Anglo-Saxons (or English, as they had begun to call themselves) were prevented from further advance, though they still held – apparently by agreement – Kent, Sussex, most of East Anglia and Lincolnshire, and parts of east Yorkshire and Northumbria.

Recent archaeological discoveries, combined with passing references in the very sparse contemporary records, give us some idea of the part played by fortifications during the first Saxon onslaught. Many Roman towns, especially those refortified by Theodosius after the 'barbarian conspiracy' of 367–69, still possessed walls formidable enough to repel enemies who knew nothing of siegecraft. One such was Verulamium, which, though uncomfortably close to the area of early English settlement, managed to hold out until at least 450, perhaps because its defences were still manned by troops who wore some form of Roman equipment and presumably maintained a semblance of the old

efficiency. The decline of urban life there, however, is demonstrated by the fact that in about 430 a corn-drying oven was dug through a fine mosaic floor in one of the principal houses, and afterwards the house itself was replaced by a barn. Paradoxically the town's piped water supply was kept in working order. Even the best Roman walls did not always prove secure, and the British population who sheltered within the old Saxon Shore fort of Pevensey were massacred to the last man by Aelle and his South Saxons, while the inhabitants of Caistor-by-Norwich may have suffered a similar fate at the hands of the East Angles.

Most Roman towns, however, were gradually abandoned rather then stormed and sacked. Conditions varied from place to place, but in general the main factors for decay were the collapse of the economy, followed by widespread famine and disease. With barbarian raiders roaming the countryside trade became impossible and farming increasingly difficult, even when (as at Verulamium) crops were stored within the city walls. The resultant famines weakened the urban population, lowering their resistance to epidemics of bubonic plague, typhus and scarlet fever. Though we shall probably never know for sure why unburied bodies lay in the main street of abandoned Cirencester in Gloucestershire, or why several unwounded people (including an old man clutching his savings) crawled to die in the heating system beneath the town baths of Wroxeter in Salop, it is fairly certain that organized urban life had come to an end in lowland Britain by about 500, and soon afterwards towns could be described by Gildas as 'squalid deserted ruins', occupied only by a few squatters.

What happened when walled towns, haunted by famine and disease, became (in the words of a contemporary, Ammianus Marcellinus) 'tombs surrounded by nets'? In some places, at least, their fleeing inhabitants (following a tendency traceable all over Europe at this time) took temporary refuge in nearby pre-Roman hill-forts, several of which, like the Caburn, were re-used during the fifth century. Other old forts, especially in western Britain, were re-occupied as the defended homesteads of the petty rulers who arose when Roman civilization, essentially urban, dissolved into chaos with the decay of the towns.

Amongst such strongholds was the Iron Age fort of Castle Dore in Cornwall, which after lying derelict since the Roman conquest was refurbished and provided with three large wooden halls within a repaired rampart. Here, it seems, flourished the

36 The Iron Age hill-fort of Castle Dore, Cornwall, re-occupied during the heroic age as the stronghold of Cynvawr, and traditionally the scene of the romance of Tristan and Isolde.

court of a certain Cynvawr or Cunomorus, whose son Drustan lies buried under an inscribed stone nearby. Thus – as so often during the heroic age – fact is inextricably mixed with legend, for the site is traditionally linked in the Welsh Annals with the Arthurian romance of Tristan (or Drustan) and his fatal love for Isolde, the wife of 'King' Mark – 'whom by another name they call Cynvawr'.

A few chieftains of this period preferred to build 37 new strongholds, like the post-Roman hill-fort at Dinas Emrys, near Beddgelert in Gwynedd, where a rocky crag was fortified with rather feeble dry-stone walls. There too legends cluster thick, for the fort is said to have been built by Vortigern, but handed over to his rival Ambrosius or Emrys – sometimes identified with Merlin – after the latter had revealed a pool containing warring dragons, symbolizing the struggle between Britons and Saxons. The dragons may be legendary, but the pool remains, as does evidence of metal-working, often associated with the households of warlords who needed armaments.

In general, the makeshift hill-forts of this period (whether new or refurbished) are both smaller and less strongly defended than their pre-Roman ancestors. A major exception to this rule is Cadbury Castle, near Wincanton in Somerset, which is associated with no less a person than Arthur himself and is traditionally the site of the legendary Camelot. Though the latter identification is open to question, there is no doubt that Cadbury was an important fortification of the heroic age, based on a strong but previously abandoned Iron Age hill-fort of the multi-ramparted Maiden Castle type. At the end of 14 the fifth century (about the time of Arthur's battles) the innermost of the four ancient banks was greatly strengthened by the addition of an entirely new rampart made of earth and rubble, held together 38 with timber framing and faced with dry-stone work. This primitive method of construction clearly relates more to prehistoric times than to the late Roman tradition of mortared stone walls, and demonstrates the extent to which Roman technology and specialist skills had fallen victim to the chaos of barbarian invasion. The mixed ancestry of Cadbury's fifth-century defences, however, appears in the new gateway: surmounted by a single wooden tower, it was similar to the type found in some small Roman auxiliary forts.

Cadbury itself is far from being small, for its defensive perimeter 1,200 yards (1,100 metres) long encloses an area of 18 acres (7.3 hectares) and is capable of accommodating a thousand men – a large army in fifth-century terms. It was quite different in purpose, therefore, from contemporary defended homesteads like Castle Dore, and Leslie Alcock, the 36 Cadbury excavator, has speculated that it was in fact the main military base and headquarters of the armies of Ambrosius Aurelianus and Arthur himself. If this is so we might expect communications with other fortresses, and sight lines would indeed carry a message by beacon from Cadbury to Glastonbury Tor and thence northwards via Brent Knoll ('burnt knoll') to the contemporary hill-fort of Dinas Powys across the Severn in south Wales.

There is no evidence that Cadbury itself was ever besieged, but some of Arthur's battles were apparently fought in or near fortifications. Castle Guinnion, the site of his eighth victory, may possibly be the Saxon Shore fort of Burgh or 31 Gariannonum; 'the City of the Legion', his ninth fight, was at Chester or Caerleon, both walled and 22 former legionary bases; and Breguoin, where the eleventh battle took place, may perhaps be identifiable with either Bremenium (High Rochester, Northumberland) or Bravonium (Leintwardine, Herefordshire), both the sites of Roman forts.

37 *The ruined dry-stone ramparts of Dinas Emrys in Snowdonia.*

38 Reconstruction of the 'Arthurian' defences of Cadbury Castle in Somerset, showing the timber-framed and stone-faced rampart with its wooden battlements and the timber and wickerwork gate-tower. (From Leslie Alcock, 'By South Cadbury is that Camelot . . .', 1972)

Arthur's last and greatest victory, at Mount Badon, is described as a siege, and one source makes it last three days. The most likely site is a hill-fort near Bath, but the Iron Age works of Liddington (near Badbury in Wiltshire) and Badbury Rings in Dorset are also possibilities. Who besieged whom, and under what circumstances, is completely unknown, but a victorious British charge played a part in the battle, and it has been suggested that Arthur was using a hill-fort as a refuge for his cavalry, it being easier for horse to charge out of a fort than into it. The other fortifications mentioned above may also have been employed in a similar way, as temporary strongholds for a mobile force which more often fought on river-crossings, where seven of Arthur's other battles took place. Such battles for fords, common during the whole of the heroic age, are said by some authorities to point to the prevalence of an essentially open and fast-moving type of warfare at this period hence, the theory runs, the general lack of formidable fortifications.

Arthur himself died in battle with fellow-Britons in about 515, a victim of the civil strife which bedevilled the last days of Celtic Britain, splitting it once again into warring kingdoms. Amongst the greatest of these was Gwynedd in north Wales, ruled by Prince Maelgwyn the Dragon, whose stronghold was the rock of Degannwy above the river Conwy. He may have claimed paramount rule over all the Britons, who now called themselves 'Combrogi' or fellow-countrymen, a name from which both Cymru – the modern Wales – and Cumbria are derived.

For a generation after Arthur's death the Saxons remained quiet, but thereafter they began a new assault on a Britain weakened by the great plague which killed Maelgwyn in 547. At first their advance was slow, but during the 550s they gained victories at Old Sarum near Salisbury and Barbury near Swindon – both the sites of ancient hill-forts, presumably now being re-used – and by 614 they had overrun southern England as far west as the Wye and the Exe.

Northern Britain, hitherto largely immune, now also felt the weight of English attack, which began when Ida, leader of a small group of Anglian settlers on the Northumberland coast, seized the rock of Bamburgh and fortified it 'first with a stockade and later with a rampart'. Nothing remains above ground

54

of Ida's defences (now covered by a magnificent if over-restored medieval castle), but they are remarkable as the only recorded instance of the construction of fortifications by the earliest English. From its base at Bamburgh the Anglian kingdom of Bernicia expanded rapidly, though successfully opposed at first by the British rulers of Rheged, whose influence dominated north-west England and whose capital was the old Roman city of Carlisle. The greatest of these were Urbgen (immortalized as Sir Urien of Arthur's Round Table) and his son Owain, who killed Ida's son Aethelric Firebrand and in the 590s led an alliance of British kingdoms which came near to driving the Bernicians into the eastern sea.

The British victory was soon marred by the old evil spirit of internal discord, for Urbgen was murdered by a jealous neighbour and his alliance broke up to allow Aethelric's son Aethelferth to overrun and destroy Rheged. The Celtic kingdoms north of Hadrian's Wall were now threatened, and in about 600 King Mynyddawg of Gododdin sent an army of picked heroes from his fortress of Dun Edin – the rock of Edinburgh – to attack Aethelferth at the old Roman fort of Catterick in North Yorkshire. In the battle which raged round the ancient ramparts the British were totally annihilated, leaving as their record one of the oldest surviving Scottish laments:

> From the army of Mynyddawg, grief unbounded,
> Of three hundred men, but one returned.

Alarmed by Anglian successes, King Aedan of Argyll now led an alliance of Scots and Ulster Irish against them, only to be crushed in his turn at the battle of Degsastan in 603.

Having become, in a startlingly short space of time, a dominant power in the north, Aethelferth absorbed his fellow-Anglians in Yorkshire and set up the kingdom of Northumbria, stretching from the Humber to the Tweed. Next he occupied the abandoned legionary base at Chester, defeating a north Welsh army sent to oppose him in 614 and severing forever the Britons of Wales from their remaining countrymen in the north. To these last remained only the kingdom of Strathclyde, covering south-west Scotland and part of Cumbria. Here the chief fortress was (like Bamburgh and Edinburgh) an

90

39

39 Dumbarton rock, 'the most strongly defended city of the Britons' and the capital of their kingdom of Strathclyde. Its natural strength guaranteed its use as a fortress up until the Napoleonic Wars, and the visible structures date from the seventeenth to nineteenth centuries.

impregnable rock, towering 240 feet (73 metres) above the confluence of the rivers Clyde and Leven: known originally as Alcluith, 'the rock of Clyde', it later became Dumbarton, 'the fort of the Britons'. Occupied since at least the fifth century BC, it remained the capital of an independent British state until 1018, when Strathclyde was reluctantly absorbed into Scotland.

Meanwhile, though Northumbria was now so strong that her rulers were recognized as overlords of all the English kingdoms in the island, the British

40 *Four stages of fortification at York. The heroic age 'Anglian Tower' (right) blocked a breach in Constantius' Roman wall (foreground, and see p. 37). These early works were then covered in turn by a Norman rampart bank (here cut away) and by a later bank supporting the thirteenth-century city wall (top).*

of Wales launched a devastating counterattack. In 633 Cadwallawn of Gwynedd, a descendant of Maelgwyn the Dragon, allied himself with the Angles of west midland Mercia and invaded Northumbria, ravaging and burning as far north as Hadrian's Wall. At one stage during the campaign the Northumbrians besieged him in 'a strong city', but he suddenly sallied out and utterly routed them. The city in question may well have been York, whose Roman walls were still defensible: at roughly this time, too, a breach in them was repaired by the construction of a small rubble-built tower, now dwarfed by the medieval defences. For all its insignificant appearance, the 'Anglian Tower' is important as virtually the only fortification of the heroic age to survive in anything like its original form: its exact date, however, is still a matter for dispute.

40

Cadwallawn's brief period of glory came to an end with his death in battle near Hexham, Northumberland, in 634, and with him died the last British hope of recovering their lost inheritance. Soon afterwards their only remaining lowland kingdom, the area round Wroxeter and Shrewsbury, fell to the English, leaving Britons ruling only in the highland zones of Wales, Strathclyde and the doomed princedoms of Devon and Cornwall. From now on the heirs of Roman Britain would forever be the 'Welsh' – the Saxon word for 'foreigners'. Their downfall had been as much due to their own faults of dissension and disunity as to the efforts of their enemies, and it was perhaps inevitable that their mounted warbands of aristocratic warriors should one day go down before the steadier infantry of a whole people in arms. The two-hundred-year-long defence of the British lowlands had nevertheless been a remarkable achievement, and even now the military successes of the Cymry – the 'fellow countrymen' – were by no means at an end.

Welsh attacks, as we must now call them, naturally fell most heavily on the English of the west midlands, the Mercians or people of the 'march' or borderlands. At the beginning of the eighth century Welsh raids penetrated as far as Lincolnshire, and in the 740s King Eliseg, a descendant of Vortigern, 'seized the inheritance of Powys' (perhaps the Shropshire lowlands) 'and held it from the power of the English for nine years with fire and sword' – an exploit proudly recorded on his memorial pillar at Llantysilio-yn-Ial, Clwyd.

To guard against such incursions, the Mercians began to build short dykes – earthwork banks and ditches – across the principal routes leading into their kingdom from the mountains. Manned by guards in times of crisis, these dykes could turn back minor raids and give warning of more serious ones. (They have parallels in the Cambridgeshire dykes which control access to the lands of the East Angles.) Next, at about the time of Eliseg's invasion, the Mercians constructed a much longer work called Wat's Dyke, running for 38 miles (60 kilometres) along the boundary of the English lowlands from the north coast of Wales at Holywell, Clwyd, to a point just beyond the hill-fort of Old Oswestry in northern Salop.

Such was the background against which Offa, greatest of the Mercian kings, 'caused a dyke to be made as a boundary between him and Wales, to enable him the more easily to withstand the attacks of his enemies . . . And it extends from one sea to the other.' The Anglo-Welsh border from the Irish Sea to the Bristol Channel is 149 miles (240 kilometres) long, and Offa's earthwork covers 81 miles (130 kilometres) of this distance, the gaps in the dyke being originally filled by impenetrable woods, marshes or rivers. Further west than Wat's Dyke, Offa's frontier line is most striking where it marches along the hillcrests of the mountainous central borderland, always positioned to give a good view towards Wales.

Offa's Dyke, easily the most impressive of Anglo-Saxon monuments, is comparable in the grandeur of its conception to Hadrian's Wall, though its form – a single bank and ditch with an average overall width of 60 feet (18 metres) – is a great deal simpler. Nevertheless the Mercian achievement, involving a massive labour force and engineering techniques capable of producing straight alignments up to 12 miles (20 kilometres) long, is a most remarkable one for a state in a far less developed condition than the Rome which built the wall. Unlike the latter, the dyke was not strictly a military defence, but rather a clearly visible frontier-line drawn up (apparently by peaceful agreement) between English and Welsh: though it would doubtless act as an obstacle to cattle-rustlers, it could clearly not be manned or defended along its whole length. The main routes into Mercia, marked by gaps in the bank and ditch, could however be controlled by frontier guards, who may also have patrolled the dyke on horseback to give notice of approaching raiders.

When King Offa died in 796 his frontier was virtually complete, but by now events were stirring which would shortly relegate the struggles of Welsh and English to a subordinate place in British history. The first sign of the new danger came quite unexpectedly in 787, when the Anglo-Saxon Chronicle records that the King's Reeve of West Saxon Dorchester heard that three strange ships had landed at Portland on the Dorset coast. Taking a few men with him, he rode to meet the foreign merchants (as he supposed them to be) and escort them to the King. Instead, the strangers slaughtered him and all his men, for they were Norwegians from Hardanger fjord, 'the first ships of the Northmen to come into England'. The Vikings – men of the *viks* or fjords – had begun as they meant to go on, and during the next three centuries no-one would again mistake them for peaceful visitors.

1 The massive Iron Age hill-fort of Old Oswestry, Salop, an isolated hill entirely surrounded by multiple banks and ditches (p. 8). Abandoned under the Romans, and re-occupied by fifth-century squatters (p. 41), it formed the southern anchor of the eighth-century Wat's Dyke (p. 47).

2 The Devil's Dyke, part of the western defences of Cassivellaunus' great oppidum at Wheathampstead, Hert-fordshire (pp. 16, 18), stormed by Julius Caesar in 54 BC.

3 Corfe in Dorset, a favourite royal castle developed and beautified by successive medieval kings and slighted by Parliament after the Civil War siege (p. 183). Henry I's great tower-keep stands at its centre, flanked by King John's western bailey and private apartments (p. 90), while the southern bailey (foreground) was walled by Henry III and given its drum-towered gatehouse by Edward I.

4 A view across the Swindale beck of Brough Castle in Cumbria, on the site of the Roman fort of Verterae. William the Lion of Scotland stormed its untowered bailey wall (left) in 1174 (pp. 88–89) and destroyed the keep on whose foundations the present great tower now stands.

5 Dover Castle, the 'key of England', from the north-east. On the left is Henry II's great keep, and just to the right of it two of the mural towers of the inner bailey are grouped to form the King's Gate (p. 89). Beyond are the concentric defences of the outer bailey, and on the extreme right stands the Constable's Gate, raised by Henry III (p. 92). In the foreground are reminders of a more recent threat, 'dragon's teeth' tank obstacles of 1940.

6 The view from Tutshill – 'the look-out's hill' – of Chepstow Castle, Gwent. In the foreground are the gatehouse and lower bailey built by the sons and grandson of William the Marshal (p. 98 and ill. 70) and beyond are the Marshal's own middle bailey tower and fitz Osbern's Norman keep (p. 95 and ill. 67), flanked on the far side by the upper bailey.

7 The fortified town and castle of Caernarfon, Gwynedd, overlooking the Menai Strait. Intended by Edward I as the capital of conquered north Wales, Caernarfon was at once the fulfilment of a Welsh legend and the embodiment of a Roman imperial past, and the 'Golden Gate' of the town (centre) and the tile-banded and triple-turretted Eagle Tower of the castle (right) were both intended to recall Constantinople (see pp. 105–106).

8 The fortress-tower of St Cynllo's church at Llanbister in the hills of central Powys, one of many such built along the troubled Welsh border (p. 108). Now topped by a wooden belfry, the tower was originally one or two storeys higher.

9 Edward I's fortified town of Conwy from the north-west corner of its walls with the upper town gateway in the foreground. In the distance is the castle, whose turretted inner ward overlooks the estuary (see pp. 104–105).

10 The triangular red sandstone castle of Caerlaverock, Dumfries (p. 113). It suffered many sieges, including a famous one in 1300 (p. 115), and the keep-gatehouse was several times rebuilt, gaining its narrow entrance and machicolated tower-tops during the fifteenth century and its wide-mouthed gunloops in the sixteenth.

11 The almost impregnable castle of Dunnottar, Grampian, built on the site of a Pictish promontory fort (p. 127). The only landward approach is by a narrow path (foreground) which drops almost to the sea before climbing to the heavily-defended gateway (ill. 132) and the L-shaped tower-house keep of 1394 (centre). The last Scottish fortress to hold out against the Parliamentarians during the Civil War, it was finally reduced by mortar-fire (p. 188).

12 Some of the wall-paintings in the Great Chamber of Longthorpe tower, near Peterborough (p. 142 and ill. 118), probably executed c. 1330. At top left is a hermit (perhaps St Anthony) watching a young man making a withy basket and another praying, with God the Father in the clouds above: below is a seated philosopher teaching a pupil. On the right-hand wall a pair of Apostles stand above two fenland birds.

13 The gatehouse of Daundelyon Manor near Margate in Kent, wasp-striped in flint and yellow Thanet brick, was built by the disreputable John Daundelyon c. 1440 to ward off foreign raiders and local rivals. Notice the cross-loops and round gunports flanking the entrance (p. 135).

14 The mouth of Dartmouth haven in Devon, showing several generations of defences. Far left is the ruined wall of a fourteenth-century 'fortalice' (p. 134), with a Victorian battery re-used in 1940 below it. Just to the right, by the church, is the earliest artillery fort in Britain, begun in 1481 (p. 136). In the foreground is the companion fort of Kingswear 'Castle', with its lower cannon ports clearly visible.

15 The great hall of Lord Cromwell's luxurious fortified mansion at South Wingfield, Derbyshire, begun c. 1440, seen from the refuge tower (p. 150). Notice the battlemented porch and the oriel window lighting the high table.

16 The sixteenth-century tower-house at Corgarff, Gram-pian, where Lady Forbes and her household were burnt alive in 1571 (p. 168). Its loopholed and star-shaped curtain wall was added after the 'Forty-five, when it became a fortified barracks guarding the Pass of Lecht (background) and the military road from Fort George to Blairgowrie.

17 Yanwath Hall, Cumbria, demonstrates how a fortified manor house near the Anglo-Scottish border developed and softened over the years. The tower (left) is of the fourteenth century, and the hall-block (with its traceried bow window to light the high table) was added during the fifteenth, while the extension to the right and the mullioned window in the tower are Elizabethan.

18 The elegant bridge, built in 1733, carrying one of General Wade's military roads over the Tay at Aberfeldy. The plaque on the parapet records Wade's road-building, intended to give government troops access to the potentially Jacobite Highlands but also earning the thanks of more peaceful travellers:

Had you seen these roads before they were made
You would lift up your hands and bless General Wade.

19 The fairy-tale castle of Craigievar, Grampian, with its riot of turrets, domes and gables. One of the last Scottish tower-houses, it was completed for William Forbes, a successful Baltic trader, in 1626 (see pp. 173–74).

20 The finest British fortification of the age of smooth-bored artillery, Fort George juts into the Moray Firth near Inverness. Built in 1748–69 as part of the final solution to the problem of the Jacobite Highlands, it never saw action. For the plan and description see p. 194.

5

6

7

8

9

10

11

12

14

13

17   18   19

41 *A tombstone at Lindisfarne Priory,*
Northumberland, said to depict the
Vikings who ravaged the place in 793.

5 'The fury of the Northmen', 800–1066

. . . from the fury of the Northmen, Good Lord deliver us.

NINTH-CENTURY PRAYER

At the time of the first serious Viking raids in the early ninth century, England was enjoying a period of comparative peace and prosperity. It was not yet one nation, being divided amongst the large kingdoms of Northumbria, Mercia and Wessex and several lesser states – East Anglia, Middlesex, Essex, Sussex, Surrey and Kent. Despite frequent minor wars between these kingdoms (from which Wessex was emerging as the dominant power), England was at this time a land largely without effective fortifications, for the early English were not by tradition fortress-builders, seeming generally to have contented themselves with rudimentary defences like the wooden stockade which the Northumbrian kings built near their summer palace at Yeavering, Northumberland. Nor did the pagan Saxons often re-use Roman sites (which they viewed with suspicion as the work of giants and the haunts of ghosts and demons), though several of the earliest Christian missionaries chose abandoned Saxon Shore forts as the sites of their first churches. One such still stands at Reculver, and Richborough, Burgh and Bradwell also served as spiritual fortresses of the new faith, to which all the English kingdoms had been converted by about 685. Their Celtic neighbours in Scotland and Wales, though long since Christianized, were no better physically protected, for there too fortifications were sparse and rudimentary.

It was, then, on a comparatively defenceless Britain that the initial Viking attacks fell. These formed part of the great Scandinavian expansion of the eighth to eleventh centuries, which took Norwegians, Swedes and Danes to Russia and Constantinople or westwards to Iceland, Greenland and the coast of America. Its root causes are still not fully understood, but overpopulation, land-hunger and political upheaval all played a part, combined perhaps with a basic lust for adventure. Its instruments were the finest sea-going ships of the age, steered by unrivalled navigators.

The first raiders to reach Britain were Norwegians tired of scratching a living from their narrow mountain farmlands. It was they who killed the Reeve of Dorchester in 787, and who in 793 attacked Lindisfarne, the Holy Island of Northumbria, slaying monks and nuns and plundering shrines. The horror with which they were regarded may be reflected in a contemporary Lindisfarne tombstone, which shows men advancing with swords and axes raised.

The main force of the Norwegian attack, however, fell on Scotland, where colonies were founded in the Orkneys, Shetlands and Hebrides as well as the northern mainland, and Ireland, which the Norwegians effectively dominated for over a century.

A greater menace to England, and one which nearly overwhelmed her, came from the Danish Vikings, who began large-scale raiding in about 835 and thereafter descended in increasing numbers on the undefended coastline. In 850 a force of Danes wintered in the Isle of Thanet instead of returning home, and in the following year an army of no less than 350 ships' companies – probably over 10,000 men – stormed Canterbury and London. According to the Anglo-Saxon Chronicle, this particular force was defeated at Ockley in Surrey by King Aethelwulf of Wessex 'with the greatest slaughter of the heathen men that we ever heard tell of'; but more often than not the Vikings routed the local levies which, in the absence of a co-ordinated system of national defence, were the only opposition to their unpredictable attacks.

The situation became still more serious in 865, when the first of the Danish 'Great Armies' appeared, led by Ivar the Boneless and Halfdan, the sons of the notorious Ragnar Leatherbreeches. Such armies, consisting of thousands of professional warriors, were no mere seasonal raiders, but were organized for systematic plunder over a period of years. Each autumn they would seize and fortify a defensible position and (having mounted themselves on stolen horses) set about ravaging the surrounding countryside until it was quite devastated or until the inhabitants bribed them heavily to desist. Next autumn they moved to winter quarters in a new area, and in the following spring the whole process began again.

Danish winter bases were usually established on or near navigable rivers, which provided access for shipborne reinforcements and also a means of escape should the Vikings be seriously threatened. Easily defended sites, like mid-stream islands, would be chosen when possible, and the Danes also made use of the stone Roman walls of York (occupied in 866), Exeter (seized in 876), and deserted Chester (in 893). For the most part, however, their camps – of which no substantial remains survive – must have been defended by stout wooden palisades, perhaps accompanied by a ditch. Simple though these fortresses were, they were apparently effective, for

42

41

42 *All but swept away by the sea, the ruins of King Egbert of Kent's church at Reculver, founded in 669 and adorned with twin towers in the twelfth century, stand within the walls (foreground) of the Roman fort of Regulbium (see p. 34).*

the English only rarely attempted to storm them, perhaps because they were resolutely defended by large numbers of men.

By 877 the whole eastern half of England was in the power of the Great Army, which had colonized Northumbria and reduced Mercia to a puppet kingdom. Only Wessex, through a combination of bribes and hard fighting, remained free, and in January 878 it too was overrun by an unexpected midwinter attack. Its king, Alfred son of Aethelwulf, took refuge in the inaccessible marshes around Athelney in Somerset, where he built himself a stronghold and engaged the Danes in guerrilla warfare. The example of his resistance (combined with the morale-boosting capture of the magic raven banner of Ragnar) enabled Alfred to gather together a new West Saxon army in the early summer, and with this he inflicted a major defeat on the Danes at Edington in Wiltshire. After a two-week blockade of their fortress at Chippenham, the Vikings surrendered, not only agreeing to leave Wessex but also allowing their leaders to be baptized as Christians.

Edington, the first major reverse suffered by the Great Army, proved to be a turning point in the war, for in showing that the Danes could be decisively beaten it inspired the English with new hope. A few years later, for example, the men of Rochester stood firm behind their Roman walls against a Viking attack, fighting off the besiegers until a relief force drove them in disorder to their ships. Alfred's successes, however, gained him no more than a breathing space, for the remnants of the Great Army still held much of England, while a new force of Danes hovered about the Channel and threatened the south-east.

The King therefore set about ensuring that Wessex should never again be completely overrun. First he laid the foundations of a royal navy, constructing ships that were not only bigger but faster and steadier than those of the Vikings, whom the English now began to attack at sea. Next – prompted perhaps by the success of the resistance at Rochester and of his own operations from Athelney – he initiated a system of national defence based on fortified towns. Each of these *burhs* (later 'boroughs') was intended to be 'a fortress for all the folk' of the surrounding countryside, behind whose walls they could shelter from enemy raiders.

It was only just, therefore, that the new fortresses should be built, maintained, and garrisoned by the 'folk' they were to defend, and the villages protected by a burh were required to provide men for this task, on the basis of one man for each 'hide' of land (about 40 acres, or 16 hectares) the village contained. Each of these militiamen was responsible for repairing and manning just over 4 feet (about 1.25 metres) of wall, so that 160 hides of land, representing about 30 small villages, would provide defenders for 220 yards (200 metres) of fortifications. The number of hides assigned to a burh varied, of course, with the size of the fortress.

The design of burhs also varied widely. Some, like Bath, Exeter and Portchester, were based on repaired Roman defences. Others, such as Lydford in Devon, Christchurch in Hampshire and Burpham in Sussex, were constructed, like prehistoric promontory forts, by building an earthwork rampart across the neck of a steep-sided headland. Others again, like Wareham in Dorset or Oxford and Wallingford in Oxfordshire, were rectangular, being defended by an earthwork bank faced with wood or stone and surrounded by a deep ditch. Where possible, the area inside the walls was divided into residential plots, whose gridlike pattern survives in the modern layout of both Wareham and Wallingford. Here merchants and tradesmen were encouraged to settle, and burhs frequently developed into prosperous market towns with permanent inhabitants ready to assist in their defence.

The construction of burhs had probably begun by about 890, and within a decade or so no village in Wessex, Surrey or Sussex was more than 20 miles (some 30 kilometres) from a place of refuge. Alfred's system apparently proved successful in discouraging Viking attacks on his kingdom, for the new Danish Great Army which landed in 892 ravaged mainly in the midlands. There the newcomers encountered stiff resistance, and their fortified camps were frequently stormed or surrounded and starved out by Alfred and his allies. Among the more spectacular English successes was the capture of the entire Danish fleet, which was trapped on the river Lea in Hertfordshire: a boom, strung between forts on either bank, was thrown across the river downstream from the enemy ships, whose crews were forced to make off overland.

By the end of Alfred's reign in 899 England was safe from Viking domination, and the next twenty-five years saw an English offensive which reasserted control over all the Danish-occupied lands south of the Humber. This was the work of Alfred's son Edward and of his daughter Aethelfleda, the remarkable 'Lady of the Mercians' who planned her own campaigns and led her army in person. The struggle was very much a war of fortresses, for the English consolidated their gains with strategically placed new burhs, while the Danish settlers, now on the defensive, began to fortify the towns in their own lands east of Watling Street. At Hertford, Bedford, Buckingham, Stamford, Nottingham and elsewhere, King Edward (remembering the capture of the Viking fleet) built twin riverside forts to control strategic waterways, and his sister guarded the entrances to Mercia with burhs at Bridgnorth on the Severn crossing and Runcorn at the mouth of the Mersey. Overlaid by later buildings, the Saxon walls of these towns are no longer visible, save for the remains at Witham in Essex, blocking the old Roman road to London from Danish East Anglia. They must, however, have been strongly built and well defended, for they repeatedly held off enemy attacks, while their Danish counterparts, including Roman-walled Colchester, were one by one reduced to English rule.

Edward's successors, now undoubted kings of all England, had completed the reconquest of their country by the 950s, when they subdued Erik Bloodaxe's Norwegian kingdom based on York. Comparatively little is heard of fortifications during these campaigns, and though established burhs may have been kept in repair no new ones are known to have been built. The Scandinavian threat to Britain seemed to be fast receding.

It revived in full strength, however, towards the end of the tenth century, during the disastrous reign of the weak and incompetent Aethelred Unraed – 'Aethelred No-counsel' rather than 'Aethelred the Unready'. Under his spiritless leadership English resistance collapsed before the onslaught of successive Viking armies, culminating in 1013–16 in a full-scale invasion by King Sweyn Forkbeard of Denmark and his son Canute. The annals of this time are full of sacked or surrendered burhs, whose collapse may have been as much due to the demoralization of their defenders as to the dilapidation of their walls. Aethelred did indeed build some new fortresses, including one at Cadbury on the site of Arthur's old stronghold, but these were short-lived and soon abandoned. Only London, the key-point of the war, beat off attack after Danish attack, even when the Vikings encircled it with a blockading earthwork. Its resistance, however, was ultimately in vain, for in 1016 Canute displaced the heirs of Aethelred to become the first Danish king of England, which for the next twenty-five years formed part of a Scandinavian empire.

43
44

43, 44 *King Alfred's rectangular burh at Wareham,
Dorset. The air view, from the north, shows the earthen
ramparts and the grid-pattern of the planned Saxon town
still surviving. Below: the north-east corner of the*
*ramparts (at the left in the air view), once faced in stone,
with the river Piddle forming an additional defence beyond.
The ancient earthworks were re-used during the Civil War,
when Wareham was held by the Royalists (p. 180).*

The heirs of Alfred were restored in 1042 in the person of Edward 'the Confessor', the half-Norman younger son of Aethelred Unraed, but when the saintly Edward died childless in January 1066 the succession again became an open question. The choice of the English council fell on Earl Harold Godwinson, a powerful nobleman who, though not of the blood royal, was a popular and successful general. Such a warrior-king was needed, for two mighty foreign rulers, King Harald Hardrada ('Hard Ruler') of Norway and Duke William the Bastard of Normandy, were preparing to assert their right to the English throne by force. Hardrada, the last of the great Vikings, saw himself as the successor of Canute, while William had a rather better claim to be the chosen heir of his cousin the Confessor.

The short reign of Harold Godwinson, therefore, was mainly taken up with measures for national defence. Seeing the Normans as the greatest threat, the King concentrated his fleet off the Isle of Wight and stationed his large army – the pick of the county levies stiffened with noblemen and professional 'housecarles' – along the Channel coast. Fortifications, however, played little part in his plans: no new ones were built, and the old system of garrisoning burhs with local militia had fallen into disuse during the Confessor's long and comparatively peaceful reign. Throughout the summer the defenders watched and waited, but as autumn drew near an extraordinary series of misfortunes began to dog the English when their bored levies ran out of supplies. No power on earth could keep them at their posts, and on 8 September the army was disbanded and the navy sent back to London, losing many of its ships to the northerly gales which were now the only obstacle in the way of Duke William's invasion fleet. Even as his forces broke up, Harold learnt that the same northerly winds had carried Hardrada across the North Sea, and that a massive Norwegian army was ravaging Yorkshire.

Raising what troops he could, the King marched northward to deal with the new threat, but meanwhile Hardrada defeated the levies of Northumbria and Mercia and made terms with the still basically Scandinavian town of York. The speed of Harold's advance, however, took the Vikings by surprise as they lay resting at Stamford Bridge to the east of York, and on 25 September 1066, after a hard and bloody fight, Hardrada was defeated.

Two days later, as ill-luck would have it, the Channel winds changed direction, and the Norman fleet at last set sail, landing unopposed at the derelict Saxon Shore fort of Pevensey and shortly afterwards moving eastward to Hastings. On hearing the news, Harold at once turned his battered and depleted forces southward and marched with startling speed to London, picking up some reinforcements on the way. Without pausing until the levies of the more distant shires could join him, he made straight for Hastings, ill-advisedly hoping to repeat the surprise he had achieved at Stamford Bridge. But the Normans marched out to meet him 'at the hoar apple tree', and by the evening of 14 October 1066 the English infantry had been utterly routed by the mounted knights and massed archers of William the Conqueror.

45 *Archbishop William of Corbeil's mighty keep at Rochester, Kent, from the north-east, showing the attached forebuilding (centre) guarding the entrance. Begun under Henry I in 1127 (pp. 82–83), it fell to King John's miners in 1215 (p. 90).*

6 'All the land filled with castles': the Normans, 1066–1154

. . . they filled the whole land with these castles; and when the castles were built they filled them with devils and wicked men.

ANGLO-SAXON CHRONICLE FOR 1137

The Normans' victory at Hastings was complete, but it was very far from guaranteeing them the mastery of England, for Harold's beaten army constituted only a proportion – albeit an important one – of the military capacity of a nation whose potentially hostile population numbered nearly a million and a half. For the task of conquest, moreover, William commanded no more than 7,000 men, a force no greater than a large Viking raiding party (such as that from which the Normans themselves were descended) and one which compares most unfavourably with the 40,000 soldiers available to the Romans. Yet in the two months after Hastings he overran south-eastern England, entered London, and had himself crowned king. Thereafter four short years of campaigning served to crush permanently all English resistance and to establish an alien ruling class whose security was only really threatened by disputes within itself.

Such a remarkable achievement clearly requires explanation. Politically, the roots of the English collapse lay in a kind of national defeatism, reminiscent of the attitude current in France during the fall of that country in 1940. Saxon chroniclers record endless indecision and delay 'until matters went from bad to worse, as everything did in the end', and state that resistance was pointless 'for God would not remedy matters because of our sins'. Nor did any great leader emerge to encourage them. The earls of Mercia and Northumbria were still recovering from their mauling by Hardrada, and though the nobility chose a new king in Prince Edgar (the Confessor's great-nephew) he proved too young and inexperienced to deal with the situation, while his advisers were only too ready to throw in their lot with the invader.

But even a well-led and determined nation might have been daunted by the military problems which now faced the English. Their armies, in the old Germanic tradition, invariably fought on foot with axe and sword, the principal tactic being to meet the enemy hand to hand and beat hell out of him. Little use was made of archers or cavalry, though horses were often ridden to the battlefield. Such old-fashioned methods, effective enough against Vikings who fought in much the same way, proved quite inadequate against the new invaders and the military innovations they brought from Latin Europe. Most immediately devastating of these were the mail-clad knights who formed the kernel and

striking force of William's army. Mounted on heavy warhorses and armed with lances, they could deliver a crashing charge which would break all but the steadiest infantry, especially if these had suffered a preliminary volley of arrows from the Norman archers and crossbowmen. Harold's defeat at Hastings had shown that even the best-led and bravest Saxon infantry could not cope with the combination of archers and heavy cavalry, and in open warfare William's fast-moving mounted force would be virtually impossible to counter with foot-soldiers alone.

Against good fortifications, however, cavalry would be next to useless, and behind defences the dogged Saxon infantry would come into their own. Yet, whether because of a failure of morale or because the old system of garrisoning and maintaining them had irreparably broken down, the English signally failed to make effective use of the fortresses they certainly possessed in the form of Alfredian burhs. During all the campaigns of the conquest only one town – Exeter – put up a serious resistance to the Normans, holding out against storming parties for eighteen days and surrendering only on favourable terms (see p. 75). Had other strong places followed this example, William's advance must have been much less swift and triumphant than it was, and might even have become altogether bogged down in a series of sieges. But this was not to be, and the failure of English fortifications was probably the greatest military factor in the national collapse.

Ordericus Vitalis, a principal chronicler of the Conquest, is more specific, ascribing the English defeat to their lack of one particular type of fortification: 'For the strongholds which the French call castles were very few in England, and for this reason the English, though warlike and courageous, were too weak to resist their enemies.' What the chronicler meant by a 'castle' had better be defined at once (borrowing a phrase from Professor Allen Brown) as 'a strongly fortified residence belonging to one man', be he king, baron or knight. In this it differed from the majority of earlier fortifications in Britain, which were either communal fortresses 'for all the folk' (like prehistoric hill-forts or Saxon burhs) or strongholds belonging to the state (like Roman forts). The castle's antecedents, rather, were the fortresses of Dark Age princes, places like Castle Dore or Dinas Emrys. Like them, it had its origins in a period of anarchy, that which followed the break-

46 *The motte of Drogo de Bevrière's castle of Skipsea,
North Humberside (see p. 80), built in 1086 on a natural
island surrounded by a marshy lake, seen from the bailey to*
*which it was originally connected by a causeway. In the left
background is the partly contemporary parish church,
reflecting the interdependence of priest and lord.*

down of the Frankish empire of Charlemagne, when
'private' fortresses grew up as the power of the
central state declined.

Though this definition as a private (rather than
communal or public) fortress is valid for the castles
of all periods, their actual form and construction
went through many changes during the five centuries of their heyday. All included one or both of
the characteristic features of castle construction: the
fortified enclosure, usually called the bailey, and the
strong citadel, also called the great tower, keep or
donjon – a name afterwards mutated to 'dungeon'
and applied to the prisons such towers often
contained. We shall see that at some times and places
the keep appears without the bailey (as in the peel-
towers of the Scottish border), or the bailey without
the keep (as in some of Edward III's Welsh castles),
but more often than not the two are employed in
concert. This was the case, indeed, in the first castles
which concern us, the 'motte and bailey' type which
played such a large part in the Norman conquest of
England.

The most important feature of these castles is the
motte, constructed like a sand-castle by digging a
circular ditch and throwing the excavated earth
inwards to form a steep-sided conical mound. Built
up and levelled off with extra material brought from

elsewhere, the motte might reach a height of 40 feet
(12 metres) or more, with its base defended by the
encircling ditch. Such artificial hillocks are common
in most parts of Britain: good examples are at Skipsea
in Humberside and Almeley in Herefordshire. The
Bayeux Tapestry shows one in course of construction, the layers of earth and rammed stones by
which it was raised being clearly seen.

The flattened top of the mound, whose area varied
from about 30 feet (9 metres) across to an exceptional
size of half an acre (2,000 square metres), would be
defended by a wooden palisade. Sometimes this
alone was considered sufficient protection, but
frequently a wooden tower was built within it, from
whose upper storey the defenders could shower
missiles on the heads of attackers. On occasions the
tower was raised on stilts to give room for manœuvre
underneath it, an arrangement which can also be
seen in the Bayeux Tapestry. The motte, then, was
the defensive kernel of the castle, and its defences
would protect the residence and headquarters of the
fortress's commander.

In the very smallest castles a motte might stand
alone, but most garrisons would require more room –
not least for their horses and stores – than the
cramped area on its palisaded top could afford. To
provide such accommodation, a more or less flat

73

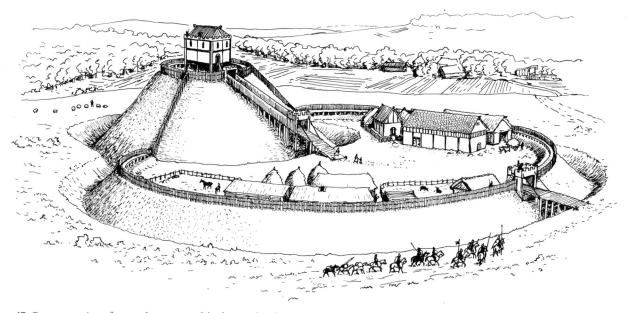

47 Reconstruction of an early motte-and-bailey castle, showing the hall, chapel and farm-buildings in the bailey, a drawbridge over the motte ditch, and a wooden keep raised on stilts crowning the motte.

47 enclosure or bailey was constructed at the foot of the motte, defended by its own ditch, bank and palisade. Occasionally the bailey surrounded the motte, but more often it was placed to one side of it, the palisade being continued up the sides of the mound until it joined the defences at the top. Larger castles might have two or even three baileys grouped round a central motte. However matters were arranged, the bailey would add to the defensive strength of the castle by keeping the attackers at a distance. Should it be hard-pressed, its defenders could retire to the motte-top, there to hurl defiance and missiles at an enemy now faced with a separate assault operation. Nor was this made easy for him, for communication between the two parts of the castle was either by an easily defensible drawbridge over the motte ditch, or
49 by a narrow 'flying bridge' thrown from the bailey straight to the top of the mound, as shown in the Bayeux Tapestry. This somewhat precarious gangway, usually supported on piles or stilts, could easily be held by a few defenders, or even demolished by them if circumstances so dictated.

Thus far we have concentrated on the defensive aspects of the motte and bailey, but we must not forget that, like a Roman fort, it could also be used as an instrument of conquest and offence. It was relatively quick and easy to construct (some of the Conqueror's castles are supposed to have been completed in a matter of weeks) and, once estab-

lished, its garrison of mounted knights could dominate the country for miles around, retiring on their fortified base if seriously threatened.

The use of the castle in both offence and defence must have been fully familiar to Duke William at the time of the Conquest, for by then he already had twenty years' experience of campaigning in castle-ridden Normandy. On the other hand, despite some recent controversy, it seems clear that the motte and bailey had never been adopted by the conservative Saxons, whose tradition of fortification was the communal burh. This is not to say that there were no castles at all in Britain before 1066, for some certainly existed on the Welsh border, where they had been established by Norman knights in the service of Edward the Confessor. Among them was Richard's Castle in Herefordshire, near Ludlow, built by a certain Richard fitz Scrob in about 1051; its overgrown and now shapeless motte still survives, perhaps the earliest of its type this side of the Channel. These few pre-Conquest castles were apparently much resented by the English, mainly because of the high-handed behaviour of their occupants, who 'inflicted all the insults and injuries they possibly could on the King's men'. In the years after Hastings, when the motte and bailey became the symbol and proof of Norman rule and Saxon subjugation, the alien castles which spread throughout the land would be hated a great deal more.

The process by which the Normans 'filled all the land with castles' was the most intensive programme of fortress-building Britain had yet experienced, and indeed the greatest she was to see until the Second World War. It began only a few hours after William's landing at Pevensey, when he ordered the repair of the old Saxon Shore fort there with 'a very strong rampart' to protect his bridgehead. Soon afterwards the invaders built their first entirely new fortification, the motte and bailey at Hastings illustrated in the Bayeux Tapestry. After the defeat of Harold garrisons were left in both these places while the Normans, cautiously hugging the coastline, marched eastwards to Dover. There the garrison of the English burh (built within an Iron Age hill-fort) capitulated at once, and William built and manned another fortress on the precipitous clifftop. Having received the surrender of Canterbury, he rested his troops at 'the Broken Tower' – probably the Saxon Shore fort at Richborough – before moving inland to probe at London with a small force of knights.

When they were repulsed, William began a march designed to isolate London by devastating a wide belt of country all around it. These 'blitzkrieg' tactics succeeded brilliantly, and the towns in the Norman path surrendered without a blow being struck. Even the strong burh of Wallingford offered no resistance when William crossed the Thames there, and he threw up a motte within the Saxon defences before marching into Hertfordshire to cut London's communications with the north. He had got no further than Berkhampstead (where another castle was built) when Prince Edgar's government capitulated and William entered London, to be crowned there on Christmas Day 1066.

The programme of castle-building continued uninterrupted. Two fortresses, one on the site of the Tower, were constructed to control the 'fierce and numerous' Londoners, and in the early months of 1067 the new King moved about the southern counties, founding castles as he went and garrisoning them with his most trusted followers. By March he felt secure enough to visit Normandy, leaving the care of England to Bishop Odo of Bayeux and Earl William fitz Osbern, 'the first and greatest of the oppressors of the English people': these two, noted the Anglo-Saxon chronicler gloomily, 'built castles far and wide throughout the land . . . and things went ever from bad to worse.'

Not all the English, however, surrendered without a fight, and when the Conqueror returned at the end of 1067 he was faced with a four-year-long series of risings brought about (according to a Norman

48 The building of the Conqueror's castle at Hastings, from the eleventh-century Bayeux Tapestry, showing the successive layers of rammed earth and stones by which the motte was raised, and the stylized palisade on its summit.

writer) partly by the brutality and exactions of the garrisons of the new castles. First to revolt was Exeter, which manned its Roman and Saxon defences and refused either to admit William or to swear allegiance to him, even when he publicly blinded a hostage outside their gates. The townsmen replied in a vulgar but graphic way, standing on the walls and farting at the besiegers 'pro contemptu Normannorum', and for eighteen days they beat off both storming parties and attempts to undermine their defences. They eventually surrendered on surprisingly generous terms, though William ordered the building of a strong castle within the town walls to ensure its future loyalty.

The suppression of further revolts during 1068 is marked by the foundation of castles at Warwick, Nottingham and York, the last being the centre of a particularly strong anti-Norman movement. There William raised a great motte over a prehistoric burial mound, before returning to London via Lincoln, Huntingdon and Cambridge, at each of which he constructed castles to secure the road to the north. It was as well that he did so, for that area was by no means subdued yet. Early in 1069 the Northumbrians penned their new Norman earl in a house at Durham and burnt him alive, and then set out to recover York. But the castle held out, and by a forced march William dispersed the rebels and relieved it, building a second and reinforcing motte (the Old Baile) on the opposite side of the river Ouse.

Later in the same year, however, York was the scene of a third northern rising. This was potentially the most dangerous of all, for it was supported by a large army of Vikings sent by King Sweyn of Denmark, to whom the rebels had offered the English crown. The garrisons of York's two castles, ill-advisedly sallying out of their defences, were cut down to the last man, and the fortresses themselves were then destroyed, for the rebels would not make use of the hated symbols of Norman rule. On the news of the Anglo-Danish victory other parts of England raised the standard of revolt, and for a while the Conqueror's hold on the nation was (for the first and only time) severely shaken. But now William's castles proved their usefulness, and Exeter, Montacute in Somerset and Shrewsbury all successfully withstood sieges, buying time for the Norman forces to destroy the rebels piecemeal. The most dangerous concentration, an Anglo-Welsh army led by Wild Edric of Mercia, was defeated at Stafford by the King himself, who then turned his attention to his enemies in Yorkshire.

By buying off the Danes, he was able to regain York and defeat the Northumbrian English, following up his victory by devastating their lands with such systematic ferocity that twenty years afterwards the north was still a depopulated wasteland. At the end of 1071, five years after Hastings, all English resistance was at an end, and the Normans could set about consolidating their conquest. During the years of crisis at least thirty-three castles had been built, and the remaining sixteen years of the Conqueror's reign, from 1071 to 1087, saw this number nearly tripled as the Normans set up a defence in depth against a renewed English rising or the more dangerous possibility of a fresh Danish invasion on behalf of the heirs of Canute.

By the end of the reign castles were fairly evenly spread over southern and midland England, with concentrations on the border with the unconquered Welsh (see Chapter 8) and along the vulnerable south and east coasts. They were scarcer north of the Humber, though some were built there to support periodical operations against the Scots. Since they were frequently constructed to control roads, river-crossings or other strategic features of changeless importance, it was inevitable that several Norman castles should occupy the sites of earlier fortifications, whose remaining defences were incorporated in the new works. At Old Sarum in Wiltshire, for instance, the ramparts of an Iron Age hill-fort formed the bailey walls of the castle, and at Pevensey the Roman defences served the same purpose, while at Wallingford, Wareham and Lydford in Devon, to name but a few cases, castles were built within Saxon burhs. Others took advantage of natural features, like Chepstow on the Welsh border or Bamburgh in Northumberland, on their towering rocks, or Skipsea in Humberside, whose motte stands on what was once an island in a lake.

172 43 6 54 46

49 The siege of Dinan in Brittany, from the Bayeux Tapestry, showing in profile the stylized bank and ditch round the base of the motte, a 'flying bridge' (p. 74), the wooden palisade with two besiegers attempting to fire it, and a curious keep on stilts.

50 The shell-keep at Restormel in Cornwall, built c.1200, with a stone gateway (centre) belonging to the earlier wooden palisade defences of c.1100.

When castles were built within existing towns dwellings were ruthlessly swept away to accommodate them, and at Lincoln 166 houses were destroyed in this way. To add insult to injury, the Normans used the pre-Conquest laws providing for the repair of burhs as an excuse to conscript forced labour for castle building, so that the English found themselves compelled to raise the instruments of their oppression with their own hands. This 'castle-work' was a particular grievance, the basis of the Saxon chronicler's lament that William

> . . . caused castles to be built
> Which were a sore burden to the poor.
> A hard man was the King.

The great majority of the castles built under the Conqueror and his successors were of the motte and bailey type, but as time went by their defences became more sophisticated than the wooden palisades and towers described earlier. Wooden defences, while convenient enough for a hastily constructed campaign fort, had many disadvantages, and it is significant that none of them has survived above ground. They were extremely vulnerable to attack by fire: the besiegers of Dinan shown in the

Bayeux Tapestry are seen igniting the castle palisade with burning torches. Such attacks could sometimes be countered by soaking the woodwork or laying wet skins over it, but even in peacetime timber structures (and especially those parts embedded in the soil) were liable to rot and need replacement within a comparatively short space of time.

The best way out of these difficulties was to build – or rebuild – the defences of the motte in stone: Restormel Castle in Cornwall is an example of one way in which this was done. When originally built to guard the crossing of the river Fowey its motte was defended by the usual wooden palisade, though even then the entrance seems to have been guarded by a stone gateway, seen in the foreground. Some time later the palisade was replaced by a circular masonry wall, producing a hollow 'shell-keep' protecting wooden buildings within it. Finally, in about the thirteenth century, these timber buildings were themselves rebuilt in stone.

Another improvement would be to replace the timber tower or keep on the motte with a stone one, which might be round or rectangular. In many cases, however, the artificial mound was too unstable a foundation for a heavy stone keep, and it was built at

49

50

51 The Conqueror's great 'Tower of London', with the
projecting apse of its chapel on the right and its only two
unrestored Norman windows on the extreme left of the top
storey. The surrounding double curtain wall and towers are
of the twelfth and thirteenth centuries.

52 The great keep at Colchester, seen – like the Tower of London, opposite – with the apse of its chapel on the near right. Its third storey and turret tops were destroyed in 1863.

ground level. Some small stone keeps, like Lydford, had low mounds built up around them, but in most cases a strong 'great tower' standing within a bailey could replace the motte altogether as the chief strongpoint of the castle.

Fortresses based on rectangular stone keeps had been known in France long before 1066, and the Conqueror and his lieutenants adopted this style for the largest and most impressive of their English castles. Certainly the best known of these 'great towers' is *the* Tower itself in London, begun in 1078 under the direction of Bishop Gundulf of Rochester, a man 'very competent and skilful at building in stone'. Built to overawe the Londoners, this massive keep (roughly 100 feet or 30 metres square, with walls 15 feet or 4.5 metres thick at their base) contained all the necessities of a royal palace, including a splendid chapel with a projecting apsed end. It stands in one corner of the old Roman city defences, which provided a ready-made bailey wall on two sides of it. Later kings added walls, towers and gates to the outer defences, but the 'White Tower' itself (so called because its masonry was once covered in gleaming whitewash) remains substantially unaltered.

An even larger keep, in fact the largest in Britain, was raised by the Conqueror at Colchester in Essex, in a strategic position near the coast most vulnerable to a new Danish invasion. Some 150 by 110 feet (46 by 34 metres) in area, it was built on the foundations of the great Roman temple of Claudius, and was originally three storeys high and turreted like the Tower. Like the Tower, too, Colchester has a semicircular projection housing a chapel, and it has been suggested that the design of both places was derived from the vanished palace of the Dukes of Normandy at Rouen: certainly nothing even approaching them in grandeur had been seen in Britain since the days of the Roman occupation. Among smaller stone keeps surviving from the Conqueror's reign is that built by William fitz Osbern on the rock of Chepstow (see p. 95) and the shattered remains at Canterbury may also date from this period.

So far we have concentrated on castles built at the King's own orders, but we must not forget that the majority of early Norman fortresses were only nominally the property of the Crown. Lacking a standing army (an element which only enters British history in the seventeenth century), the King relied for support in war on the Norman barons and

53 William de Warenne's Castle Acre in Norfolk, looking across the bailey (centre) towards the shell-wall of the motte, with the earthwork village enclosure away to the left.

knights who served him in return for hereditary grants of confiscated English lands. Upon these lands the barons fortified their own residences, which though technically 'rendable' to the King on demand were in effect their own private property. One such baronial castle was Skipsea, built by Drogo de 46 Bevriere, a Flemish adventurer to whom the Conqueror had given the east Yorkshire lands of King 53 Harold. Another was Castle Acre in Norfolk, where the new King's friend and adviser William de Warenne built a great stone keep on a motte, flanking it on one side by a bailey and on the other by an earth-ramparted village enclosure. There were very many others, and some magnates held five or six strongholds scattered throughout the country.

While the Norman hold on England was endangered by Saxon risings or Danish invasion these private castles, backing up the fortresses of the King, were an indispensable part of the system of national defence. As soon as these perils were passed, however, and King and barons ceased to work together for a common cause, they appeared in a rather different light. Even before the Conqueror's death in 1087 rebellious barons were holding their castles against the Crown, and in the following century the strongholds which filled the land became the focus of struggles between Norman and Norman.

Most of these wars turned on the royal succession, and they originated with the Conqueror's death-bed decision to divide his dominions: Robert, his good-natured but incompetent elder son, became Duke of Normandy, while England passed to his favourite second son William, called Rufus from his flaming red hair. The Anglo-Norman barons whose lands lay on both sides of the Channel thus found themselves involved in a conflict of interests, and of their two masters many preferred the easy-going Robert to his 'very hard and severe' brother, who by all contemporary accounts was a very unpleasant character indeed. The baronial revolt of 1088 was designed to depose William and make Robert ruler of all the Norman lands. Castles all over the country declared for the rebels, but their main strength was in the south-east, where they held the Conqueror's landing place at Pevensey as a bridgehead for expected reinforcements from Duke Robert in Normandy. With a curious irony, the rebel strongholds were reduced principally by King William Rufus's employment of a large army of Englishmen, recruited on false promises but doubtless glad of the chance for a licensed crack at their Norman overlords. Amongst the last places to fall was Pevensey itself, which held out for six weeks but surrendered after Robert's advance guard had been slaughtered by the King's Englishmen as they attempted to get ashore.

By dividing their forces into garrisons for scattered castles the rebels of 1088 had allowed themselves to be defeated piecemeal, and the same miscalculation was made by the barons who rose against William seven years later in 1095. This insurrection culminated in the siege of Bamburgh, 54

54 *Bamburgh Castle, Northumberland, built on a basalt rock first fortified by Ida of Bernicia in the sixth century (pp. 44–45) and besieged by William Rufus in 1095. The* *present castle, centring on the twelfth-century keep, fell to Edward IV's heavy artillery in 1464 (p. 154).*

55 *Carlisle Castle, Cumbria, one of the chief bastions of England's northern frontiers, though its twelfth-century keep (right) was probably built by King David I of Scotland, who occupied the castle during Stephen's troubled reign. Back in English hands, it was unsuccessfully* *attacked by the Scots in 1315 (p. 119) but failed to hold Kinmont Willie Armstrong in 1596 (pp. 170–71) and in 1745 became the last English fortress to sustain a siege (p. 193). The 'shot-deflecting' battlements of the keep date from 1541 (compare ill. 114).*

56, 57 Rochester Castle keep. Above: interior at second and third-storey level, looking through the arcaded cross-wall; notice the fireplace and below it the joist holes for a wooden floor. Below: plan of the first floor, showing the cross-wall, the forebuilding (bottom right) and the corner (bottom left) destroyed by King John's miners (p. 90) and rebuilt with a more modern semi-circular turret under Henry III (p. 92).

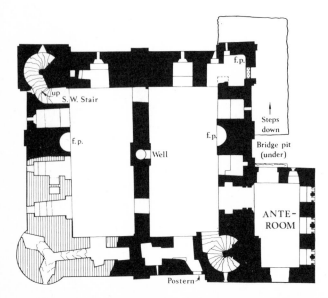

the virtually impregnable stronghold of the rebel leader Robert de Mowbray. Called away from the long siege by trouble in Wales, the King ordered the construction of an earthwork fort – named 'Malvoisin' or 'bad neighbour' – designed to blockade the approaches to the castle, which eventually fell only after Mowbray had been lured out with a false message from his supporters and captured by the King's men. He was paraded outside the castle walls, and his wife (now commanding the garrison) was told that he would be blinded with hot irons unless she surrendered, which she not surprisingly did forthwith.

William Rufus was no great castle-builder, but it was he who founded the fortress at Carlisle, which was to play such a large part in border history. Whether the squat keep there is his is uncertain: it may perhaps be a little later. The Red King died mysteriously in the New Forest in 1100, and his younger brother Henry at once seized the throne. Duke Robert of Normandy, cheated once again of the crown, was less than pleased, and in 1101 he landed an invasion force at Portsmouth, receiving the immediate support of a number of Anglo-Norman barons. Henry's army (assembled to repel an expected landing at Pevensey) was outflanked, but the King outmarched his sluggish brother, whose efforts in the end came to nothing. The vengeful Henry then set about dealing with his disloyal barons, the chief of whom was the quite exceptionally vicious Robert of Belleme, called 'the Devil'. Belleme was famous for two things, his interest in fortresses and his love of torture (among his jollier exploits was scratching out the eyes of his own godson), and he held no less than six strong castles. With the enthusiastic help of English levies these strongholds fell one by one, and when Belleme was finally exiled popular songs of rejoicing were written.

For the remainder of Henry I's long reign (1100–1135) England was at peace, and the King was himself able to build a number of impressive fortresses. To prevent any further enemy landings at Portsmouth he refurbished the abandoned Saxon Shore fort at nearby Portchester, sealing off one corner of the interior with a stone wall and raising a four-storey stone keep on the site of the Roman angle tower. Further west along the same coast he built the lofty great tower at Corfe in Dorset, and at Rochester in the south-east he encouraged William of Corbeil, Archbishop of Canterbury, to construct one of the strongest keeps in Britain as the centrepiece of an already existing castle. All these buildings had their

58, 59 *The hall-keep at Castle Rising, Norfolk, built within a formidable earthwork (seen in the background) by William d'Albini in about 1140, to mark his marriage to* the widow of Henry I. Below: *the ornate carving over the entrance, via the forebuilding, to the keep.*

56   interiors divided in half by a sturdy cross-wall,
57   forming a keep within a keep which could hold out (as was later proved at Rochester: see p. 90) even after the other section of the building had been taken. They also had their entrances protected by a 'forebuilding', a porch that would have to be carried before an attacker could reach the inner door of the castle.

Though the King fathered no less than twenty-one children only two of them – William and Matilda – were legitimate. William died in the midst of a drunken debauch when his 'White Ship' sank in 1120, and Matilda was recognized as heir-apparent, but on Henry's death many of the barons (who disliked the notion of a female ruler) chose instead to crown his nephew Stephen. What followed was a devastating civil war, which lasted almost uninterruptedly for the full nineteen years (1135–54) of Stephen's 'reign'. Neither the King's supporters nor the allies of Matilda and her son Henry of Anjou could achieve decisive victory, and both sides wooed the robber barons who became the real power in the land. Thus, according to an English witness,

every great man built him castles and held them against the King, and they filled the whole land with these castles; and

when the castles were built they filled them with devils and wicked men. By night and by day they seized those whom they believed to have any wealth . . . and tortured them with unspeakable tortures. . . . They hung them up by the feet and smoked them with foul smoke. They strung them up by the thumbs or by the head, and hung coats of mail on their feet. They tied knotted cords round their heads and twisted them till they entered the brain . . . and so destroyed them . . . At regular intervals they levied a tax known as protection money upon the villages. When the wretched people had no more to give, they plundered and burned all the villages, so that you could easily go a days journey without ever finding a village inhabited or a field cultivated . . . the land was ruined by such doings, and men said openly that Christ and His saints slept.

All royal control over fortress-building ceased, and according to one contemporary authority no less than 1,115 unlicensed or 'adulterine' baronial castles sprang up during this period of anarchy. Most were of the most rudimentary kind, and bore little resemblance to the beautiful keep at Castle Rising in Norfolk, with its decorated forebuilding, which was built by one of Stephen's supporters near the beginning of the reign. Many, indeed, were probably not new at all, but were recommissioned mottes of the Conqueror's day, and even earlier fortifications like the Caburn were pressed into service. Stone churches and monasteries found themselves converted to military use, and in the heavily fought-over Thames Valley many castles were 'twinned' with earthwork counterforts built by the enemy to keep them under observation.

The whole war turned on the possession of castles and the country they controlled, and an endless series of sieges is described in contemporary chronicles. Certainly the most remarkable was the occasion when Matilda's army, besieging the two castles within the walls of Winchester, were themselves blockaded by a force of the King's men which surrounded the town. More typical, perhaps, was Stephen's attack on the motte and bailey at Winchcombe in Gloucestershire, when he ordered that 'some should advance shooting clouds of arrows, others should crawl up the mound, and everyone else should rush rapidly round the fortifications and throw in anything that came to hand'.

Eventually even the most rapacious barons tired of the interminable war, and some began to make private peace treaties amongst themselves. One such (underlining the importance of castles) stipulated that neither party should build any new fortresses within a certain radius of Leicester, and that both would join together to attack anyone else who tried to do so. Finally, in 1153, the main contenders themselves made peace, agreeing that Stephen should reign unchallenged until his death, but that Matilda's son Henry should afterwards peacefully succeed him. A principal article of the treaty stipulated that all unlicensed castles built during the war should be demolished, for the lesson had been learnt that a land filled with baronial castles could only too easily become a land filled with strife and lawlessness.

58
59

60 Henry II's revolutionary polygonal
keep at Orford, Suffolk (p. 87),
originally surrounded by a towered
curtain wall; notice the raised entrance
via the forebuilding.

7 'The bones of the kingdom': the Angevin kings of England, 1154–1272

... the bones of the kingdom, that is, the King's fortresses.

WILLIAM OF NEWBURGH, c. 1198

Henry of Anjou, the young man who in 1154 became Henry II of England, must surely rank amongst the most formidable and capable of British monarchs. Duke of Normandy and Count of Anjou by birth and Duke of Aquitaine by marriage, by the age of twenty-one he already ruled half of France, and his hereditary advantages were matched by outstanding personal qualities, not the least of them being a boundless and untiring energy. So swift were his movements about his vast domains that his contemporaries declared that 'he must fly rather than travel by horse or ship', and he was said never to have sat down except when riding or eating. On the other side of the coin he was subject to fits of violent rage, when he would throw himself on the floor and chew the rushes.

61 The keep, c.1157, of the English border castle of Norham, Northumberland, guarding a ford across the Tweed. Frequently besieged by the Scots, it held out successfully for eleven months in 1318 (p. 119), but fell to James IV's heavy artillery in 1513 (p. 162). It subsequently became a base for English border officials (p. 170).

All Henry's energies were needed to re-establish the shattered authority of the English Crown and restore order to a nation torn by twenty years of war and anarchy. His first moves, the demolition of 'unlicensed' castles and the deportation of foreign mercenaries, were almost universally welcomed, but he met with more opposition when he began to repossess the royal castles and estates which a weak government had allowed to fall into the hands of various over-mighty barons. A massive show of strength brought the recalcitrant magnates to heel, and Henry scored a further diplomatic triumph when he persuaded the Scots to restore the northern border counties (together with their strong castles) granted away by Stephen.

Even when all this was done, the new King found that his own castles were greatly outnumbered by those of barons whose support for him was at best uncertain. Throughout his reign he spared no effort to redress this balance, firstly by confiscating or demolishing any baronial fortress he could lay hands on and secondly by adding to the numbers and strength of the castles of the Crown. Castle-building, in fact, was so important a facet of Henry's royal policy that it swallowed up (on average) nearly a tenth of the annual revenues of the Crown, far outweighing any other article of expenditure. For the construction of stone fortresses was a very different matter from throwing up a simple motte and bailey, and money was needed for quarrying and transporting stone, for lime and cement, and for the wages of expert masons, carpenters, metal workers and other craftsmen, not to mention the hordes of labourers who excavated the foundations and ditches, sometimes hacking through solid rock.

The first fortresses to which Henry turned his attention were those of the northern border, which had until now proved unequal to the task of repelling Scottish invasions. Carlisle and Bamburgh were strengthened, the Bishop of Durham was encouraged to improve his motte and bailey at Norham in Northumberland with a stone keep, and Henry himself raised new donjons at nearby Wark on the Tweed and Newcastle on the Tyne: the last of these, rectangular and turreted like Rochester, still survives to its original height of 80 feet (25 metres). Further south, at Scarborough in North Yorkshire, the King killed two birds with one stone by confiscating the chief stronghold of the most powerful local baron, William of Aumale, and building there a lofty tower-keep of his own. Its site, a rock 'stupendous alike in height and area and surrounded by inaccessible cliffs rising out of the

54
55
61
45
62

sea', had a long history, for it had previously served as a Roman signal station and a Danish settlement.

East Anglia, with its long exposed coastline, was another potential danger area for the King, not least because at the beginning of his reign he possessed no castles of his own there. Baronial strongholds, on the other hand, were numerous, the most formidable group – Framlingham, Bungay, Walton and Thetford – being the possession of the powerful and shifty Hugh Bigod, Earl of Norfolk. Henry dealt with this problem in a characteristic and entirely admirable manner, confiscating Bigod's castles and only returning them on payment of a massive fine. The money so raised covered two-thirds of the cost of building an entirely new royal castle at Orford, positioned so as to cut Earl Hugh's Framlingham off from the sea.

Unique among Henry's castles in being raised on a previously unfortified site, Orford was also revolutionary in design. Its keep was not the conventional cubic shape, but was a polygonal tower flanked by three tall turrets and a forebuilding. This arrangement gave the garrison a much improved field of fire, and went some way towards disposing of the principal weakness of the rectangular donjon, namely its right-angled corners. Such corners were vulnerable to battering by siege-engines and (since they could not be properly covered by fire from the wall-tops) also to undermining, as we shall see when we consider the siege of Rochester later in this chapter. The ultimate answer to the problem was, of course, to build keeps which were completely cylindrical, and polygonal structures like Orford were a half-way stage in this process. King Henry's later polygonal keeps (like Chilham in Kent and Tickhill in South Yorkshire) went one step further by dispensing with rectangular turrets on the exterior, and before the end of his reign the barons of the Welsh March – where everything had to be up to date – had begun to build round keeps proper.

It should perhaps be emphasized here that, despite these developments in design, the conventional rectangular keep continued to flourish, as is evidenced by Henry's own massive donjon at Dover, begun ten years after Orford was finished. No tidy progression of design can in fact be traced, and there were certainly times when rectangular, polygonal, and round keeps were all under construction at the same time.

Side by side with improvements in keep design went the development of the defences of the surrounding bailey. The wooden palisade of early Norman times suffered from the same disadvantages

62 The shattered tower-keep of Scarborough, North Yorkshire, looking across the rock-cut ditch from the barbican. Built by Henry II between 1159 and 1168, the keep was partially demolished in 1645, after a long Civil War siege (p. 183).

63 *The moated inner bailey of White Castle or Castell Gwyn in Gwent, so named from the gleaming plaster which once covered its walls, and which now survives only in a* *few sheltered crannies. Built c.1185 with a plain curtain wall, it was given flanking towers when the castle was threatened by Prince Llywelyn in the 1260s (pp. 99–100).*

as a timber keep, and before long it began to be replaced by a stone 'curtain wall' like the one which surrounded the bailey at Brough in Cumbria, a castle built on the site of the Roman fort of Verterae. Such plain curtain walls, however lofty, were nevertheless difficult to defend, for they lacked the protruding towers which had allowed the Roman defenders of Pevensey or Portchester to direct cross-fire onto an enemy assaulting the base of the wall. The Classical system of mutually supporting towers (which also divided the defences into separate and more manageable sections) seems, indeed, only to have been rediscovered in Britain in the late twelfth century. It was employed to good effect by Henry II on the inner bailey wall immediately below his keep at Dover, where, as in most early examples, the

towers are rectangular. These towers, however, shared the same 'corner problem' as rectangular keeps, and in later castles mural towers were usually semicircular. So necessary were they considered to be for the defence of the bailey that in some instances they were added to existing defences: this happened at White Castle, Gwent, where the join between the original plain curtain wall and the towers added a century later can be clearly seen.

King Henry's firm rule and his challenge to baronial power – not least in the matter of castle-building – made him many enemies, and in 1173–74 he found himself faced with a dangerous revolt throughout his dominions. Masterminded by the King of France (who was jealous of the vast Angevin empire) and led by Henry's son, Henry 'the Young

King', it was supported by King William the Lion of Scotland and by a number of English barons including the resentful Hugh Bigod. While the King campaigned in France, the war in England was skilfully conducted by his Justiciar, Richard de Lucy, who held the south coast castles against a French landing and defeated the rebel barons in the midlands and East Anglia. Two successive invasions by the Scots were foiled by their inability to take the border fortresses of Wark, Alnwick and Carlisle, even though at the last place King William threatened to throw the castellan off the keep unless he surrendered at once.

Brough, garrisoned by only six knights and their retainers, was less fortunate, and held out for no more than a few hours. First the untowered bailey wall was stormed, and when the defenders retired to the keep the Scots stacked brushwood around it and burnt them out. According to the chronicler Jordan Fantosme, however, one brave knight retired to the top of the keep with two shields, and held out there until the flames overtook him.

> He hung shields on the battlements, stayed there a
>   long time,
> And hurled at the Scots three sharp javelins:
> With each of the javelins he struck a man dead.
> When those failed him, he takes sharp stakes
> And hurls them at the Scots . . .
> And ever he goes on shouting, 'Soon shall you all be
>   vanquished.'

His prophecy was fulfilled, for the King of Scots was surprised and taken outside the walls of besieged Alnwick, and the revolts elsewhere ended in complete victory for Henry. The barons who had rebelled paid dearly for their disloyalty: their castles were confiscated and (where they were not needed by the King) 'slighted' to make them useless. Earl Hugh Bigod's Bungay was undermined, Framlingham was systematically razed to the ground, and in places even the earthen mottes of baronial fortresses were dug away so that no new structures could be built on them. Two years after the war ended the King felt strong enough to take a further step towards the 'nationalization' of fortresses, and he 'took into his own hand all the castles in England . . . and put his own custodians in them'. Even his supporters were compelled to hand over their strongholds, and from now on the defence of the realm would turn more and more on the forces and fortresses of the Crown and less and less on those of the barons.

Though the baronial castle became increasingly irrelevant to national defence after the end of the twelfth century, it remained important as a centre of resistance at times of civil unrest. The nobility, therefore, having regained control of their castles from Henry's successors, continued to rebuild and modernize them, though few entirely new non-royal fortresses were raised. Nor could the barons hope to match in strength the greatest fortresses of the Crown, whose progressively more sophisticated defences called for expenditure which only the central government could produce.

The most spectacular demonstration of Henry II's determination to outdo his barons was his conversion of the Conqueror's castle at Dover into the strongest fortress in the land, rightly called the 'key of England'. The works there cost a total of £7,000, a sum whose magnitude can only be appreciated if we consider that the wages of a contemporary workman amounted to less than £1.50 a year. At the heart of the castle stands the great cubic keep, just under 100 feet (30 metres) square and a little less in height: designed by Maurice 'the Engineer', its immense walls vary between 17 and 21 feet (5–6.5 metres) in thickness. Surrounding it is the curtain wall of the inner bailey, studded with fourteen rectangular towers, four of which are paired to form two gatehouses. If Dover's towered bailey wall was in the forefront of military fashion, these gatehouses were something quite new to British medieval fortress design, nothing like them having been seen since late Roman times. They are, in fact, the earliest surviving examples of the long line of twin-towered gatehouses which protected and adorned castle and town walls throughout the Middle Ages and beyond.

Still more revolutionary, however, was Henry's decision to begin building an outer curtain wall, also protected by towers, surrounding the inner one. This outer bailey wall, completed by Henry's son and grandson, made Dover (as Allen Brown observed) 'the first known castle in Western Europe to employ concentric lines of fortification, one inside the other'. Attackers, in other words, would first have to assault the outer wall, running the gauntlet of flanking fire from the defenders on its towers. Any portion of wall they took could be sealed off by the towers on each side of it, which would have to be systematically reduced before the enemy could go on to repeat the process of attack on the defences of the inner bailey. The latter were well within range of supporting fire from the top of the keep, which was in itself more than capable of holding out even if both sets of bailey walls should fall. The three concentric lines of mutually supporting defences, then, were designed to inflict maximum casualties on any foe bold enough to storm them, and their appearance alone was enough to daunt any but the most determined attacker.

For all his fine castles, the great King Henry died a broken man in 1189, hounded to death by an alliance of the ever-jealous King of France and his own faithless wife and sons. He was succeeded by Richard, his eldest surviving son, who as the 'Lionheart' became one of the great heroes of Victorian legend. His contemporaries thought rather less of him ('bad to all, worse to his own people, worst of all to himself'), and there can be no doubt that, though a brave and expert soldier, he was an unmitigated disaster as King of England. He spent only six months of his ten-year reign in the country, which he milked dry to pay for his crusading campaigns and later for his ransom when the German Emperor captured him on the way back from Palestine. Nor did he add much to the defences of Britain, though he lavished care on his favourite castle of Château Gaillard, on the borders of Normandy. An expert in siege-craft, he employed an ingenious prefabricated wooden fort during his Mediterranean campaigns, and it is ironic that it was a chance arrow from a petty castle in France that ended his life in the last year of the twelfth century.

The crown then passed to his younger brother, the much-maligned King John, who had been Henry II's favourite son and who inherited his father's restless energy, though his character was marred by a streak of cruelty. He was, incidentally, much remarked on for his frequent baths, as well as for his possession of a dressing gown or 'overtunic for getting up at night'. The upheavals of his reign (1199–1216) were principally due to the machinations of King Philip Augustus of France, who finally succeeded in conquering Normandy in 1204 and went on to threaten the invasion of England. Faced with this danger, John strengthened the south coast castles, especially Dover and his favourite Corfe, and built himself a new octagonal keep at Odiham in Hampshire. Yet the blow, when it arrived in 1215, came from within rather than without, and from a familiar direction, namely a group of rebel English barons abetted and encouraged by the French. Having forced Magna Carta on John, these dubious characters (far removed from the democratic champions of liberty so often portrayed) refused to be satisfied with the settlement, and raised open war on behalf of King Philip and his son Prince Louis (later Louis VIII), to whom, hoping to enhance their own power, they offered the crown of England.

John's response was swift, and on 11 October 1215 he appeared before the important enemy stronghold of Rochester Castle, which blocked the road from London to the vulnerable Channel coast. What followed was the most notable siege to take place in England since the Conquest. The garrison consisted of about a hundred of the 'best and strongest knights', supported by archers and crossbowmen, and their fortress (though by no means new) was amongst the most formidable in the land: they therefore had little immediate cause for alarm, especially since the barons had sworn faithfully to relieve them. John, however, broke down the bridge which linked Rochester with the London road and settled down to bombard the castle with stones from five great siege engines, while the royal infantry fired showers of arrows to clear the battlements. Relieving his men in shifts, the King kept up the barrage by night and day, but it apparently had little real effect, and the royal miners were sent for.

These miners began a process to which all castles not founded on rock or surrounded by water were vulnerable. Tunnelling until they reached a point immediately under the bailey wall, they propped up their shaft with wooden posts, and when the mine was finished they filled it with brushwood, oil, and other combustibles which were then set ablaze. As the pit-props burnt through the tunnel collapsed, dislocating the foundations above so that the stone wall resting on them came crashing and rumbling down. The only real defences against mining would be either to flood the shaft or to dig a countermine and attack the enemy below ground, but both these courses were liable in themselves to weaken the foundations, and at Rochester neither was attempted.

Instead the garrison, when John's men stormed into the bailey, retired into their strong keep: its walls, 12 feet (3.6 metres) thick, were virtually impervious to siege engines, and though one relieving force had turned back another could still be hoped for. But by now the siege had dragged on for nearly six weeks, and the King was losing patience. Once again the 'underwallers' were set to work to undermine a corner of the keep, and John sent for 'forty of the fattest pigs of the sort least good for eating to bring fire under the tower': their fat was to be used to ignite the mine. Soon a whole section of the keep collapsed in ruins, but still the garrison held out behind the strong cross-wall 'which separated the half that had fallen from the other'. Reduced to a meagre diet of horse-flesh and water, the defenders expelled the injured and sick amongst them, and

64 *Dover Castle from the north, showing the huge extent of the defences (see also pl. 5). At the core is the twelfth-century keep, surrounded by the square-towered inner bailey wall. In the centre of the outer bailey wall is the old north gate, breached during the siege of 1216 and thereafter blocked by a solid beaked tower. Henry III* *further defended this angle of the castle with a bulwark (foreground), the ditch between it and the castle being guarded by the sunken St John's Tower – whose circular top can just be seen – and also added the massive Constable's Gate on the far right.*

these unfortunates are said to have had their hands and feet cut off by the King's men. The end was in sight, and within a few days – after a resistance which had lasted nearly two months – the garrison finally gave in, meeting with surprisingly lenient treatment from King John. The fall of Rochester, however, and more especially the failure to relieve it, was a grievous blow to the morale of the baronial party, and afterwards 'few they were who put their trust in castles'.

During the next six months John had comparatively little trouble in subduing his English opponents, and he was on the point of attacking their last strongholds round London when, in May 1216, the situation was radically changed by the landing there of Prince Louis and a large army of Frenchmen. Now the rebels took new heart, and within a short time almost the whole of eastern England was once again in the hands of the King's enemies. Castle after castle surrendered, some without resistance and others (like little Odiham, whose thirteen-man garrison held off the French for a week) after a stiff fight. Only a handful of royal strongholds, including Windsor, Lincoln and Dover, held out behind Prince Louis' lines, but it was these that quite literally saved England for the descendants of the Conqueror and prevented her from becoming a mere province of France. By far the most important of them was

Dover, which sat astride the shortest cross-Channel supply route. Fortunately it was also the strongest fortress in England, manned by Hubert de Burgh with 140 knights and many more infantrymen, and the story of its ten-months' intermittent siege presents a sharp contrast to the destruction of Rochester.

The attack began on Midsummer Day 1216, when Louis' entire army surrounded the landward side of the castle while his fleet blockaded the approaches by sea. Siege-engines (including one particularly large one brought especially from France) began to batter the walls at close range, but the garrison made continual sallies out against them, killing so many of their expert operators that they had to be moved further away. Prince Louis, it is said, then swore to take the castle and hang every man in it. He concentrated his efforts on the north gate of the outer bailey, but before he could assault it he had first to take the ditched and palisaded outwork, or 'barbican', that stood before it as an additional defence. This was done, not without loss, by a party of French knights, while Louis' carpenters prepared engines to breach the wall itself. Amongst these was a 'belfry', a movable wooden tower from whose top storey the attackers could swarm directly onto the battlements, and a 'cat', a battering ram protected by a kind of hut on wheels.

65 A tunnel through the chalk at the northern end of Dover Castle, cut by Prince Louis' sappers during the siege in 1216. It was later intersected by one of the underground passages linking the new defence works built by Henry III c.1221–27 (see ill. 64).

In the end, however, it was the Prince's miners who brought down one of the towers of the gatehouse. (Their tunnel cut through the solid chalk can still be seen.) But the defenders were prepared, and the Frenchmen who rushed triumphantly through the breach met with such a hot reception that they were forced to retire at once, leaving the garrison to fill up the hole with a hastily constructed barricade of boulders and tree-trunks. This setback seriously demoralized Louis, whose main army had by now been tied down before Dover for nearly four fruitless months. Then, in mid-October 1216, the news came of the sudden death of King John, and the Frenchman imagined that all England was his for the taking. He therefore made a truce with the garrison and marched off northwards, leaving a small force to watch the untaken fortress.

Though Prince Louis succeeeded in taking several royal castles, including Colchester and Orford, the tide of war was beginning to turn against him, and more and more English barons rallied to the cause of John's infant son Henry III and his guardian William the Marshal. Louis' failure to capture Dover was a constant reproach to him and an encouragement to his enemies, and in the spring of 1217 he returned there for a further attempt. He met only with more frustration, for the French siege lines came under continual harassment from an army of Kentish guerrillas led by 'Willikin of the Weald', while their supply ships were sunk by the piratical mariners of the Cinque Ports. Eventually Louis found himself virtually trapped in the town of Dover, with English ships anchored outside cutting off his communications with France.

While Dover sapped the strength of his main army, Louis' allies were investing another royal fortress, Lincoln, held by the redoubtable Lady Nicola de la Haye. On 20 May 1217, when the besiegers were tightly packed into the space between the castle wall and the cathedral, they were caught between a surprise attack by the army of William the Marshal and a simultaneous sally by the garrison. Utterly routed, they left behind them so much valuable baggage that the battle was called 'The Fair of Lincoln'.

This was effectively the end of the war, and a few months later the last European invaders to gain a real foothold on English soil made peace and went home. Though other factors were involved, Prince Louis' failure to conquer the land was in practical terms due to the resistance of a few strong fortresses, the royal castles which the Angevin kings had made the 'bones of the kingdom'.

During the long reign of Henry III (1216–72) considerable care and expense was devoted to keeping the 'bones' in good condition. War damage was repaired, at Rochester by rebuilding the undermined corner of the keep and at Dover by blocking the breached gateway with a solid tower with a wedge-shaped outer face. This gate was replaced by a new and immensely strong entrance, the Constable's Gate, which funnelled an enemy attack through a narrow passage between and beneath a complex of five towers with arrow-slits for archers. The strengthening of the gatehouse, and of the defences of the curtain wall in general, was the main feature of English thirteenth-century castle-building, reaching its apogee in the great 'concentric' Welsh castles of Edward I described in the next chapter. At the same time the 'houses within the castle' – the halls, chambers, chapels and kitchens that made up the residential accom-

66 *'Clifford's Tower', Henry III's clover-leaf keep at York, built c.1245 on William the Conqueror's first motte (see p. 75).*

modation – were becoming increasingly elaborate and Henry III (whose artistic taste was highly developed) took a personal interest in the design of new windows, fireplaces and ceilings.

The emphasis on the features of the bailey meant that less importance was being attached to the keep, though some new ones were built both at royal castles and elsewhere. Many of these, especially as we shall see in Wales and the Marches, were round, but at York the King replaced the ruined defences on the Conqueror's motte with a keep shaped like a quatrefoil or four-leafed flower. Derived from French models, the design of 'Clifford's Tower' was unique in England: it was, however, remarkably efficient in providing the maximum all round field of fire, and something like it was much later adopted for the artillery fortresses of the Tudors.

The most important military event of Henry III's reign was the struggle between the Crown and a group of barons, led by Simon de Montfort, who desired a greater share in government both for themselves and for the newly-established institution of Parliament. Among the barons' demands, significantly, was the custody of the principal royal castles (including Bamburgh, Corfe, Scarborough and Dover) as a guarantee that their constitutional reforms would be carried out. Fortifications, however, played a comparatively minor role in the war itself, though there were notable sieges of Kenilworth in Warwickshire and (yet again) of Rochester: instead, the outcome was dictated by two major field battles, de Montfort's victory at Lewes, Sussex, in 1264 and the royalist success at Evesham, Worcestershire, in the following year. The King's party eventually emerged triumphant, thanks to the leadership of Henry's soldierly son Edward, who on his father's death in 1272 succeeded peacefully to the throne. During the next thirty-five years Edward I was to establish English domination over virtually the whole island of Britain, building as he did so one of the most spectacular series of castles anywhere in Europe. His first expansionist efforts were directed at Wales, and it is there that we must ourselves turn next.

93

67 *William fitz Osbern's hall-keep at Chepstow, Gwent, built c.1070, straddles the narrowest point of a rocky ridge above the Wye (right). Entered by the Romanesque door seen here, which incorporates Roman bricks in its arch, it originally consisted of a cellar and two storeys. The now ruined top floor was added, like the upper bailey (left), during the thirteenth century.*

8   The conquest of Wales, 1066–1415

Be ware of Wales, Christ Jesu must us keep,
That it make not our child's child to weep.
For to rebel, that Christ it forbid
Look well about, for God wot we have need.

The Libelle of English Policy, c. 1436

The subjugation of Wales, unlike the Norman conquest of England, was not completed in a matter of years, but was a piecemeal affair spread over several centuries. Two factors were of prime importance. The first was a curse inherited from the Britain of the heroic age, namely the chronic inability of the Welsh to unite behind one ruler. The advantage this gave to an invader, however, was more than counterbalanced by the natural defences of the country, whose mountains made it difficult of access and ideal for guerrilla warfare, as well as rendering it quite unsuitable for the introduction of any kind of settled society on the English pattern. Thus the only way in which an intruder could survive was to build strongholds to defend himself and his property, and expansion could only be carried out from securely fortified bases.

The great number of castles in Wales, far exceeding the count for any other comparable area of Britain, need not therefore surprise us. Even before 1066 Norman knights in the service of Edward the Confessor were building mottes (like Richard's Castle) in the disputed Welsh borderlands, and when the Conqueror came he gave lands there to the most warlike of his followers. The greatest of these 'Marchers', or 'frontiersmen', were the Earls of Chester, Shrewsbury, and Hereford, whose border strongholds served as staging-points for every major invasion force. From Chester the Conqueror's deputies Hugh of Avranches and Robert of Rhuddlan marched into the north Welsh principality of Gwynedd, while the lords of Shrewsbury threatened Powys in central Wales and Gwent in the south was assailed by the great Earl of Hereford, William fitz Osbern. A renowned fortress-builder (see p. 75), fitz Osbern established his forward base on a bend in the Wye at Chepstow. There, in about 1070, he raised

67 the first stone castle in Wales, a two-storey rectangular keep built across the narrow neck of a towering spur of rock. A steep gully on one side and a sheer drop to the river on the other provided natural defences, and stone walls enclosed sections of the ridge to form baileys on either side of the keep.

6 Several times added to by later generations, fitz Osbern's stronghold proved so impregnable that throughout the border wars of the next four centuries it was never once seriously threatened.

68 Another of fitz Osbern's castles, Wigmore, now presents a sad contrast to the glories of Chepstow. The most important link in a chain of fortresses guarding Herefordshire from Welsh incursions, it too utilized a steep-sided ridge (overlooking a Roman road) as a site for a motte and bailey surrounded by a double ditch. In the later Middle Ages it became the chief stronghold of the mighty Mortimer family (who built the stone keep and curtain wall) but now it stands strangely forlorn, covered with undergrowth and populated only by sheep.

Following in the footsteps of the Conqueror's Earls, the Normans succeeded in overrunning almost the whole of south and west Wales during the latter part of the eleventh century. These conquests were achieved, not by the King's armies, but by the private enterprise of the Marcher barons, supported by landless adventurers anxious to win estates for themselves by the sword. In each area the pattern of invasion was similar, with bands of heavily armed knights and foot soldiers moving up the river valleys or old Roman roads, harried as they went by sudden Welsh raids from the inaccessible hilltops: 'the French [wrote a native chronicler] dared not penetrate the rocks or the woods, where the Britons had their fastnesses'. The leaders of these land-grabbing expeditions threw up the familiar palisaded mottes and baileys to consolidate their new conquests, and when firmly established they distributed estates to their followers, who in turn built small castles of their own. Thus the Marchers set up what amounted to private kingdoms, virtually free from interference by the English Crown but constantly under threat of attack by Welsh guerrillas or their own rapacious Norman neighbours.

It is hardly surprising, then, to find more Norman mottes in Wales and the Marches (where they often occur one or two to a parish) than in the whole of the rest of Britain. The vast majority of them are now no more than grassy mounds, whose detailed history is unknown or long forgotten. One such is Almeley in Herefordshire, whose close proximity to the church, reflecting the interreliance of the parish priest and the lord of the manor, is a common feature of these defences.

By the beginning of the twelfth century it seemed that, despite occasional reverses, the Anglo-Norman invaders were on the verge of conquering all Wales. Then, when the Marchers were distracted by the long civil wars of Stephen's reign (1135–54), the beleaguered Welsh princes seized the opportunity to launch a massive counterattack. Led by Owain Gwynedd in the north and Rhys ap Gruffydd in the

68 *The rapidly-decaying ruins of Wigmore Castle, Herefordshire, founded by William fitz Osbern. Its surviving masonry is mainly the work of the great Marcher family of Mortimer, one of whom ruled England as the lover of Queen Isabella. The keep crowns the hill; below it on the left is the gatehouse of the bailey wall.*

south, they fell on the intruders and overran their castles, until at one stage only Pembrokeshire remained in Norman hands. Even the mighty Henry II was unable to retrieve the situation fully, but he did succeed in containing the princes' advance, and by the end of the century an uneasy peace had been patched up, with the Welsh holding most of the mountainous north and west and the Anglo-Normans occupying the lower-lying south and east of the country.

It was at this time, in 1194, that Giraldus Cambrensis (himself of mixed Norman and Welsh descent) wrote his account of Wales, describing a society which had changed little since the heroic age. The Welsh, he declared, have no castles or towns, but live in huts in the woods. They are inured to war, the men of north Wales being especially skilled with the spear and those of the south excelling with the longbow. In battle their first charge is devastating, but if resolutely opposed they will flee – only to return and fight again another day. Advising the Normans on how best to defeat them, Giraldus first of all urges the exploitation of quarrels between the native princes. The invaders must be prepared for

campaigns lasting up to a year, and should take care to employ only experienced frontiersmen as their commanders. Above all, if Wales is to be permanently subjugated, the invaders must build strong stone castles both on the borders and in the interior, and must keep them well provisioned and garrisoned in times of apparent peace as well as during open war.

The unsettled years which followed the death of Henry II, however, and indeed the first three-quarters of the thirteenth century, saw a general curbing of English expansion in Wales. The comparative instability of the English Crown at this time coincided with the growth in strength of the north Welsh princes of Gwynedd, who never failed to attack the conquered territories whenever the invaders were weakened or preoccupied by events east of the border.

The Marchers reacted to this state of permanent crisis by strengthening or rebuilding their castles, employing all the latest devices of military engineering to make them as impregnable as possible. One innovation which found particular favour was the round keep, which, apart from its effectiveness as a

96

69 Pembroke Castle, Dyfed, showing William the Marshal's great round keep (left) and the towered outer bailey raised by his descendants. Cromwell declared it a place 'not to be had without fit instruments for battering', and its resistance in 1648 played a notable part in the Second Civil War (p. 188).

defence, had the advantage of being easily constructed from roughly coursed rubble, without the use of the shaped corner stones required for a square tower. Whatever the reason, twelve of the twenty or so surviving British round keeps are in Wales or the Marches, the earliest being probably those at Longtown (built in 1186–87) and nearby Lyonshall, both in Herefordshire. The largest and most impressive, however, is the massive keep of Pembroke, raised by William the Marshal in about 1200 on the site of an earlier earth and timber fortress. Its walls, still 75 feet (23 metres) high, were originally crowned by a battlemented wall-walk and topped by a dome carrying a still higher 'crow's nest': from here crossbowmen and archers could command both the bailey and the surrounding curtain wall. Should the bailey be taken, moreover, the keep was ringed by a projecting wooden gallery, or 'brattice' (supported on beams whose put-holes can still be seen) from which the defenders could shower down missiles on the heads of an enemy attacking the base of its massive walls.

The Marshal's great tower provided the inspiration for several later round keeps, like little

69

70 The lower bailey and gatehouse of Chepstow Castle were built c. 1225–45 by the sons of William the Marshal, and Marten's Tower (left), with its spur-buttresses and loopholed battlements, was added by his grandson Roger Bigod in 1287–93. (See also pl. 6.)

Bronllys and its big brother at Tretower, both in southern Powys and apparently the work of the same designer. Nearby, at Skenfrith in Gwent, our old acquaintance Hubert de Burgh followed the fashion with a similar keep: remembering, perhaps, his experience of enemy miners at Dover, he not only thickened its walls at their base – a usual feature of such towers – but further strengthened them by piling 6 feet (some 2 metres) of earth around the bottom. Nor did the Marchers neglect the outer defences of their castles. Hubert's keep was surrounded by a bailey wall with four round towers, while at Chepstow the sons of the Marshal extended fitz Osbern's old castle by adding long stretches of curtain wall, complete with a powerful gatehouse.

By no means all the castles in Wales, however, were the work of the Anglo-Norman invaders, for despite Giraldus' contention that the Welsh had no castles in his day, it is clear that by the beginning of the thirteenth century the native princes had in fact begun to build such fortresses for themselves. Rhys ap Gruffydd, ruler of Deheubarth in south-west Wales during the time of Henry II, is credited with the foundation of several castles there, including Kidwelly, but nothing of his work now remains, and for surviving Welsh-built fortresses we must look to the north, the territory of the princes of Gwynedd. Amongst the mightiest of these was Llywelyn the Great (1200–1240) who not only dominated his fellow princes but (by marrying the daughter of King John and taking advantage of every twist and turn of contemporary English politics) made himself a power to be reckoned with in Britain as a whole. His castles in Gwynedd, at Criccieth, Castell-y-Bere, Dolwyddelan and Dolbadarn, are all sited on the summits of rocky crags, which were surrounded by stone walls to form irregular enclosures somewhat reminiscent of hill-forts. All of them, however, had keeps, and there is certainly nothing old-fashioned about the fine cylindrical tower at Dolbadarn, which commands the road through the pass of Llanberis in Snowdonia.

A more characteristically Welsh type of keep was rectangular with one rounded end. Several of these were built (for instance at Castell-y-Bere near Towyn and at Castell Carn Dochan near Dolgellau, also in

71 *Hubert de Burgh's round-keeped castle of Skenfrith, by the river Monnow in Gwent, was built c.1230 to command one of the main routes between England and Wales.*

72 *The Welsh-built round keep at Dolbadarn Castle, which controls the pass of Llanberis in Snowdonia, was probably raised by Prince Llywelyn the Great. The curved stair to the* first floor entrance is modern, but the projection to the left of it originally housed the keep's garderobes or latrines.

Gwynedd): the best surviving specimen is the 'Welsh Tower' at Ewloe, Clwyd, a few scant miles from English Chester. Its position so close to the border reflects the continuing decline of English power in Wales which took place during the time of Llywelyn ap Gruffydd (1257–82), grandson and eventual successor of Llywelyn the Great. Building on his grandfather's achievements, he declared himself Prince of a united Wales, and intervened in the wars between Henry III and Simon de Montfort to such effect that in 1267 the English King had no alternative but to recognize him as the independent ruler of all the northern and central parts of the country, leaving only a strip to the south in the hands of the Marchers.

Llywelyn's dramatic success was resented by the many lesser Welsh princes whose estates he had swallowed up, and still more so by the Marcher barons whom he had expelled from their lands. Those that remained feared, with good reason, that it was only a matter of time before he moved to overrun the rest of the country, and in the years after 1267 hurried preparations were made to resist him. At about this time, for instance, four round towers and a great gatehouse were added to the previously

73 *The 'Welsh Tower', the D-shaped or apsidal keep of the little castle of Ewloe, Clwyd, built in the woods near Chester by Llywelyn ap Gruffydd in 1256.*

99

63 plain curtain wall of White Castle in Gwent (see p. 88) while Gilbert de Clare, most powerful of the southern Marchers, began a completely new castle at Caerphilly to protect his threatened lands in Glamorgan. Llywelyn's expansionist aims were confirmed by his reaction to this new fortress, whose half-built works he attacked and demolished in 1270. 'Red Gilbert', however, was not to be discouraged, and in the following year he made a
74 fresh start on what was to be the largest castle in
75 Wales, with the most complex water defences anywhere in Britain.

These defences were produced by blocking streams flowing through a marshy valley with a great coffer dam (itself later fortified) so that two artificial lakes were formed, one on each side of a central ridge. The ridge itself was then cut through with wet ditches to make two islands, one constituting the outer bailey and the other containing the main works of the castle, which could thus only be reached by crossing either the lake or a series of heavily defended drawbridges. Those who did so found themselves faced with a carefully planned concentric fortress, a contracted and developed version of the type
5 initiated by Dover a century earlier (see p. 89), with a low platform-like outer ward dominated by the high towered walls of the inner ward. Instead of a separate keep, however, the easternmost of the two inner gatehouses was designed to act as the defensive kernel of the fortress, strong enough to hold out independently when all else had fallen. Such keep-gatehouses (the direct descendants of structures like the Constable's Tower at Dover) were the very latest thing in thirteenth-century military engineering, and we shall hear a great deal more of them in the following pages.

Caerphilly never felt the weight of Llywelyn's attack, for within a few years of its building that prince had troubles enough of his own. With enemies to spare in his own lands, the Welshman made the mistake of antagonizing the new king of England, Edward I, by stirring up trouble among the barons and building a new castle at Dolforwyn, Powys, deliberately and uncomfortably close to the royal border fortress of Montgomery. Such policies were all very well when English affairs were unsettled, but the warlike Edward stood at the head of a united nation, and in November 1276 he declared full-scale war on Llywelyn. In the twenty years of intermittent fighting which followed Welsh independence was virtually extinguished, the house of Llywelyn was wiped out, and Gwynedd itself became the personal property of the English Crown.

Edward's conquest of Wales, having been achieved by a series of carefully planned campaigns, was accompanied by a concentrated programme of fortress-building unequalled in grandeur since the days of Rome. By the end of the wars in 1296 Gwynedd was ringed by no less than ten new royal castles, the majority of them larger and stronger than anything (save only Caerphilly, Dover and the Tower) hitherto seen in Britain, and all except one freely accessible to the supply-fleets on which English military policy largely depended: they were Builth, Flint, Aberystwyth, Rhuddlan, Ruthin, 76– Hope, Conwy, Caernarfon, Harlech and Beaumaris. 80 They were backed up by four new Marcher castles 83 (Hawarden, Denbigh, Holt and Chirk) and by three rebuilt Welsh fortresses (Dolwyddelan, Criccieth and Castell-y-Bere), and together they formed a unified system which ensured that no native leader would ever again completely expel the invaders. The expenditure of manpower and money on them was enormous, with craftsmen and labourers conscripted from virtually every shire in England and a sum equivalent in modern terms to £10,000,000 disbursed by the royal treasury before all were made defensible. Raised under the directing hand of James of St George, the King's brilliant Italian Master of the Works, they represent the highest point of castle development in Britain, and half of them survive unchanged enough to provide (along with the remarkably complete accounts of their construction) a stone textbook of medieval fortress-building.

Scarcely less important, in political terms, were the fortified towns which Edward attached to many of his new castles. Populated by immigrant English burgesses attracted by low rents and trading concessions, they not only acted as a reliable source of supplies and manpower in times of crisis but also assisted in the insidious Anglicization of the conquered territories. If their immediate inspiration was the fortress-towns or *bastides* which King Edward built to defend the frontiers of his dominions in southern France or James of St George designed for the dukes of Savoy, they had an ancestry nearer home in the ramparted villages attached to Marcher castles like Wigmore or 68 Richard's Castle and in the planned burhs by which the Saxon kings consolidated their gains from the Scandinavian invaders.

Unlike the uncoordinated land-grabbing of the early Marcher barons, Edward's enterprise involved the resources of a whole nation, and was highly organized from the very beginning. When he declared war in November 1276, the King's ultimate

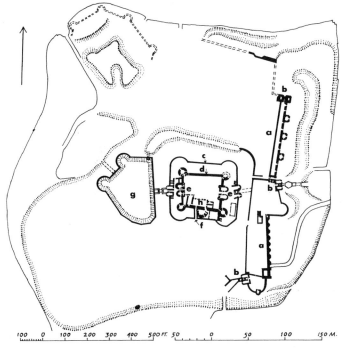

74, 75 *Caerphilly Castle, Glamorgan, begun by the Marcher lord Gilbert de Clare in 1271, seen in plan and from the air. (a) eastern barbican and fortified coffer dam, (b) gates, (c) outer ward of castle, (d) inner ward of castle, (e) gatehouses of castle, with keep-gatehouse on the right, (f) sally-port, (g) outer bailey or hornwork, (h) hall. In the air view we are looking east, from the outer bailey island to the coffer dam (its moat silted up). Note the powerful keep-gatehouse on the far side of the castle's inner ward (compare Harlech, ill. 77).*

100 0 100 200 300 400 500 FT. 50 0 50 100 150 M.

aim was an attack on Snowdonia, the heartland of Gwynedd, but this could not possibly be attempted before the next summer campaigning system: during the intervening winter and spring, therefore, Edward's clerks prepared the writs of summons to the feudal-levy and his agents recruited mercenaries and bought warhorses in France. Meanwhile three small task-forces, each led by a Marcher baron, operated out of Chester in the north, Montgomery in the centre and Carmarthen in the south-west, their purpose being to neutralize the minor Welsh principalities which surrounded Llywelyn's homeland. Their work was not always arduous, for many of the native princelings, whose attitude to Llywelyn was lukewarm if not actually hostile, made little or no resistance, and by the time the King mustered his main army at Worcester on 1 July 1277 only north-west Wales remained in enemy hands.

Edward's first march was to Chester, where he met with his fleet, twenty-seven ships drawn mainly from the freebooting confederacy of the Cinque Ports. They were an essential part of his plan of campaign, for they were to carry the supplies and baggage of his army while it pushed its way along the flat coastal strip of north Wales, thus avoiding the narrow mountain tracks where Llywelyn's guerrillas lurked in ambush. Three great rivers barred his path to Snowdonia: on about 21 July the army crossed the first of them, the Dee, to set up its field headquarters on the far bank at Flint. The force was already accompanied by a large number of diggers, woodcutters, carpenters and other workmen conscripted from the northern and midland shires, and more contingents came marching in daily (in one case at least accompanied by armed guards to prevent them from deserting en route) until the diggers alone numbered over three thousand.

As they laboured on a great double bank and ditch around the camp which grew into the fortified town of Flint, and laid the foundations of the castle which was to rise within it, word came in that the Marcher forces pushing up from west Wales had reached Aberystwyth and begun another castle there. Soon afterwards, on 16 August, Edward himself drew the net round Gwynedd tighter by advancing to the river Clwyd – his way cleared by woodcutters and pioneers – and setting up a second camp and embryo castle at Rhuddlan near the head of Offa's Dyke. From there, less than two weeks later, he advanced to Deganwy, where only the river Conwy separated him from the mountains of inner Gwynedd.

Instead of a frontal attack, however, the King used his fleet to outflank Llywelyn by carrying a powerful force to the island of Anglesey, the granary of north Wales. There the soldiers confiscated or destroyed the ripened harvest, denying the Welsh the food they needed for the coming winter, and then stood poised to cross the Menai Strait and attack Llywelyn from behind. With this force in his rear, the Marchers at Aberystwyth in the south and the King across the Conwy, the Welsh Prince was now completely surrounded, and rather than face a hungry campaign in barren Snowdonia he began to negotiate terms for surrender.

The terms agreed upon were comparatively generous, for Edward had no wish to annexe Gwynedd, though Llywelyn was shorn of all his other lands, including the buffer-zone between the two new castles rising at Flint and Rhuddlan. Flint, washed by the tidal waters of the Dee, is comparatively simple in design, with a square inner bailey defended by round towers at three of its corners. Outside the fourth, and surrounded by its own sea-filled moat, is a much larger circular tower, apparently intended both to act as a keep and to protect the harbour whose entrance lay at its foot.

The lengths to which Edward would go to maintain close contact between his new fortresses and his all-important fleet are even better exemplified at Rhuddlan Castle, which stands nearly 3 miles (5 kilometres) inland, on the then shallow and meandering river Clwyd. In order to make the river navigable, the King ordered a new deep-water channel to be cut between the castle and the sea, a work which occupied an average of sixty-six labourers for three years. When it was finished, the largest of Edward's ships could anchor under the shelter of the castle's outer bailey or moor to unload stores at a dock constructed in the moat.

The inner defences at Rhuddlan are diamond-shaped and perfectly symmetrical, with a pair of double-towered gatehouses at diagonally opposite corners and single round towers of the same pattern at the other two angles. As at Caerphilly and at most of Edward's other new castles, these gatehouses replaced the keep as the chief strongpoint. At Aberystwyth, the third new castle, Master James made do with one gatehouse in a fortress which otherwise resembled Rhuddlan. It is now almost completely ruined, while its southern companion at Builth in the Wye valley has disappeared altogether.

Two further castles, at Ruthin on the upper Clwyd and Hawarden (a Marcher fortress) near Chester, completed Edward's first scheme of fortresses for the protection of his conquests. Long before work on any of them was finished, however, another and far

76

76

76 *Rhuddlan Castle, Clwyd, displaying its western keep-gatehouse across the deep-water channel cut by Edward I's labourers. On the right is the fortified entry to the dock in the moat.*

more serious war broke out. Goaded by their loss of independence, by the high-handed behaviour of the English officials sent to rule them, and perhaps most of all by the alien castles rising on every side, the Welsh of both north and south rose in general rebellion. The signal was given by David, brother of Llywelyn, who surprised and captured Hawarden one stormy night in March 1282, and within a month the half-finished works at Aberystwyth had been destroyed, several Marcher castles in the south had 76 fallen, and Flint and Rhuddlan were under siege.

The struggle which followed, by contrast with Edward's triumphal progress in 1277, dragged on for fifteen bitter months. At first the unprepared English suffered several serious reverses, and an attempt to invade Gwynedd from Anglesey over a specially built bridge of boats was repulsed with heavy loss. Refusing to be discouraged, the King called up a force of Gascon mercenaries and fought on, and in December 1282 he was rewarded by the head of Llywelyn, killed in an obscure skirmish near Builth. But brother David still held out in Snowdonia, and it was not until the English had fought their way into the heart of the mountains and

reduced his strongholds of Dolwyddelan, Dolbadarn 72 and Castell-y-Bere that, in June 1283, he was taken by Welsh soldiers in the English service and handed over for execution.

Edward's victory was complete, and this time there was no talk of terms. Gwynedd was annexed to the personal estates of the English Crown, and steps were immediately taken to ensure her complete and permanent submission. Employing conscripted labour from as far afield as Norfolk and Kent, the King ordered the repair of the castles damaged in the war, and the addition of a further ten to their number. A royal castle at Hope, and Marcher castles at Holt, Denbigh and Chirk reinforced the frontier lands between Rhuddlan and Chester, while the captured Welsh strongholds of Dolwyddelan, Castell-y-Bere and Criccieth were rebuilt to provide English bases amongst the mountain passes. Most important of all, the encirclement of Snowdonia was completed by the construction of four more royal 77– fortresses on the coast, at Harlech, Conwy, Caernar- 80 fon and (last of all, in 1294) Beaumaris. 83

Immediately to the south-west of the mountains, the old Welsh fortress on the crag of Criccieth was

103

given a strong inner bailey with a massive gatehouse, and a few miles away, across Tremadoc Bay, another rocky outcrop became the site of the completely new castle of Harlech. Seen against the background of the Snowdon range, Harlech is the most dramatically sited of Edward's castles, and the strength of its position is attested by three and a half centuries of resistance to Welsh and English, Yorkists and Parliamentarians. The crag on which it stands was originally washed on two sides by the sea, and sheltered a harbour guarded by stone-throwing engines and connected to the castle by a walled and loopholed stairway. The fortress itself bears more than a passing resemblance to Caerphilly, with the same platform-like outer bailey dominated by massive inner defences, two of whose four corner towers are surmounted by watch-turrets looking out over the sea.

Harlech's most striking feature, however, is the great keep-gatehouse, the best example of the type in Britain, which protrudes towards the landward side, overlooking and reinforcing the rock-cut ditch which defends the castle's only practicable approach. As well as the private apartments of the constable (an office once held by Master James the architect himself) it contained within its four storeys room for enough supplies to enable it to hold out independently. Through its vitals passed the main passage into the fortress, within which an intruder could be trapped by a series of doors and portcullises and done to death by missiles dropped through 'murder holes' in the roof. All this took over seven years to complete, even though at one time 227 masons, 115 quarriers, 30 smiths, 22 carpenters and 546 labourers were all at work simultaneously, and the total cost, in modern terms, was something like £2,000,000.

Ambitious though the works at Harlech were, it was the smallest of the three new royal castles begun in 1283. In March of that year, while the war was still in progress, King Edward established his headquarters at Conwy, on the Welsh side of the river of that name. There, on an eminently defensible spit of land washed on two sides by the tidal estuary and on the third by a small stream, stood a great abbey, the spiritual centre of Gwynedd and the burial place of Llywelyn the Great. Within days of his arrival the King decided to transfer the abbey to a new position (thus emphasizing the downfall of Llywelyn's dynasty) and to use its site for a new castle to guard the easternmost boundary of Snowdonia. To underline further the finality of conquest, a new fortified town inhabited by English immigrant traders was to

77 *The inner face of the keep-gatehouse of Harlech Castle, Gwynedd, showing the large windows (originally traceried) of its principal rooms.*

be attached to the castle, acting as both a supply centre and a massive outer bailey.

The town walls of Conwy were accorded as much attention as the castle itself, and they remain virtually unaltered to this day, the most impressive work of urban defence in Wales, if not the whole of Britain. Over three-quarters of a mile (1.2 kilometres) long, they are reinforced every fifty yards (46 metres) by hollow round towers, twenty-one in number, each containing a wooden bridge whose removal would break the circuit of the wall-walk and isolate any section taken by the enemy. Three strong gateways pierce the defences, the largest of them fitted out as an office for the King's private secretariat. Its staff were provided with the last word in thirteenth-century toilets, twelve separate cubicles or 'gonges' projecting from the walls and discharging into the stream below.

Unlike the Edwardian fortresses previously dealt with, Conwy Castle itself is neither symmetrical nor concentric in plan, but follows the roughly pentagonal shape of the rock on which it stands. Nor does it boast a keep-gatehouse, though the eight round towers distributed at regular intervals round its

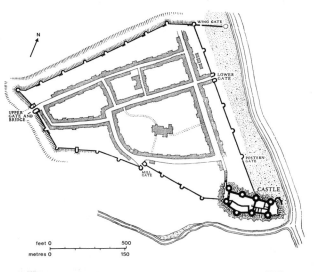

78 *Harlech Castle from the south, with the mountains of Snowdonia in the distance: note the watch-turrets on the two left-hand corner towers. Perenially the fortress of lost causes, Harlech was in turn the last stronghold of Owen Glendower (pp. 109–10), the Lancastrians (p. 154) and the Civil War Royalists (p. 187).*

79 *Plan of the fortified town and castle of Conwy, Gwynedd, showing the principal medieval streets (see also pl. 9). Mill Gate, west of the castle, housed the King's secretariat.*

walls are in themselves keep-like in size and strength. It represents, in fact, the final development of the towered bailey wall, so strong as to require no special 'great tower' as an ultimate defence. The river-side end of the castle, however, is cut off from the rest by an internal dividing wall to form a square inmost ward, intended as the chief Welsh residence of the King himself, and the four towers which flank it are distinguished by small watch turrets from which the royal banners could fly. Yet, though Conwy was substantially completed in the remarkably short period of four years, it was never destined to fulfil its planned role as the capital of north Wales. The focus of English power moved westwards to the third new fortress, Caernarfon.

The two places are markedly similar in plan. Like Conwy, Caernarfon stands on a peninsula, washed on the north by the Menai Strait and on the west by the river Seiont, with a brook protecting the eastern approach. The walled town occupies the whole of this area, with the irregularly-shaped and keepless castle again forming the innermost defence. But if Conwy was significant as Llywelyn's burial place, the associations of Caernarfon were even more

80 *A wall-walk at Caernarfon Castle, Gwynedd. The outer face (right) is pierced with defensive embrasures.*

81 *The keep-gatehouse of the little border castle of Brampton Bryan, Herefordshire, built in the early fourteenth century: notice the portcullis slot above the entrance and the elaborate chimney-stack of the chamber within. (See also p. 183.)*

ancient and powerful. According to a persistent Welsh tradition recorded in the *Mabinogion*, the nearby Roman fort of Segontium or Caer-yn-Arfon had been the home of the 'Emperor' Magnus Maximus, in reality a fourth-century Dux Britanniarum (pp. 38, 40). He, so the story went, had been led there by a dream of

a great city at the mouth of a river, and in the city a great castle, and he saw many great towers of various colours on the castle . . . Inside the castle he saw a fair hall and . . . a man seated in a chair of ivory, with the images of two eagles in red gold thereon . . .

Within the hall was a maiden, Elen of the Hosts, and from her union with Maximus supposedly sprang not only many of the Welsh noble families but also – in defiance of historical fact – the first Christian Emperor, Constantine the Great.

King Edward, who occupied Caernarfon in May 1283, was quick to foster the traditions which made it the fountainhead of Western Christendom, and soon after his arrival the body of 'Maximus father of Constantine' was conveniently brought to light. The fortress that Edward then began, moreover, set out 7 to embody in stone both the legend itself and, by implication, the King's own claim to quasi-imperial power. An eleventh-century motte, marking the westernmost limit of Norman penetration in North Wales, already stood on the site, and this was carefully preserved as a reminder of Edward's descent from the earlier conquerors. Around it rose a castle which, though it resembled Conwy in design, was very different in appearance, for its mural towers were polygonal rather than round and its walls were decorated with horizontal bands of contrastingly coloured stone. With these features, the first rare and the second unique in British medieval castle-building, the King deliberately recalled the mighty walls of Constantinople, Constantine's own city, and the more familiar defences built by that Emperor and his descendants at York and Pevensey. Not content with this, he gave 32 the new town a 'Golden Gate' to the sea, named after 172 a similarly positioned entrance at Constantinople, and decorated the principal tower of the castle with turrets topped by the eagles of Maximus' vision.

The work on Caernarfon had scarcely begun when Edward's Queen was brought there to bear a son (later Edward II) who was introduced to the Welsh as their new prince, 'born in Wales and speaking not a word of English'. This bad joke understandably failed to impress, and in 1294 the Welsh again rose in rebellion, capturing the still uncompleted works at

82 Kidwelly Castle, Dyfed, seen across the marshy valley of the Gwendraeth, with the four towers of Payne de Chaworth's inner bailey (1275) to the right, the buttressed and loopholed chapel protruding at the centre, the concentric outer bailey of c.1300, and on the left the massive keep-gatehouse, rebuilt after the sieges of 1403 and 1405 (pp. 109–10).

83 Ground plan of Beaumaris, Anglesey, the ultimate in concentric castles, with its fortified dock leading off the Menai Strait (bottom). The castle's core (shown in cross-hatching) stands within a lower curtain wall (solid black). The southern keep-gatehouse was later given added protection by a barbican across its entrance.

Caernarfon and besieging the other new castles. Reinforced and supplied by sea, these more than proved their worth by tying down the rebels until English reinforcements could be brought up, and when the rising was crushed Edward decided to add one final fortress to their number.

This was Beaumaris – 'the beautiful marsh' – built on the north shore of the Menai Strait to control previously undefended Anglesey. With its concentric defences, its two symmetrically placed keep-gatehouses and its defended dock capable of holding a ship of 40 tons (36 tonnes), Beaumaris is perhaps the most technically perfect of Master James's castles. It was, however, never fully completed, despite the architect's plea to the royal council: 'Sirs, for God's sake be quick with the money for the works . . . otherwise everything done up till now will be of no avail.' Having effectively subjugated Wales, Edward's gaze and his imperial ambition were now directed towards Scotland (see Chapter 9). All the same, the King realized that 'Welshmen are Welshmen, and we shall need to watch them', so the royal fortress system in north and central Wales continued to be adequately maintained and garrisoned.

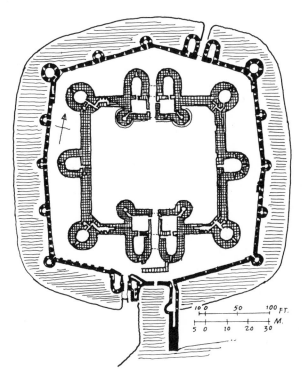

84 *The fortified cathedral close of St David's, Dyfed, looking from the ruined great hall of the quadrangular bishop's palace, with its rose window, towards the cathedral and Porth y Twr gatehouse (centre distance).*

In south Wales and the borders, meanwhile, the Marcher barons played their part in the consolidation of Edward's conquests by raising new 'private' fortresses. By their very nature, these did not form part of a coordinated system, but individually many of them are scarcely less advanced than the royal castles of the north. Even little 81 Brampton Bryan, in Herefordshire, boasts a strong keep-gatehouse, but the most magnificent of these Marcher fortresses of the turn of the thirteenth and 82 fourteenth centuries is certainly Kidwelly, Dyfed. Its site, near the mouth of the river Gwendraeth, was used by the Normans, but the present castle was begun about the time of King Edward's first Welsh war, when Payne de Chaworth built a square inner bailey with four corner towers. To this was added a massively buttressed chapel, whose spiritual purpose was belied by arrow slits commanding the steep slope up from the river. Next, in about 1300, the three more approachable sides of the castle were provided with concentric defences by the construction of a towered outer wall, and finally a great gatehouse was built over the fortress's main entrance.

Again following the example of the royal fortress-boroughs of the north, the lords of Kidwelly fortified the town attached to their fortress, and the same process was repeated at Chepstow, Cardigan, Tenby and the other principal English outposts in south Wales. Even the mother church of Wales, St David's 84 in Dyfed, found a place in the series of fortifications triggered by Edward's Welsh wars, for the English bishops who ruled there surrounded their cathedral, their palace and the houses of their clergy with an enclosing wall and defended gatehouses, including the double-towered Porth y Twr. Ordinary parish churches built or altered at this time, and especially those on the border, also took on the character of fortresses, with massively strong towers like that of 8 St Cynllo's at Llanbister in central Powys.

The new or refurbished defences from Snowdonia to the Bristol Channel did much to preserve English rule virtually unchallenged throughout the fourteenth century, but in the first year of the fifteenth a revolt occurred which all but succeeded in re-establishing Welsh independence. It began as a private quarrel between Owen of Glyndfrdwy, who claimed descent from the rulers of both north and south Wales, and one of his Marcher neighbours, but grew into a full-scale national movement when Glendower (as the English named him) declared himself Prince of Wales and called on Scotland and France for support. He had chosen his time well, for Henry IV of England was fully occupied with unrest at home, and such expeditions as he was able to send met with scant success against Owen's guerrilla tactics. By 1403 the English were virtually confined to their fortresses, scarcely able to communicate with each other for fear of the rebels holding the open country: in one case a verbal call for help was conveyed by a woman, 'because there was no man who dared to come, and neither man nor woman dare carry letters'.

The great castles of the north were seriously undermanned, and their lifelines from the sea threatened by the lurking French warships which patrolled the coast and landed forces to assist the
7 Welsh. Caernarfon, held at one time by only twenty-eight men, beat off several rebel attacks, but Harlech was in even worse case. Two successive governors were lured out and kidnapped by the besiegers, and in April 1404 the garrison, reduced by wounds and disease to five Englishmen and sixteen Welsh, was forced to surrender. Shortly afterwards Aberystwyth also fell, giving Owen a pair of strong bases. The situation elsewhere was just as serious, and every defensible place on the border, including several ancient and dilapidated mottes, was victualled and garrisoned. In the south-west castle after
82 castle fell to the rebels, but Kidwelly held out, and its financial accounts show us a vivid picture of life in a threatened fortress.

In the autumn of 1403 a large force of rebels, led by Glendower's lieutenant Henry Don and reinforced by French and Bretons, were ravaging the area round Kidwelly Castle and cutting off all communication by land. Fearing an attack, the garrison sent two messengers in 'a little boat' to Bristol with a plea for help, and laid in stocks of bread, honey, wheat and oats, as well as buying a cow at an extortionate rate and salting down its flesh. They also cleared the choked ditch outside the castle gate, and cut extra loopholes in the walls. Most of the townspeople had fled, but some took shelter in the castle 'in despair of their lives', and thirteen civilians (including a priest and a skinner) were drafted in to augment the tiny garrison of two men-at-arms and six archers. These precautions were not in vain, for though a force of rebels succeeded in breaching the town defences and battering the castle walls and roofs, the garrison were able to hold out until they drew off in search of easier prey.

The next year, 1404, was quieter, and the damage caused by the attack was repaired using the timbers from the wrecked town hall. The stock of armour was cleaned and mended, much-needed wine, ale and cider were brought in by a merchant named John Sweteapull, and the defenders were reinforced by a band of archers and a gunner. This was as well,

85 The only surviving fortified bridge in Britain, protecting the road over the Monnow into the border town of Monmouth in Gwent. The bridge tower is equipped with machicolations from which missiles could be dropped on enemies attacking the gate, and its portcullis groove can be seen next to the cross arrow-slit on the left.

for in August 1405, when a force of 2,500 Frenchmen landed 25 miles (40 kilometres) to the west at Milford Haven and were joined by some 10,000 Welsh, 82 Kidwelly was in greater peril than ever. Extra wooden towers and fighting tops had to be hastily constructed, but though several desultory attacks were repulsed the main enemy force marched on northwards and into England, where they encamped at the prehistoric hill-fort of Woodbury, only 8 miles (13 kilometres) from Worcester.

The invasion, however, turned out to be a flop. Faced with an English army, the Franco-Welsh retired, and during the next few months French support melted away. From now on Glendower's fortunes took a rapid downward turn, and the forces under Prince Henry – the future victor of Agincourt – gained more and more ground, relieving the beleaguered castles and returning the countryside to English rule. But the Welsh were far from finished, 78 and they still held Aberystwyth and Harlech. The first beat off the Prince's army for a year before surrendering in September 1408, and Harlech hung on even longer, only succumbing after a prolonged

bombardment by a great gun firing stone balls 22 inches (56 centimetres) in diameter. At its surrender Glendower's family fell into English hands, and he himself was reduced to the status of a homeless outlaw, finally disappearing into hiding in about 1415. With him passed away the last hope, until our own time, of an independent Wales.

Like the Welsh princes in the twelfth century and the two Llywelyns in the thirteenth, Glendower had very nearly succeeded in ousting the invaders, but like them he was baulked by that old enemy of his nation, the English castle. The resistance of Kidwelly, Caernarfon and a source of other fortresses had been a continual thorn in his side, cheating him of the complete victory he needed to keep the loyalty of his countrymen and attract essential help from abroad. They had held on long enough to allow the tide to turn, and provided a focus for the English counter-measures which eventually brought about his downfall. They had, in short, fulfilled the purpose for which the English policy of fortress-building in Wales, so long pursued, had always been intended.

9   Castles to 'lord it over the land':
Scotland and the Borders, 1066 – c. 1400

86 The cluster of towers which form the main strength of Dirleton Castle in Lothian, built c.1225, covering the raised entrance (right) reached by a drawbridge over the rock-cut moat: notice the protruding garderobe to the left of the gateway.

In 1314 King Robert Bruce ordered the destruction of Roxburgh, Linlithgow and Edinburgh castles 'lest the English ever afterwards might lord it over the land by holding the castles'.

JOHN OF FORDUN, *Cronica Gentis Scotorum*

While the first castles in England can be securely dated just before the Norman conquest, and those in Wales not long after it, the origins and early history of the castle in Scotland are to a far greater extent shrouded in obscurity. We can be certain, however, that the Conqueror's landing in 1066 was in the end scarcely less momentous for Scotland than for the countries to the south. At that time five loosely-knit peoples occupied the land: the most numerous were the mingled Picts and Gaels who held the Scottish heartlands, flanked to the south-east by the Angles of Lothian and to the south-west by the Britons of Strathclyde, while the descendants of Norse Vikings ruled and populated much of the far north and the western isles. Over all these peoples except the last the 'King of Scots', Malcolm Canmore, exercised a somewhat uneasy suzerainty, very much less cohesive than the feudal monarchy which the Conqueror soon established in England.

The changes wrought by the Normans, however, did not go unremarked by Canmore or his wife, the pious St Margaret, great-granddaughter of Aethelred Unraed (p. 69). Despite her Saxon birth, she was an enthusiastic upholder of the new Norman order in both Church and State, and it is significant that none of their three sons, Edgar, Alexander and David, bore the Celtic names of Malcolm's predecessors. Ruling successively from 1097 until 1153, these three worked dedicatedly towards converting their kingdom into a feudal state on English lines, pursuing a policy of inviting Norman knights to support them in war in return for estates in Scotland. Such families as the Maxwells, Gordons, Chisholms, Sinclairs, Frasers and Bruces – names we now think of as typically 'Scottish' – are descended from the Norman incomers of this period, who brought with them their own special type of fortification, the motte-and-bailey castle.

In Scotland, then, as in England and Wales, the earliest castles were most probably the earth and timber fortresses raised by these Normans some half-century after the battle of Hastings. Their remains, now no more than mounds, cluster thickest in Galloway in the south-west and Aberdeenshire (Grampian Region) in the north-east, two Celtic areas where Normans were settled to control violent local opposition to the centralizing policies of the monarchy. The alien fortresses were as unpopular there as in Saxon England, and given the opportunity the Scots rose and burnt their defences, only to have them rebuilt when the King's Norman cavalry crushed the revolt.

There are no mottes in the far north and west, where the King's power was feeble and his mailed cavalry were of little use amongst the mountains and islands, and such early castles as remain there owe little or nothing to the Norman tradition. Just how old these remote fortresses are, and whether they predate the mottes, is impossible to say, but it is certain that the Norsemen of the Orkneys – who also made use of prehistoric brochs when danger threatened – were building their own stone strongholds by the early twelfth century. One such is 'Cubbie Roo's Castle', the stump of a tower 20 feet (6 metres) square within an oval ditch, built on the island of Wyre in about 1148 by a certain Kolbein Hruga, whom the *Orkneyinga Saga* calls 'the most outstanding of men'.

Much more difficult to date are the castles of the north-western seaboard, ruled until the middle of the thirteenth century by the lieutenants of the king of Norway. Both before and after Alexander III of Scotland wrested suzerainty from him in 1263, however, real power in the islands and sea-lochs lay with the Gaelic chieftains of the area, men like the MacSweens and the MacDougalls who held most of Argyll. Neither were behindhand in building castles, and the former guarded the narrowest part of Loch Sween with a sizeable rectangular keep of a type rare in Scotland, and perhaps derived from the Norman donjons of nearby Ireland. It has been claimed as the earliest stone castle in Scotland, but its date remains problematic. Other western strongholds, constructed by building a wall round an irregular rocky outcrop, were (like some Welsh-built castles) doubtless derived from prehistoric fortresses. This was certainly the case with Dunstaff- 88 nage, near Oban, where the first Gaelic invaders of Argyll had established a stronghold overlooking Loch Etive. Here, it was said, they had brought from the Hill of Tara the coronation stone of the High Kings of Ireland, later transferred to Scone and stolen by Edward I for his throne at Westminster. At this place, called in the sixteenth century 'the eldest fortification in Scotland', a strong castle was built in the early 1200s by the MacDougall lords of Lorne, who equipped it with corner towers and a gateway whose entrance was raised high above ground level.

Returning to the lands held by the Normans in the lowland south and east, we find mottes continuing to be built throughout the twelfth century. Perhaps the most impressive of all is the 'Bass of Inverurie', Aberdeenshire, raised in about 1180 by the younger brother of the William the Lion who besieged Brough (p. 89). Nothing like the great tower-keep there, still less like the massive donjon at Dover – begun, incidentally, at the same time as Inverurie – seems however to have existed in Scotland. Though our knowledge is limited by the wholesale destruction of fortresses during the Wars of Independence, there is little doubt that Scottish castles of the twelfth and thirteenth centuries were generally much less up to date than those south of the border, and certainly there were no fortresses built to the fully concentric plan of Caerphilly.

Towards the end of the thirteenth century, nevertheless, a handful of Scottish castles were built which would pass muster anywhere. All have curtain walls with round towers, and in the case of Kildrummy in Aberdeenshire and Bothwell near Glasgow one of these towers, larger than the rest, forms a cylindrical keep. At Dirleton, Lothian, the strength of the castle consists of a whole cluster of towers, both round and square, placed immediately next to the raised entrance so as to form a kind of keep-gatehouse.

There is a keep-gatehouse proper at Caerlaverock, Dumfries, perhaps one of the most pleasing of all Scottish castles. Though much altered in later times – the corbelled-out machicolations on the tower tops are fifteenth-century – it presents substantially the same picture as it did in 1300, when an observer described its triangular shape as

> like that of a shield, for it only had three sides all round, with a tower at each angle, but one of them was a double one, so high, so long and so large that under it was the gate with a drawbridge . . . And I think you will never see a more finely situated castle, for on one side can be seen the Irish sea . . . and to the north a fair moorland, surrounded by an arm of the sea . . . so that no creature living can approach it on two sides without putting himself in danger of the sea.

A third side was covered by woods and marshes, and the walls themselves are immediately surrounded by two wet moats separated by a bank. Facing the only practicable approach is the great gatehouse, inescapably reminding us of Edward I's Welsh castles in its position and design. Indeed, Caerlaverock, ideally situated to act as a bridgehead for an English invasion force crossing the Solway Firth, may well have been built at Edward I's orders by a Scottish knight in his service during the last decade of the thirteenth century. At that time, certainly, invasion

87 The interior of the sixteenth-century dovecot at Dirleton, which provided a useful source of food for the castle's occupants.

88 Dunstaffnage Castle near Oban, built in the thirteenth century on the site of an ancient Gaelic stronghold. The tower-house within is seventeenth-century.

was in the air, and the long period of comparative amity between England and Scotland was about to erupt into centuries of bloody and destructive war.

The first and greatest of these conflicts, the War of Independence which lasted from 1296 until 1328, was at the same time a triumph of Scottish arms and a signal failure of the castle as an instrument of conquest. It was occasioned by a series of those unhappy accidents which dogged the northern monarchy throughout its existence. On the dark and stormy night of March 1286, with seers prophesying the approaching end of the world, Alexander III, last of the house of Canmore, broke his neck in a fall from his horse, leaving as his only heir an infant grand-daughter in Norway. Four uneasy years later she too died, and the succession lay open to the claims of no less than fourteen 'Competitors', mainly men descended in the female line from the royal house. Before war could break out between the two most determined of them – Robert Bruce, Lord of Annandale, and John Balliol, Lord of Galloway, both of Norman descent – the Scots lords called upon King Edward of England to adjudge the rightful heir.

> Ah, blind folk full of folly
> Had ye bethought you thoroughly
> What peril to you might appear
> Ye had not done in that manner.
> Wales example might have been
> To you, had you it foreseen.

So lamented, with the benefit of hindsight, the fourteenth-century poet John Barbour. But in 1291 Edward was regarded as a friendly prince, and most Scots allowed his claim to be Lord Paramount of Scotland – though what he and they meant by this vague title turned out to be quite different things. At any rate, Edward demanded and obtained the homage of all the claimants as well, ominously, as custody of all the major Scottish castles while judgment was pending. He decided for Balliol, who indeed had the better title, and the latter was crowned as King John I. All might then have been well had not Edward insisted on treating his fellow-king as a subservient vassal, and in 1294 demanding the service of Scotsmen for his French wars. Instead of concurring, the exasperated nobles forced Balliol into an alliance with France, undertaking to attack England should Edward leave his country.

It was a foolish and disastrous move, and in March 1296 armies were mustering on both sides of the border. The Scots struck the first blow, attacking 55 Wark Castle and besieging Carlisle. Edward in- 143 stantly replied by sacking ill-defended Berwick-on-Tweed, then in Scotland and her largest and richest

town. While he set about converting Berwick into a fortified borough on the lines of Conwy or Caernarfon, the Scots (in the first of a series of raids whose effects on border fortifications we shall consider later) ravaged Northumberland, allegedly burning alive a party of schoolboys and monks at Corbridge. Refusing to be distracted, in late April the English routed an army sent against them at Dunbar and moved on into Scotland. Edinburgh Castle fell to 90 Edward's siege engines after three days, Stirling was 89 abandoned without a blow, and the invaders marched triumphantly as far north as the Moray Firth. Just twenty-one weeks after crossing the border, Edward was in total control of Scotland: her coronation stone and her holiest relics were sent to London, Balliol was formally stripped of his crown, and almost every man of note swore allegiance to the conqueror. Most important for us, every important Scottish fortress was taken over, 'and stuffyt [stuffed] all with Inglis men'.

It was upon these Scottish castles, now the fortified bases of the invader, that the fate of the nation was largely to turn for the next quarter century. Less than a year after Edward's contemptuously easy conquest, risings began to break out against his lieutenants. They were led at first not by a nobleman but by the son of a Lanarkshire knight, William Wallace or Waleys, whose name may indicate that he came of the old Strathclyde Welsh stock. With the help of Andrew Moray in the north, and the support of a few barons like young Robert Bruce of Carrick, grandson of the 'Competitor' of 1291, he raised an army consisting largely of spear-armed infantry. With them, flying in the face of military orthodoxy, he routed the mounted English army of occupation at Stirling Bridge in September 1297, flaying the body of one of its leaders and using his skin as a sword-belt. Neither this nor the atrocities of Wallace's ill-controlled men when they raided northern England in the following months would be forgiven by King Edward, and in the summer of 1298 he crossed the border to take his revenge. His task was made easier by the fact that, though the Scots had retaken many of their castles (including Dirleton), they had been unable to reduce the key 86 fortresses of Stirling, Edinburgh, Roxburgh and Berwick. Dirleton too was soon back in English hands, after a ferocious assault directed by the warrior-bishop of Durham, and not long afterwards English knights and Welsh archers crushed Wallace's army at Falkirk – among the first of the many great victories of the longbow. Wallace and Bruce escaped and the latter, prophetically, de-

The precipitous western face of Stirling Castle, the 'Key of Scotland'. Scene of a famous siege in 1304, it held off Cromwell during the Civil War (p. 188) and Prince Charles Edward Stuart in 1746 (p. 193). The present castle is fifteenth-century and later: in the foreground is James V's palace, of the 1530s, and beyond it a much-altered older range used in the late seventeenth century as officers' lodgings.

liberately destroyed his own castle of Ayr so that it should be of no use to the enemy.

Despite Falkirk, the Scots fought on after 1298, and for the next five years the fortunes of war swayed this way and that. The English garrison of Stirling was starved out in 1299, but Edward's men still held the other major fortresses, and in July 1300 he laid siege to Caerlaverock, which at some time unknown had fallen into Scottish hands. A poet with the army described – as if it were a tournament or a knightly game – how the attackers, having failed to take the castle by storm, made short work of its walls with the fire of three siege-engines: when the garrison of sixty men surrendered, he claimed, the King pardoned them and gave them new clothes. Other sources say he hanged them from the nearest tree.

In May 1303 Edward, determined to make an end of Scots resistance, launched a third full-scale invasion. With him now was Robert Bruce, who for reasons not entirely clear had changed sides. As in 1296, the King planned to march right up the east coast of Scotland, relieving or recovering the fortresses on the way. Across his path lay the Forth, whose only practicable bridge was guarded by the enemy-held 'key of Scotland', Stirling Castle. Rather than commit himself to a long siege early in the campaign, and remembering the crossing of the Menai Strait during the Welsh wars (p. 103), he ordered three remarkable prefabricated bridges to be built, complete with drawbridges at each end and defensive towers equipped with machine-operated crossbows or 'springalds'. Towed up from Norfolk by sea, they were a triumphant success, and by the time Edward went into winter quarters within the shelter of a ditched and palisaded camp at Dunfermline most of his aims had been achieved and many of the Scots nobles had already surrendered.

Stirling, whose keeper proudly claimed to hold it for 'the Lion' (the heraldic personification of Scotland), remained to be taken, and to do so Edward gathered together the largest collection of catapults and other siege engines that Britain had ever seen. Whole woods were cut down to provide their timbers, church roofs were stripped of lead for their counterweights, and by 22 April 1304, when the siege began, at least thirteen of them were ready. The largest fired stones weighting 200–300 pounds (90–140 kilograms), and others shot sealed pots of 'Greek fire' – which broke and ignited as the substances within reacted with the air – into the castle, while the Queen and her attendants watched from a specially constructed window in their lodgings. Yet Stirling, placed on 'the strongest of rocks', provided no easy triumph for the ladies to applaud. The garrison had engines of their own, and gave almost as good as they got, and the King himself was struck by a spent bolt from a springald which stuck between the plates of his leg armour without piercing the flesh. This 'miracle' (as the chroniclers interpreted it) did little to improve Edward's temper, and he ordered the construction of yet another engine, named 'War Wolf', even larger than all the rest. Before it could be brought into play the garrison, who had resisted gallantly for twelve weeks, capitulated, but Edward insisted that they remain in the castle to defend themselves as best they could against his new machine, which demolished an entire wall with a single shot.

With the surrender of Stirling all effective Scots resistance came to an end, and it seemed that the war was finally over. Displaying more tact than in 1296, Edward allowed the Scottish nobles a part in the ruling of their nation, though an English lieutenant had the final say and Englishmen garrisoned the major fortresses. These fortresses were, where necessary, repaired, and several towns and manor houses (including Linlithgow, Selkirk and Perth) were defended by new 'peels' – elaborate wooden stockades, complete with gates and towers and surrounded by banks and ditches. No great new 'Edwardian' castles like those of north Wales, however, rose in subjugated Scotland, though had they done so the final outcome of the war might have been very different. Doubtless the existing fortresses were deemed to be sufficient and, though Edward planned a chain of strongholds along the line of the Forth, no scheme of maritime fortifications could command Scotland as they had the much smaller area of Snowdonia. Besides, the still uncompleted Welsh castles had cost so much that the English exchequer could not easily afford another such programme, and before one could be seriously contemplated the fighting – just eighteen months after the fall of Stirling – had broken out anew.

It began suddenly and unexpectedly on 10 February 1306 when Robert Bruce, latterly a trusted ally of England, murdered his rival John Comyn of Badenoch on the very steps of the altar of the Greyfriars Kirk at Dumfries. This was the prelude to a carefully planned *coup d'état*. Supported by the clergy, and especially Bishop Wishart of Glasgow (who turned the timbers given to him by Edward for his cathedral into siege-engines to batter English garrisons), Bruce quickly gathered together an army, and six weeks after the murder had himself crowned king of Scotland at Scone. Pitted against him were not only the English, led by Aymer de Valence, Edward's lieutenant and Comyn's brother-in-law, but also the powerful Scottish connections of the murdered man, notably John MacDougall, lord of Dunstaffnage Castle. They inflicted two successive defeats on King Robert in June and July 1306, and by September he had no alternative but to flee the country, leaving his family to be captured when their refuge of Kildrummy Castle was set afire by a traitor within the walls. With three of his brothers and many of his chief supporters executed, his female relations sent to English nunneries or kept in iron cages in English castles, and he himself 'lurking in the outermost isles of Scotland', it seemed that the brief reign of 'King Hob' had been no more than a summer's dream.

But Bruce, encouraged perhaps by the famous spider, was not to be daunted, and in February 1307 he was back in Galloway. From now on his policy, dictated by his enemy's superiority in cavalry, castles and siege-engines, was to be one of relentless guerrilla warfare:

> On foot should be all Scottish war
> By hill and moss themselves to lair . . .
> In strait places keep all store
> And burn the plain land them before
> Then shall they pass away in haste
> When that they find nothing but waste
> With wiles and wakening in the night
> And sudden noises made on heights
> Then shall they turn with great affrai [fear]
> As they were chased with sword away.
> *(Good King Robert's Testament)*

Above all, woods and hidden glens were to serve instead of fortress walls, no men were to be wasted in vulnerable garrisons, and castles captured were to be utterly destroyed so that the English could not again use them 'to lord it over the land'. Soon successful ambushes were making the south-west too hot for the English, who were further demoralized when the sixty-eight-year-old King Edward, leading a new invasion force, died of dysentery and exhaustion at Burgh-by-Sands in Cumbria on 7 July 1307.

The great 'Hammer of the Scots' was succeeded by his ineffective son, Edward II, whose campaigns in Scotland were to be a chapter of disasters and whose reign in England was from the beginning plagued by baronial opposition and later by outright civil war. Now he did no more than show his face across the border before leading his army home, leaving Bruce to fight his own Scottish enemies and reduce the small English-held castles in the far north. Meanwhile King Robert's most loyal supporter, the pale-faced lisping Sir James Douglas, was mounting a terrorist campaign against the enemy garrisons in the south, starting with the one which occupied his own family's stronghold of Castle Douglas, near Lanark. Learning from an old retainer that the defenders would be in church on Palm Sunday, Sir James's men disguised themselves as labourers and slaughtered them at their devotions. He then easily took the fortress, poisoned the well with salt and the bodies of dead horses, carried off the movable booty and, locking the prisoners and the remaining supplies in the cellar, burnt the keep over their heads: with savage humour, the Scots named the exploit 'the Douglas larder'.

Bruce's victory at the Pass of Brander, Argyll, over his chief remaining enemy, John MacDougall (whose fortress at Dunstaffnage was soon afterwards taken), meant that he and Douglas were increasingly able to concentrate on the destruction of the greater English-held castles. Not one of these was to be taken by a conventional assault, and treachery, courage and surprise night-attacks were aided only by the Scots substitute for a siege-engine, the rope-ladder. One of these was described by a curious English chronicler as having wooden steps 30 inches (75 centimetres) long, set at intervals of 18 inches (45 centimetres) and secured with knots in the rope; at the top was an iron hook with rings on each side, so that it could be lifted on the point of a lance and placed on the battlements with a minimum of noise: 'Thus they can go up the wooden steps as if climbing an ordinary stair, and the heavier the weight going up, thus more will the iron hook adhere to the wall.'

The first castle to fall victim to these scaling-ladders was perhaps Forfar, which was surprised on Christmas night 1308. The garrison paid for their 'want of watch' by being slaughtered to a man and (following the new policy) the fortress was razed to the ground, even its well being filled in. A half-hearted invasion of southern Scotland in 1310 did little more than provoke Bruce into raiding the long-peaceful English Borders in the succeeding two years, though a Scots night attack on Berwick in December 1312 was foiled by a dog which barked loudly as the first ladders struck the wall. The important town of Perth, besieged by Bruce in the following month, was less fortunate: finding its stone walls too strong for conventional assault, he lulled the garrison into complacency by marching away, only to return one 'mirk night' a week later. The King himself led the hushed attackers, wading chin-deep across the moat and carrying his own ladder while he tested the bottom with his spear. When the place was taken all the Scots who had opposed him were slain (though the English were spared) and 'he leavit not about that toune, tower standing, stone nor wall'.

During the remainder of 1313 Dumfries and Caerlaverock were starved out, and the peel of Linlithgow was taken when a farmer hid eight soldiers in a haycart and, cutting the traces, jammed it in the entrance so that the gates could not be shut against the concealed Scots outside. A still more cunning ruse was employed by James Douglas in his assault on Roxburgh Castle on the dark night of Shrove Tuesday 1314. His men, with their ladders, wrapped themselves in black cloaks and approached the walls on all fours, so that the watch mistook them for wandering cattle. Nevertheless, a grappling-hook rattling against the battlements attracted attention, and the leading Scot had to stab an Englishman who tried to kill him as he mounted the wall. The remainder of the garrison were surprised carousing in their hall, though a few of them escaped when Douglas burst in and held out in the keep until they saw resistance was hopeless.

The capture of Roxburgh spurred Douglas's comrade and rival, Thomas Randolph, then besieging Edinburgh Castle, to the most daring exploit of the whole war. Despairing of taking the fortress by conventional methods, he made discreet enquiries for any man 'that knew any good enterprise to climb the walls privily'. A certain William Francois came forward, who had lived in the castle as a youth 'and loved a wench here in the town'; he used to visit his sweetheart secretly by climbing up and down the precipitous rock, and claimed to know his way even on the darkest night. Arranging a diversionary attack on the castle's east gate to draw off the garrison, Randolph set out with thirty picked men to scale the northern face of the 270-foot (80-metre) crag on which it stands. Barbour's poem *The Bruce* (rendered here into modern English) gives a vivid account of the attack:

> Then William Francois leading them
> Clung to the crags before them aye
> And at his back him followed they
> With mickle pain, while to, while fro
> They scrambled up the footholds so
> Till half the crag they conquered had
> And there a ledge they found so broad
> They could just barely sit to rest

90 Edinburgh Castle from the north, showing the crag-face scaled by Thomas Randolph's men during their surprise attack in 1314. Dominating the Scottish capital, the castle was never taken by open assault, but was several times bombarded into submission. The bastioned outworks date mainly from the seventeenth century. (See pp. 45, 114, 165, 168, 192.)

For they were tired and scant of breath . . .
Just then above them on the wall
The night-watchmen assembled all
Now help them God that all things may
For in full great peril are they
For might they see them, there should none
Escape out of that place unslain
To death with stones they would them ding
And they could help themselves nothing
Yet wonder mirk was all the night
So that they had of them no sight
But nonetheless yet was there one
Of them that dropped right down a stone
And said 'Away, I see you all'
Although he saw them not at all
Out over their heads flew the stone
And they sat silent every one
The watchmen when they heard nought stir
From that part passed together were
And chattering onward went their way . . .

The second half of the climb was worse than the first, but the Scots reached the wall and, using the inevitable rope-ladders, climbed in. After a sharp fight they gained the east gate, set upon the defenders from behind, and let in their companions to complete the rout of the garrison.

Edinburgh, like Roxburgh and Linlithgow, was dismantled, and in March 1314 only one effective fortress north of Berwick remained in enemy hands. This was Stirling, which, significantly, was the only one to be attempted by purely orthodox methods of

siege-craft, being beleaguered by the King's brother Edward Bruce for four months in 1313. More chivalrous than politic, he abandoned the siege on the understanding that the castle would surrender if it was not 'rescued by battle' by the King of England before Midsummer 1314. It was a fateful agreement, for Edward II dared not for his crown and credit refuse the challenge, and King Robert was forced willy-nilly to abandon guerrilla tactics and fight a pitched battle at Bannockburn below the rock of Stirling. The result was a crushing and ignominious defeat for the invaders, which set the seal on the liberation of all Scotland save Berwick from English rule. Such an end could never have been achieved, however, without the painstaking reduction over the past six years of the English-held castles, an achievement without parallel in the annals of British fortification, and one which must surely rank amongst the most successful guerrilla campaigns in British history.

After Bannockburn Bruce was free to carry the war into the enemy camp by intensifying his devastating attacks on northern England, aiming not only 'for to enriche his men' but also to force a peace which recognized an independent Scotland. Year after year Thomas Randolph and James Douglas led their horsemen over the border for two- or three-week raids, ravaging Northumberland and Cumbria and at times penetrating into Yorkshire and Lancashire. Like the Viking armies of four centuries earlier, they burnt or trampled crops, lifted livestock and drove off men and women for ransom, sparing only those areas which paid them vast sums in 'protection money'. In 1318, for instance, they plundered Ripon in Yorkshire, and would have burnt it to the ground had not the burgesses – who had barricaded themselves in the minster – offered them a ransom of more than £600 and handed over hostages for its payment. Nor were churches or abbeys exempted from the choice between ransom and destruction, and in ten years of raiding the Scots extorted more than £20,000 in cash alone, not to mention the value of their booty. Famine and gangs of freelance bandits soon added to the miseries of the borderlands, and English counter-raids usually met with a bloody nose at the hands of the 'Black Douglas', whose very name was so dreaded that mothers used it to frighten wilful children.

The only hope for the hapless northern English, whose King was too inept or too occupied with his own troubles to defend them, was to take refuge in a castle or a fortified town. These, on the whole, the lightly-armed raiders avoided, preferring the easier prey to be found in the open country. On the occasions when the Scots did bring the panoply of a siege against a border fortress they met with a spirited resistance. Norham, for instance, held out successfully for eleven months in 1318 and again for seven months in the following year, while an attack on Carlisle in 1315 ended in utter disaster for the invaders. Inexperienced in formal sieges, the Scots had only one 'engine', which was soon put out of action by the fire of the defenders, and a siege-tower built to overtop the battlements sank immovably in the mud. Two general assaults on the defences were repulsed with heavy loss, as was an attempt by Douglas to scale the walls with ladders under cover (as at Edinburgh) of a diversionary attack. Finally, after eleven days during which only two of the garrison were slain, the disconsolate Scots retired, leaving all their baggage and several important prisoners to fall into the hands of the exultant defenders. As a reward for their gallant defence, the citizens of Carlisle were granted a charter of civic liberties, and the events of the siege are graphically illustrated in its initial letter.

These local English successes, however, were more than offset by the fall of Berwick, betrayed to the Scots by a disgruntled townsman in 1318. In the changed circumstances Bruce did not destroy its defences, but rather garrisoned it strongly, drawing Edward II at last northwards in an attempt at recapture which collapsed when Douglas and

91 *The initial letter of the Carlisle charter, 1315, showing (left to right) the Scottish trebuchet or siege-sling, a defender hurling spears and another winding a crossbow, a man dropping boulders on an enemy miner, and the spearing of an axe-wielding attacker at the top of a scaling ladder.*

Randolph led a diversionary raid almost up to the walls of York. Edward's own attempt at raiding, in 1322, was an ignominious failure, for Bruce's scorched-earth policy ensured that the English found, it was said, only one lame cow in the whole of Lothian. Meanwhile King Robert had outflanked him, leading an army including wild Gaels from the Isles into Cumbria and catching the retiring English in northern Yorkshire. Edward's precipitous flight on this occasion was the final blow to his prestige and in 1323, with his subjects declaring that he 'neither knew how to rule his kingdom nor how to defend it', he agreed to a truce.

Four years later Edward paid for his many faults by his deposition and murder at the instigation of his wife Isabella and her lover Roger Mortimer, who crowned his fourteen-year-old son in his stead. Bruce marked the occasion by launching a new series of raids, against which a costly campaign led by the young Edward III achieved absolutely nothing. He was showing signs of annexing Northumberland when Isabella's government, acceding to the general English war-weariness, began to negotiate a formal peace. By the Treaty of Edinburgh, signed in 1328, an English government at long last recognized that Scotland was a separate and independent kingdom, over which it had no rights, and that King Robert Bruce was her lawful ruler.

Though the thirty-two-year-long war had seen the mass destruction of major castles in the Scottish

92 *The large fourteenth-century tower-house of the Umfraville family at Chipchase, Northumberland (left), much altered by the addition of a mansion and Georgian casements. The top stage and the nearside face, however, retain their original form (ill. 96).*

93 *Opposite: Halton Tower, Northumberland, with its corbelled-out corner turrets (compare Chipchase, ill. 92), built in the fourteenth century of stone from a nearby Roman fort. In the foreground is part of the original barmkin wall, but the house (right) and large window are later additions.*

heartlands, it also gave rise to the proliferation of a rather different type of fortress on the borderlands, and more particularly, at first, on the English side. There were, it is true, already castles enough there, and together with walled towns like York and Newcastle they had more than played their part in preventing Scots annexation of English territory. As we have already seen, however, they had done little or nothing to protect the population from the systematic robbery and devastation which began in 1296 and reached a crescendo in the years after Bannockburn. What resulted was a devolution of border fortress-building from kings and great lords, building for national defence, downwards to knights, small landholders and lesser churchmen, building for personal protection. These men did not need, and could not afford, expensive curtain-walled castles capable of withstanding a full-dress siege, but rather required a place of temporary refuge, where they could hold out with their families, servants and (if possible) livestock until the lightly-armed raiders passed on in search of easier prey.

This situation produced the tower-house, which is nothing more or less than a miniature stone keep, a scaled down version of the twelfth-century donjons which form the centrepiece of border castles like Brough or Appleby. No two towers are exactly alike, but they tend to be two or three times as tall as they are broad, having only one room on each floor in the smaller examples like that at Corbridge, though the larger and later Chipchase, also in Northumberland, has several chambers in each upper storey. Almost invariably the ground floor has a stone-vaulted roof as a precaution against an intruder setting fire to the rooms above. The lower floors generally have very small windows, or none at all. (The large casements at Chipchase and Halton Tower are seventeenth-century alterations made after mansions had been attached to the old towers.) Entrance is either at ground level – when a thick oak door was often accompanied by a hinged iron grille or 'yett' (gate) which acted as a secondary defence – or, for added safety, one storey up and gained by an easily removable ladder. Yet another precaution was incorporated in the spiral staircase or 'turnpike'

120

94 *Below: Section of a small tower-house, Liberton in Lothian, showing (top to bottom) the ladder to the battlements; men removing the outside ladder leading to the main entrance; and the vaulted and slit-windowed lower storey, with defenders blocking the trap-door from the cattle-byre before retreating up the stair to the second floor.*

95 *Below: Section of a large and luxurious L-shaped tower-house, Craigmillar, Edinburgh (see pp. 126–27 and ill. 102). The projecting wing or 'jamb' on the left houses small private rooms, while the principal bed-chamber, great hall (with window-seat) and store-rooms are in the main block to the right.*

121

96 *Looking up the tower wall of Chipchase (ill. 92) at the two projecting garderobes, corbelled-out corner turrets and machicolated parapet.*

97 *Below: the 'vicar's peel' in the churchyard at Corbridge, Northumberland, built c.1300 of Roman stone, equipped with corbelled-out corners and a garderobe (left).*

98 *Opposite: the fortress-tower of Newton Arlosh in Cumbria, c.1305, accessible only from within the church.*

within the tower, which twisted clockwise so as to give a defender maximum play for his sword arm and maximum protection for his unguarded left side. Usually these stairs are within the thickness of the wall, but in larger towers like Chipchase they occupy a small projecting wing of their own.

External defences were concentrated at the top of the tower, which often has battlements and small corner turrets, one of which carried a beacon to pass on warning of raiders or to call for help against them. At both Halton and Chipchase the turrets project on 92 corbels to give a better command of the base of the 93 tower, and Chipchase has its whole parapet machico- 96 lated so that missiles could be dropped directly on the head of an attacker who ventured too close to the walls.

The tower-house, then, was equipped with as many devices as possible to provide safe accommodation for the owner and his dependents, and for as many others as could be squeezed inside during an emergency. The less fortunate, together with the owner's livestock and farm-buildings, would find some protection within the walled or stockaded courtyard which surrounded the tower, constituting the equivalent of a weak bailey. These walled courtyards, alias 'barmkins' or 'peels' (cf. p. 116), were never very elaborately defended, being intended only as a deterrent to small bands of marauders or casual thieves. In many cases they have now completely disappeared, leaving the tower – the 'peel-tower' – to stand alone.

Tower-houses of a sort seem to have been in existence before the outbreak of the War of Independence, and their spread was rapid after the raiding began. Among the early builders were churchmen like the vicar of Corbridge who, mindful 97 of the fate of the schoolboys and monks burnt alive there in 1296, used stone from the nearby Roman fort to make himself a sturdy tower in his churchyard. At least a dozen more 'vicar's peels' remain in Northumberland and Cumbria, apart from church towers built (as in the Welsh Marches, p. 108) as refuges. One of the strongest of these last is at Newton Arlosh 98 in Cumbria, built in about 1305 by the monks of Holmcultram Abbey for the parish church of their 'new town' founded at this time. More of a fortress than a place of worship, the massive tower has no windows near the ground and is equipped with an overhanging turret: it could only be entered by climbing a ladder to a door at first floor level inside the body of the church, which thus acted as a second line of defence. Most tower-houses, however, were built by laymen, like the Haltons who raised the tower 93

named after them or the much more powerful Umfravilles who built Chipchase. With its area of 53 by
38 feet (16 by 11.5 metres), the latter is among the
most imposing of border towers, and belongs
probably to the middle rather than the beginning of
the fourteenth century. For neither the Anglo-
Scottish wars nor the building of tower-houses
ended with the Treaty of Edinburgh in 1328: both,
in fact, were only just beginning, and had nearly
three centuries yet to run.

In the four years after the Treaty events moved
rapidly towards the complete reversal of the Anglo-
Scottish balance of power. King Robert and many of
his captains died, leaving the kingdom to the five-
year-old David Bruce, while in England Edward III,
who had inherited both the ambition and the
military ability of his grandfather, the Hammer of
the Scots, seized the reins of government. He had
never cordially assented to the 'Shameful Peace',
with its clause retaining Scotland's by now traditional alliance with France, and in 1332 he began a
new attack, first through the agency of Edward
Balliol, son of the unlucky King John, and soon
afterwards in his own person.

The third Edward's Scottish wars bear an as-
tonishing resemblance to those of his grandfather.
They began with smashing defeats for the Scots at
Dupplin Moor in 1332 and Halidon Hill in 1333, and
with the recapture of Berwick in 1333, using an
arsenal of siege weapons including, probably for the
first time in Britain, a few small cannon. 'King'
Balliol, in gratitude for English support, ceded
virtually the whole of southern Scotland to Edward

who, despite some reverses, had by 1336 occupied
and begun to rebuild most of the major Scottish
fortresses from Stirling to Caerlaverock. But if the
English followed the strategy of the previous war, so
too did the Scots, and the castles were scarcely
garrisoned when Sir Andrew Moray (son of
Wallace's ally) and William Douglas (a distant cousin
of Sir James) began to capture and 'kest them doun',
employing both guerrilla attacks and a siege-engine
named 'Boaster'. Soon the Scots were again raiding
over the border, and English morale was further
damaged by their own failure to take Dunbar, where
the formidable Black Agnes conducted the defence
with such gusto that Edward's exasperated lieutenant exclaimed 'Came I early, came I late, I found
Agnes at the gate.' By April 1341, when Edinburgh
Castle fell to a party of Scots disguised as merchants,
the war was effectively over, and two months later
David Bruce returned in triumph from his exile in
France.

Long before this, and indeed since about the time
that Moray and Douglas's destruction of castles had
shown that Scotland was still neither easily taken
nor lightly held, King Edward's attention had been
diverted towards the nation which had given David
shelter. Preparations for a struggle with France, at
least partially prompted by a desire to cut off her
help and encouragement to the Scots, were well
under way by 1337, and the first major campaign of
what became the Hundred Years' War began two
years later.

Though for the next century and more the main
military efforts of England were directed across the

99, 100 One of the earliest Scottish tower-houses, the stronghold of the Irvines at Drum in Aberdeenshire. Above: the round-cornered tower, later enlarged by the mansion on the left. Below: the vaulted second storey, *showing the supporting corbels (left) for the wooden floor which divided the main hall from the bedrooms above (compare ill. 95).*

Channel rather than across the Tweed, Scotland's continuing alliance with France ensured that there would be little peace on the border. Sometimes raid and counter-raid flared into full-scale war, as when King David Bruce, shortly after the French defeat at Crécy in 1346, answered his ally's call for help by invading England, only to meet with disaster and capture at the battle of Neville's Cross near Durham. Even in time of truce Scotland was rarely at peace within herself during the fourteenth century. The misfortunes of her successive monarchs – the eleven year captivity of David Bruce, the advanced years and timid nature of his nephew and successor Robert II (1371–90), and the almost total incapacity of the crippled Robert III (1390–1406) – meant that the central government could exercise scant control over the ambitions and murderous feuds of her squabbling nobility. Such conditions dictated the building of new strongholds to replace those destroyed in the Wars of Independence and the later struggle with Edward III. In Scotland proper as well as in the Borders, the dominant form was to be the tower-house.

Whether or not, as some patriotic Scots writers maintain, the tower-house in fact originated in Scotland rather than in the northern English Marches, one of the earliest surviving examples north of the Tweed stands far away from the border

99 at Drum in Aberdeenshire. Its date is much disputed, but it seems likeliest to have been built no earlier than 1323 by the Irvine family who were then granted lands at Drum by King Robert Bruce: certainly Irvines have held it ever since, adding the Renaissance mansion attached to it in 1619. Whatever its origins, the tower is a splendid piece of work, with both its walls and its battlemented parapet elegantly rounded at the corners. The raised entrance was originally gained by a ladder rather than the modern stair, and the interior is stone-

100 vaulted as a fire precaution, not only on the ground floor but also in the two upper storeys.

101 Threave, in Dumfries and Galloway, is a far less elegant tower, a sheer stone rectangle rising 70 feet (21 metres) above an island in the Dee. Perhaps the most significant thing about it is the rock-cut well in the basement, an indication of preparedness for a

long siege. To winkle out the occupants, indeed, the attackers would first have to negotiate the surrounding river, and then brave the missiles dropped on their heads from the overhanging wooden gallery whose fittings can be seen near the top of the tower. Given that they broke through the ground floor door, they could then reach the upper storeys only by first climbing a ladder to the floor above and then cutting their way across a hall to a turnpike stair in the opposite corner. In both its strength and its subtlety, Threave is worthy of its builder, Sir Archibald Douglas, bastard son of Bruce's companion and nicknamed 'the Grim' 'because of his terrible countenance in warfare' – in which, incidentally, he was noted for wielding a sword 6 feet (nearly 2 metres) long that no other man could lift. It was built between 1369 and 1390, at a time when Douglas, as both ruler of the turbulent province of Galloway and warden of the western Borders of Scotland, needed protection from his own countrymen as well as from English raiders.

Nor was the growing power and influence of the Douglases confined to the Borders. On the death of

101 Archibald the Grim's tower-house at Threave, with the put-log holes and access ports for an overhanging wooden gallery near the top, and a fragment of the turretted and gunlooped fifteenth-century curtain wall (see p. 161).

102 *The great L-shaped tower-house of Craigmillar, Edinburgh (see ill. 95), built after 1374 and later surrounded – perhaps in 1427 – by the machicolated curtain wall which appears on the right (p. 160).*

King David Bruce in 1371 William, the first earl of Douglas, even put himself forward as a contender for the crown, and about this time his family pride and ambition were expressed in the building of Tantallon Castle in Lothian. It stands on a headland – perhaps the site of a prehistoric promontory fort – jutting into the Firth of Forth. A great dry ditch dug across the neck of the promontory forms its outermost defence, and protects an enclosure which once contained the fortress's less important ancillary buildings. Where the headland narrows towards its seaward end is an inner ditch, and behind it stands the principal strength of the castle, a wall 50 feet high and 12 feet thick (15 metres by nearly 4 metres) describing a shallow ellipse from cliff-edge to cliff-edge. Near its centre is the keep-gatehouse or Mid

Tower (with a protruding forework of a later date) and at either end is a round tower, the three towers being so positioned as to give flanking fire along the whole outer face of the curtain-wall. Three successive lines of defence thus block the landward approach to the castle, and its northern, eastern and southern sides are protected by almost vertical cliffs falling 100 feet and more (some 30 metres) into the sea.

Though the mighty curtain wall of Tantallon was imitated by Bishop Traill in his similarly situated castle of St Andrews, the tower-house remained the **dominant** Scottish form. By the end of the fourteenth century, however, there were variations on the simple rectangular theme of Threave or Drum. Craigmillar, for instance, built on the outskirts of

103

102

103 *Tantallon Castle in Lothian, looking from the outer ditch (guarded by the gunlooped sixteenth-century spurwork on the right) towards the mighty curtain wall which* *resisted James V's heavy artillery in 1528 (p. 164). The bridge on the far left leads across the inner ditch to the (later) forework of the keep-gatehouse.*

Edinburgh after 1374, has a wing or 'jamb' projecting at right angles to the main tower, making its ground plan L-shaped rather than rectangular. This jamb 95 was designed to increase the accommodation inside the tower, and contained several sets of small private rooms for the use of the owner and his family. But if comfort was the first consideration, defence was also served by placing the entrance to the tower near the angle formed by the projecting wing, so that it could be covered by cross-fire from the battlements and arrow-slits of the jamb as well as from those of the tower proper.

11 Dunnottar in Kincardineshire (Grampian Region) has another early L-shaped tower, built in the last decade of the fourteenth century when 'wyld wykkyd Heland-men', unrestrained by the weak government of Robert III, were ravaging the north-east. It stands on a rocky promontory which had been the site of a Pictish fortress and of an earlier castle destroyed by Sir Andrew Moray in 1336 (p. 123), and dominates the only landward approach, a narrow path which descends almost to the sea before climbing sharply up the crag. Two centuries later this path was further defended by a gatehouse with a 132 battery of gunports. By that time Craigmillar, Tantallon, Threave and Caerlaverock had also all 103 been adapted for defensive artillery. 10

To trace the process by which cannon first entered the calculations of British fortress-builders we must leave Scotland for southern England, there to consider the new fortifications being constructed as a result of the Hundred Years' War.

104 *The early-fourteenth-century outer gatehouse of Carisbrooke Castle, the chief stronghold of the vulnerable Isle of Wight: notice the machicolations and keyhole gunports of the top storey, added at the end of the century after the gatehouse had beaten off an attack by French raiders (p. 132).*

10 'Made in help of the country': English coastal defences and the advent of artillery, 1335 – *c.* 1600

Knouwyth that beeth and schul be
That I am mad[e] in help of the cuntre

INSCRIPTION ON COOLING CASTLE, 1381

Throughout the later Middle Ages and the subsequent age of the Tudors, England was more or less continuously at enmity with her European neighbours. For much of this time France, usually allied with Scotland and sometimes with Spain, was the principal enemy, but by the time of Queen Elizabeth Spain herself had taken over this role. Although the threat fluctuated with England's success or failure in war and diplomacy, her coastline – and especially the stretch from Cornwall eastwards to the Wash – was in fear of attack more often than not, and on three occasions at least, in 1386, 1540 and 1588, the nation was in real danger of full-scale invasion from the sea. How English coastal defences developed, or failed to develop, to counter these threats will be the theme of this chapter.

We are accustomed to thinking of the Hundred Years' War as taking place exclusively in France, but in fact some of its first blows were struck in Hampshire. During the second half of the 1330s tension between England and France had been mounting steadily. Several factors were involved, prominent amongst them being a dispute about the Plantagenet dominions in France (and notably the rich Duchy of Acquitaine) which had come to the English crown as the heritage of Henry II. These lands were held as tenants of the King of France rather than independent possessions, and the proud Edward III found this situation irksome, especially since he believed himself to have a better claim by blood to the French crown than his 'landlord', Philip VI. Philip's persistent support for Edward's enemies in Scotland did little to calm the situation, and French preparations to intervene there in 1336 made the outbreak of general hostilities virtually inevitable. Finally, in May 1337, Philip formally 'confiscated' Aquitaine and six months later Edward, equally formally, claimed the crown of France.

An important part of the English preparations for war was the overhaul of the long-disused system of coastal defence. The militia of the maritime counties were ordered to the alert, and beacons were set up both there and inland; but, apart from a new gatehouse for Carisbrooke Castle in the Isle of Wight, no new fortifications were built, and many of southern England's richest ports remained virtually undefended. The consequences of this state of affairs soon became obvious. In June 1338 French galleys, vessels whose shallow draught, manœuvrability, and speed made them ideal for inshore raiding,

suddenly descended on unprotected Portsmouth and burnt it to the ground, and four months later fifty such ships attacked Southampton. Easily penetrating the port's half-hearted defences, French soldiers and Genoese mercenaries put the townsmen to precipitate flight, hanging those they captured from the gables of their own houses. The militia were nowhere to be found, and it was nearly twenty-four hours before a force could be raised to drive the enemy back to their ships. Before they left, however, they had burnt most of the town, destroyed or carried off vast quantities of wool and wine from its warehouses, and even stolen the scales from the Customs House.

But if the material damage done was great, the blow to English pride and morale was greater, and a furious Edward III ordered a full enquiry into the 'disgraceful neglect of duty' by those responsible for the defence of Hampshire. He also ordered a stone wall to be built round Southampton, a locking of stable doors after bolted horses which we shall find characteristic of medieval coastal defences. Elsewhere the Londoners, in a panic measure, blocked the Thames with wooden piles, and churches throughout the land were told to ring only one bell for services, the full peal being reserved (as in 1940) for an invasion warning.

Such anxiety was by no means unfounded, for in 1339 French 'pyrats' were again on the rampage. Though, significantly, the new defences of Southampton deterred them from landing there, they found plenty of unprotected ports to plunder. Harwich and Hastings went up in flames and Rye was badly damaged before the raiders were chased back to Boulogne by the mariners of the Cinque Ports, who burnt the town and hanged twelve enemy captains in revenge. Perhaps chastened by this experience, the French transferred their attention to Devon in 1340, destroying Teignmouth and threatening Plymouth.

These wide-ranging and unpredictable attacks meant that no undefended place on the south coast could feel secure, and the alarm and demoralization thus created were doubtless one of the enemy's chief aims. By their destruction of English shipping the raids may also have been designed to clear the way for a full-scale invasion, and they were certainly intended to tempt King Edward to keep his forces at home rather than attacking France. In neither of these last respects, however, were the French successful, and the great English naval victory off Sluys in modern Belgium, on Midsummer Day 1340, virtually destroyed the enemy fleet.

During the next two decades a succession of victories in France (Crécy in 1346, La Roche-Derrien in 1347 and Poitiers in 1356), together with the capture of the naval base of Calais in 1347 and the defeat of another enemy fleet in 1350, ensured that the English coast was free from raiders. The lesson of Southampton had been ill-learnt, however, and during this respite little was done either to improve coastal defences or to protect exposed ports. When the 'roveres upon the sea' returned in March 1360, they were able not only to devastate Winchelsea, slaughtering and raping even in the parish church, but also to destroy over again two of the towns – Rye and Hastings – that they had attacked previously.

Luckily for the southern ports, this bout of raiding was soon ended by a peace treaty. In return for relinquishing his claim to the French crown, King Edward obtained absolute control over an enlarged Aquitaine; and he also received a promise of £500,000 (something like £100 million in modern terms) as a ransom for King John of France, taken prisoner at Poitiers. Edward's captains had also grown fat on ransoms and plunder, and both he and they were inclined to celebrate their good fortune with costly building programmes (pp. 144–47). Far too little of this building was relevant to coastal defence, though the King did spend £20,000 (less than half the cost of his new apartments at Windsor) on a completely new castle raised in 1361–75 to guard the Thames estuary against French attacks. This was Queenborough, on the Isle of Sheppey in Kent, which has now completely disappeared: it is known to have consisted of a massive circular tower or 'rotunda' with six round turrets, within an outer wall that was also perfectly circular. Such a plan, reminiscent of later artillery forts, suggests that Edward may have had cannon in mind for the defence of his new castle, and certainly it was at about this time that provision was first made for defensive artillery in British fortifications.

It is still sometimes stated that the introduction of cannon immediately revolutionized warfare and rendered the castle obsolete, but that is in fact very far from the truth. Early guns were not generally cast in one piece, but were constructed by welding iron bars together to form a tube, which was then bound with iron hoops in the manner of a barrel – hence the name still in use. This type of construction did not make for tensile strength, so it was probably just as well that early gunpowder was weak and inefficient

and did not, as a rule, project missiles with any great force or velocity. The first British cannon seem to have fired metal arrows bound round with leather to fit the bore: these were soon replaced by iron, lead, or stone balls, but in each case the rate of fire was of the slowest. Since gun carriages as such were unknown, early cannon also suffered from limited mobility, the larger types being simply clamped to hollowed-out beds of massive timber and the smaller sort generally mounted on unwieldy stands. All these demerits meant that, during the fourteenth century at least, cannon brought about few changes in the practice of war. Their immobility made them of limited value in field battles and, though some small cannon made an appearance before Berwick in 1333, they were not particularly efficacious against fortifications, having first to be transported to the siege on carts and then laboriously manœuvred close enough to take effect on the walls. The more powerful and probably more accurate 'engines', therefore, still formed the mainstay of the siege train.

Cannon were at this time far more useful to the defenders of fortresses, who could fix them in prepared and protected positions either on the battlements or behind gunports cut in the wall near ground level. From here their fire could be directed in relative safety against attackers, the flame and smoke of their explosion adding its psychological effect to the terrible damage caused by a ball or hail of bullets fired at head height. It follows that gunports would best be concentrated in or near the gatehouse – at once the most vulnerable part of the fortress and one where besiegers would cluster the thickest – and this was in fact the most favoured position for them in the fourteenth and fifteenth centuries.

The earliest surviving gunports in Britain apparently date from about 1365, and form part of the new defences then erected to protect the abbey of Quarr on the north shore of the Isle of Wight. Viewed from the outside, they are simply round holes cut into blocks of stone; but behind these facing blocks is a much larger rectangular aperture widening towards the inside of the wall, and designed to allow the defenders to operate a small gun mounted on a stand or clamped to a bed on the sill of the 'embrasure'. Such primitive ports made no allowance for sighting, but their provision, and the building of the defences in which they were contained, displays a prudence which was conspicuously lacking elsewhere.

The inevitable renewal of the French war in 1369, indeed, found the English coast little better protected than before. To make matters worse, circumstances had by now put the galleys of the mighty Castilian navy at the enemy's disposal, while English naval strength still depended on a handful of royal ships augmented by whatever merchantmen could be pressed into service. Equipped with cannon and sailed by perhaps the finest mariners of the age, the Spanish ships easily defeated a much larger English fleet in 1372. With her affairs in France going badly and political squabbles dividing the government at home, England was now more vulnerable than ever, and on 29 June 1377 – eight days after the unlamented death of Edward III – the first Spanish galleys of a new raiding force appeared off the Sussex coast.

What followed has a depressingly familiar ring. For the third time in forty years Rye and Hastings were sacked, Portsmouth went up in flames a second time, and Folkestone, Dartmouth, Plymouth and Yarmouth on the Isle of Wight were added to the tale of devastated ports. This time, however, the enemy was not to be content with hit and run raids. The French soldiers and Spanish sailors who destroyed Rottingdean proceeded to march 6 miles (10 kilometres) inland and burn Lewes, routing a scratch force raised by the local prior and carrying him and several other Sussex worthies off for ransom. On the Isle of Wight, too, the raiders stayed long enough to extort a tribute of over £600, and even attempted to take Carisbrooke Castle, where, however, they met with a sharp reverse. In 1378 there were further signs that the enemy had more than chance plunder in mind, for the Castilians who then ravaged Cornwall promised to return with a still larger force and occupy the county permanently. This threat never materialized, but in 1380 the raiders attacked Sussex yet again and ventured as far up the Thames as Gravesend, where they burnt the outlying warehouses of London merchants.

The raids of 1377–80 were, in short, by far the worst yet experienced. By the extortion of tribute, the threat of occupation and the extension of devastation to inland towns – quite apart from the material damage done – the enemy were bringing the French war to the southern English in much the same way as, sixty years before, Robert Bruce had brought the Scots war to their northern compatriots. And, just as the proliferation of towers and holds in the Borders had followed in the train of Bruce's incursion, so the years after 1377 saw a hurried programme of fortress-building in the south-east as that area was at long last forced to look seriously to its defences. Like the tower-houses, these new

105 One of the earliest keyhole gunports in Britain (right), cut through the blocked window of a seaward-facing Romanesque house converted into part of Southampton town wall.

southern fortifications have a certain family resemblance, for most of them have overhanging stone galleries (or 'machicolations') for the close-quarter defence of their gateways and many of them, significantly, are equipped with gunports.

The towns and seaports which were at once the chief prop of the region's economy and the principal enemy target were, with government encouragement that sometimes bordered on compulsion, among the first to call in the stonemasons. Rye was complimented for having 'so speedily taken order for its defence' after the raid of 1377, and it was perhaps at this time that the magnificent Landgate was built to guard the principal approach to the town. At Southampton improvements to the walls included the provision of gunports shaped like an inverted keyhole, with a round hole for the gun at the base and a slit for sighting it above – a great advance on the 'blind' gunports of Quarr Abbey. No less than seventeen of these keyhole gunports appear in the West Gate of Canterbury, a city which stood too near the coast for comfort, astride one of the most likely routes an invader might take towards London.

104

105

107

108

106

106 *The West Gate at Canterbury, Kent, completed in 1380, displaying some of its seventeen keyhole gunports.*

107 *Gunner's eye-view of Canterbury city wall, showing how the keyhole ports in this and the neighbouring tower sweep the intervening ditch.*

108 *Section of a keyhole gunport, showing a gunner aiming a barrel-forged and breech-loading cannon clamped to a wooden bed (p. 130). A spare breech-piece stands behind the gunner, whose mate is preparing a red-hot wire to fire the cannon.*

Its cathedral contained the fabulously rich shrine of St Thomas Becket, and both church and government joined with the citizens in wishing its dilapidated Roman walls to be replaced by more modern defences. Work began in 1378, and two years later the West Gate – the only survivor of four such portals – was complete. The gateway itself is guarded by a machicolated gallery above and a waist-high gunport on either side, while the fire from another two ports crossed a few yards in front of it. The remaining thirteen gunloops are distributed on all three floors so as to sweep almost every approach, and Canterbury may justly claim to possess the earliest remaining British fortress designed specifically for defence by firearms. Not long afterwards the gatehouse of Carisbrooke Castle, damaged in the siege of 1377, was converted for artillery defence, with keyhole gunloops in the new upper storey and two smaller ports to sweep the drawbridge.

Outside the towns and royal castles, the threat from the sea also prompted the clergy and gentry of the south-east to fortify their houses, and one of the first to do so was Bishop Rede of Chichester. Mindful of the sack of Lewes and the fate of its kidnapped prior, he began in 1377 to surround his ancient

106

104

palace of Amberley – 9 miles (14 kilometres) inland but situated on a navigable river – with a towering curtain wall. Its defensive value is somewhat dubious, however, for the gatehouse lacks machicolations or gunports, the wall is without flanking towers (the only projection being a massive block for garderobes or privies!), and the whole fortress is overlooked by the neighbouring church tower.

Roger Ashburnham, a Kentish gentleman, also thought it prudent to fortify his new manor house at Scotney, even though it lay nearly 20 miles (30 kilometres) inland from Rye. Diverting a small river, he created an island on which to build his hall, and further defended it by a curtain wall with four squat corner towers, each surmounted by a ring of machicolations. Only one such tower (given a picturesque roof in the seventeenth century) now remains, together with a fragment of the gatehouse which guarded the drawbridge over the moat.

Amberley and Scotney are essentially fortified houses intended primarily for the protection of their owners, but Cooling Castle in northern Kent, begun in February 1381, was designed as a positive contribution to national defence. Built for Sir John Cobham, an old soldier and a member of the royal council, it guards a desolate peninsula jutting into the Thames estuary, a tempting landing place for

109 Cooling Castle, Kent, begun 'in help of the country' by Sir John Cobham in 1381, looking from the machicolated outer gatehouse (with a small round gunport at the top left) across the now dry moat to the keyhole-ported inner ward (left).

110 Bishop Rede's 'castle' of Amberley, by the river Arun in Sussex, with the protruding garderobe block to the left and the overshadowing church tower beyond.

raiders like those who had burnt nearby Gravesend just six months before. As befits its purpose and its owner, it is a full-dress castle, with three successive lines of defence. Entrance to the inner ward, which has its own moat, gatehouse and corner towers, could only be gained across a drawbridge protected by the separate outer bailey. The machicolated outer gatehouse has small round gunports, and the inner defences are liberally supplied with loops of the keyhole type. Cooling, in short, was the very latest thing in castles, and Cobham proclaimed his patriotism in building it on a copper plate which is still fixed to the outer gatehouse:

> Knoweth that be-eth and shall be
> That I am made in help of the country
> In the knowledge of which thing
> This is charter and witnessing.

That 'the country' desperately needed such help in 1381 is past a doubt. That summer the peasants of the south-east, wrung for taxes to pay for the war, rose in general revolt, and it was only by a lucky political chance that the French were unable to take advantage. The rising was soon crushed, but the general situation continued to deteriorate, and in 1385 and 1386 there was a real danger of invasion, with a French army 35,000 strong standing poised to cross the Channel. Just how far enemy preparations had gone was revealed by the chance capture of two ships containing part of a prefabricated wooden wall intended to act as a bridgehead defence for the invaders. It was rumoured to be over 2 miles (3 kilometres) long, with a tower every twelve paces and loops for guns and arrows. England had faced no greater peril since the days of King John, and royal commissioners spurred to hasten work on the defences of Canterbury and Rye. Amongst them were the master mason Henry Yevele, Sir John Cobham and another old soldier, Sir Edward Dalyngridge, who at the end of 1385 began work at Bodiam in Sussex on 'a castle . . . in defence of the adjacent country against the King's enemies'.

111

The fortress he built was, indeed, well equipped to repulse the King's enemies, should they march the 9 miles (14 kilometres) up the Rother valley from Rye. As at nearby Scotney, Dalyngridge used the water of an artificial lake for his first line of defence. To cross it, the enemy had first to negotiate a bridge at right angles to the entrance front, exposing his flank all the way to fire from the walls. He then had to fight his way across two separate fortified islands linked by a drawbridge, and finally to deal with another drawbridge before reaching the main gatehouse – where he would be greeted with the fire of eight keyhole gunloops and a rain of missiles from the machicolated galleries. The tiny postern (or 'back door') on the opposite side of the castle is also defended by drawbridges and housed in a machicolated tower, and square towers are set midway along the other two walls of the rectangle, with round towers at each corner.

Bodiam's aggressive exterior, however, belies something of its character, for its builder was a courtier as well as a soldier, and his castle was a sumptuous residence as well as a fortress 'built in help of the country'. A rectangle of towered defences confronts the world, but the inner face of the rectangle is made up of wings of comfortable rooms – including a hall, a chapel, several private suites and no less than twenty-eight garderobes – looking inwards on to a pleasant central courtyard. This convenient arrangement was by no means unique, for quadrangular castles were the height of fashion during the last years of the fourteenth century (pp. 144–46).

In the event, neither Bodiam nor the other fortresses raised in the years of crisis had to face an invading army. The mighty French fleet suffered endless delays, and in 1387 an English naval victory pruned away much of its strength. Afterwards the war petered out, until in 1396 a twenty-eight-year truce was sealed by the marriage of Richard II to the infant daughter of the King of France. Though French hostility was again aroused when Henry IV deposed Richard and sent the princess home, the occasional raids that resulted were more of a nuisance than a threat. A force of Bretons, indeed, got a very bloody nose when they made an attempt on Dartmouth in 1404. The port (notorious for the piratical activities of its mariners) lies up an inlet whose entrance is guarded by a pair of rocky headlands. One of these had been equipped in 1388 with a small fort or 'fortalice', so the Bretons landed 5 miles (8 kilometres) away at Slapton Sands, but as they did so they were set upon by the countrymen – and countrywomen – and put to flight with the loss of their leader and twenty-three of his captains.

14

The memoirs of a Spanish galley captain who tried his luck on the south coast in 1405 bear out the impression of a general improvement in the efficiency of the English defence system. Don Pero Niño was able to plunder unprotected St Ives in Cornwall, but when he sailed to Dartmouth he dared not land for the 'troops of archers and soldiers coming up on all sides to defend the shore'. At Plymouth 'they fired so many cannon and bolts from

111 The magnificent quadrangular castle of Bodiam in Sussex, begun in 1385, showing on the left the final drawbridge to the machicolated and gunported main gateway.

the town, that those in the galleys thought they would be sunk . . . there was one ball which went twice the height of a tower and fell into the sea nearly half a league [1½ miles, or 2.5 kilometres] off'. Plainly this was fired from a fairly advanced type of gun, of the sort used to batter Harlech and Aberystwyth (p. 110) a few years later. Poole in Dorset also resisted manfully, its defenders bearing house doors before them against the Castilian crossbows, and a party put ashore on the Isle of Wight 'turned very quickly back to sea' on meeting a party of English archers. Ten years later, under the leadership of Henry V, archers like those decimated the French cavalry at Agincourt, the first of a series of victories which gave England control over more than half of France and once again lined the pockets of her soldiers with loot and ransoms.

Not until after 1435, when England's Burgundian–Flemish allies turned against her, was the coast – and especially the section from Thanet northwards to the Wash – again threatened. It was, perhaps, this new danger from Flanders that led John Daundelyon, a somewhat disreputable Kentish 'gentilman', to fortify his farmhouse-manor near Margate in the Isle of Thanet. All that now remains is the gatehouse, wasp-striped in bands of black flint **13** and local yellow brick (in that part of the country a new and prestigious material) and defended by two round gunports and a pair of cross-loops for handguns or crossbows. Its massive gate-housings, tall enough for the loaded carts which, when nights were dark, smuggled corn to foreign ships, would have made it difficult to defend against a serious assault, but it was an effective enough defence against casual attack, as well as admirably demonstrating Daundelyon's local importance. Caister Castle in Norfolk, which will be discussed more fully **124** elsewhere (p. 149), was also built with an eye on the Flemish threat and, apart from its own artillery, kept a supply of guns ready to transport to the coast on carts. But, though the Flemings made an unsuccessful descent on Norfolk in about 1440, and caused consternation there a decade later by kidnapping people walking on the beach, the next serious raiding – the first for over fifty years – emanated once again from France.

It came in 1457, after the English had suffered final defeat in Normandy and Gascony, and at a time when the nation was divided by the Wars of the Roses: some, indeed, said that the French who burnt Yorkist Sandwich did so at the invitation of the Lancastrian leaders. In the same year Fowey in Cornwall was attacked, and though the squire's wife successfully defended her manor house, much damage was done in the town. When civil order was restored by Edward IV, therefore, the Fowey men insured against another surprise attack by stretching an immense chain-boom across their harbour mouth, supported on small anchored boats and defended at each end by a small blockhouse. Dartmouth did the same, and in 1481, encouraged by a government concerned about a landing by Henry Tudor, the exiled Lancastrian heir, also began work on a coastal **14** defence of an entirely new type.

This new structure was a fort designed specifi- **106** cally for offensive artillery. Its guns were not merely **111** an aid to the close-quarter defence of a gatehouse (as at Canterbury) or a residence (as at Bodiam), but the very reason for its existence: they were to be used offensively, to sweep the estuary and sink enemy ships. For this reason they were set low down, almost on the waterline, and fired, not through old-fashioned defensive keyhole loops, but through ten much larger rectangular enclosures 2 by 2½ feet (60 by 75 centimetres) square designed to afford a wider field of fire. The floor above the main battery, which contained the pulley arrangement for the great chain-boom, is also equipped with eleven square ports for the smaller guns graphically known as 'murderers'.

As the pioneer of the artillery forts which from now on were to dominate coastal defence, we must not expect Dartmouth to be perfect. It was comparatively ill-equipped for landward defence, and its height and relatively thin walls made it vulnerable to counter-fire from enemy ships. Its gunports still had far too limited a field of traverse, and the cannon with which it was originally equipped were still fixed to clumsy wooden beds rather than mounted on carriages. Probably of the old-fashioned 'barrel' construction, they seem to have had insufficient range to reach right across the inlet, let alone cover its opposite shore against a landing. To remedy this

defect a smaller artillery fort, Kingswear 'Castle', was **14** begun there in 1491.

By this time Henry VII was on the throne, but the foreign policy of the first of the Tudors was largely pacific, and it was only after his son had (for no very good reason) re-opened hostilities with France that further coastal defences became necessary. In 1514, for instance, the French burnt and plundered Brighton, 'a poore village in Sussex'. Henry VIII's masons took up the ideas initiated at Dartmouth in several artillery forts built during the 1520s and 1530s, but it was not until 1539 that they really came to fruition. In that year, according to the Elizabethan historian John Lambarde, 'King Henrie the Eight, having shaken off the intolerable yoke of the Popish tyrannie, and espying that the Emperour was offended for the divorce of Queen Katharine [of Aragon] his wife, and that the French King had coupled the Dolphine [Dauphin] his son to the Popes niece, and married his daughter to the King of Scots, so that he might more justly suspect them all, than safely trust any one, determined (by the aide of God) to stand upon his owne gardes and defence: and therefore with all speede, and without sparing any cost, he builded Castles, platfourmes and block-houses, in all needefull places of the Realme.' 'All needefull places' included the entire coastline from Hull to Land's End, for the enmity of the Emperor meant that England was threatened from Flanders and Spain as well as from France, and the undertaking was the most thorough and extensive scheme of coastal defence since the days of the Saxon Shore – or, indeed, up until the time of the Napoleonic Wars. Unlike the coastal fortifications of the previous two centuries, raised piecemeal by private persons or town councils in reaction to purely local threats, it was directly controlled and financed by a central government grown rich on the spoils of the recent Dissolution of the Monasteries. It was, in short, the first modern scheme of national defence.

As such, it depended largely on artillery forts, eventually over twenty of them from Kent to Cornwall alone, incorporating the most up-to-date ideas on the combination of firepower and fortification. Unlike lofty Dartmouth, they were built low and thick-walled against enemy artillery, and their own guns – at first imported from the Low Countries but increasingly home-produced in Sussex – were of the latest type, cast in one piece rather than barrel-forged. They could thus take a more powerful charge, firing a larger ball for a longer distance, and they were mounted on wheeled carriages rather than immobile blocks.

Henry's first priority was to guard the coast nearest the Continent and closest to London, and the earliest forts to be built were those intended to 'keepe and beate' the landing places between Thanet and Dover. Deal, the first, largest and most complex of the whole series, has a round central 'keep' with six slightly lower semicircular bastions radiating from it. Closely surrounding it, and lower again, is a 'curtain wall', also with six semicircular bastions, and beyond is a wide dry moat and a six-lobed outermost wall. By contrast with the 21 gunports of Dartmouth, Deal has no less than 145 embrasures, and though it certainly never had so many guns, those which it did possess could be moved from port to port on their carriages with relative ease. The heaviest cannon were mounted in three tiers on the reinforced roofs of the curtain-wall bastions, the bastions of the keep, and the keep itself. These were for long range offensive use, mainly against ships, but – again unlike Dartmouth – Deal was equipped for landward defence not only by the massive strength of its concentric walls, but by multitudes of gunports cut through them. Some 54 loops for handguns cover the outer moat, and a further 30 or so defend the space between the keep and the

112, 113 *Deal, the largest of Henry VIII's coastal artillery forts, built c.1539–40, with three tiers of platforms for long-range offensive cannon and handgun embrasures low down on each level. The composite plan (below) shows the large number of handgun embrasures necessary for all-round defence.*

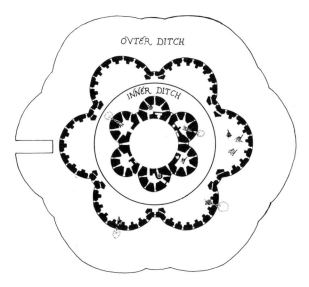

OUTER DITCH

INNER DITCH

114 *'Little Dennis' artillery blockhouse in Cornwall, built in the 1520s, with 'shot-deflecting' battlements, hand-gunports (left and centre) and a single embrasure for a long-range cannon to seaward (right). In the distance is the keep of Pendennis fort.*

curtain wall. These ports are splayed both inside and out to give the maximum field of fire, and may be the 'splaies which the king's grace hath devised', the design of Henry VIII himself, who certainly took a keen interest in artillery.

Walmer, smaller and simpler, continued the chain of forts 'buyldid by the contery' westward, followed by works at Sandown, Dover, Sandgate near Folkestone and Camber guarding Rye. Forts at Calshot and Hurst in Hampshire and at East and West Cowes on the Isle of Wight commanded the approaches to Southampton, and Portland watched the Dorset coast. All these were complete by 1540, and in the following years the chain was extended northwards and westwards, with forts at Harwich in Essex and Hull in Humberside, at Portsmouth, and at Poole and Weymouth in Dorset, while St Mawes and

Pendennis guarded each side of the entrance to the great landlocked harbour of Carrick Roads in Cornwall. Pendennis (Pen Dinas, 'the fortress headland') was the site of a prehistoric promontory fort, and during the 1520s a small artillery block-house, known as 'Little Dennis', had been erected at 114 its seaward end. Now this was brought up to date with splayed gunports and inward sloping battle-ments to deflect enemy fire, while a new fort was built at the highest point of the headland. Much less complex than Deal, this last was nevertheless capable of mounting about thirty cannon in its circular keep and surrounding fifteen-sided curtain wall. St Mawes, across the bay from Little Dennis, 115 also has the usual round keep, here surrounded by a clover-leaf of three bastions to house its heavier guns; among them (at least by Elizabethan times)

138

115 *Interior of one of the three main batteries at St Mawes fort, Cornwall, showing the widely splayed embrasures, each flanked by sockets for the beam which once secured its shutters.*

were three long 'culverins' capable of firing a ball weighing 18 pounds (8 kilograms) well over a mile (more than 1.5 kilometres).

The advent of guns like these meant that, after two centuries of development, artillery had come of age as the decisive factor in siegecraft, if not in warfare as a whole. The emphasis of the relationship between cannon and fortifications, which had hitherto moved from close-range defence to long-range offence, now swung back again to defence, and Henry's coastal forts were outmoded almost as soon as they were built. Comparatively low and thick-walled though they were, Deal and the rest were essentially medieval castles, still presenting far too large a target for enemy guns. Though useful for all-round offensive fire, their circular plan was in-efficient in defence, being basically incompatible with the straight lines described by cannon balls. A disproportionately large number of guns, therefore, had to be employed to avoid leaving 'dead ground' in which an attacker could rally under the walls.

In the end, it was necessary to discard the notion of the castle altogether, and to rethink fortification geometrically and entirely in terms of firearms. What emerged was the 'arrow-head' bastion, pro- 116 bably first brought to maturity in Italy during the 1530s. This arrangement presented the minimum target to an enemy attacking from the front, and its sides, being quite straight, could be completely covered by a mere two guns carefully sited in the neighbouring works. In return, a pair of guns in the flanks of the bastion – protected by the point of the 142 arrow – could effectively sweep the straight wall on either side of it, while further cannon in the arrowhead itself could cover a quadrant of at least 180 degrees to its front.

The first such bastions in England date from 1546–47, when, in response to a French raid on the Solent, one was erected to guard the gates of Portsmouth and another built on the landward corner of a new fort – significantly square rather than circular – at Yarmouth on the Isle of Wight. These were made of stone, but most later examples had solid walls of rammed earth faced with masonry on both sides: even if the latter were smashed away, the earth could go on absorbing fire almost indefinitely. Before long the new device swept all competitors before it, and the reconstructed defences of Berwick, begun in 1558, consisted of five large bastions, each completely covering its neighbour and the length of 100-foot (30-metre) thick curtain-wall between. The 'bastioned trace', as complete geometrical systems like this are known, increased mightily in complexity over the years, but it was to remain the basic principle behind all large-scale British fortresses for at least the next three centuries.

Apart from Berwick, however, only Portsmouth had been given a complete circuit of modern defences by the time England was next seriously threatened from the sea, and when the 'Invincible Armada' sailed in 1588 King Henry's forts still formed the mainstay of coastal defence. Feverish efforts were made to cover other likely landing places, and the medieval walls of Great Yarmouth in Norfolk were modernized with arrow-head bastions and fronted with ramparts 40 feet (12 metres) thick made of pounded earth and dung 'resistable, by God's help, against any battery whatsoever'. Elsewhere trenches were dug and ramparts raised to protect otherwise undefended stretches of coastline, and chains or booms stretched across the entrances to harbours. (The most important of these, blocking

the Thames at Gravesend, broke with its own weight at the first flood-tide!)

More vital, perhaps, than anything else was the system of coastal beacons, much more complex and efficient than in Edward III's time, which gave warning far and wide when the Armada first appeared off Cornwall. For years these beacons had been 'tedyously' watched day and night from March until October, by men who were not even allowed a dog for company and who were sheltered, at best, by a hut 'withoute any seates or place of ease lest they should fall asleape: only to stand upright in with a hoale towards the Beacon'. Now they passed their message on, via hilltops and church towers, to the inland shires, and the militia marched to their carefully allotted posts. Those from the southern maritime counties gathered at major ports, while the remainder joined the field armies – one for the defence of the Scottish border and the north-east coast, one at London to protect Queen Elizabeth, and the third and largest mustering at Tilbury to counterattack the Spaniards should they gain a foothold on land.

This, of course, they never did. The veteran Spanish army in the Low Countries, the major part of a projected invasion force some 50,000 strong, could only cross the Narrow Seas under the protection of the Armada, and the Armada was defeated by the English navy – albeit helped mightily by fireships, the Dutch, and the weather. Towards the end of Elizabeth's reign there were further alarms, and between 1597 and 1600 Carisbrooke, Pendennis and St Mawes were all surrounded by up-to-date bastioned traces. From now on, however, England's most important defensive walls would be the wooden ones of her ships, and many of her coastal fortresses were to be employed next not against a foreign invader but against fellow-Englishmen during the Civil War.

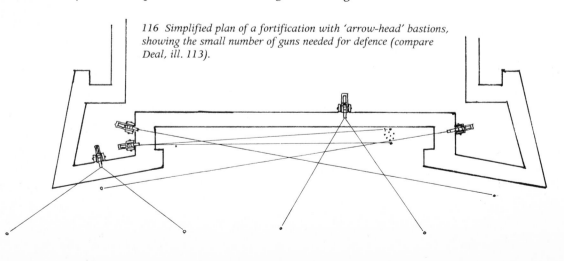

116 Simplified plan of a fortification with 'arrow-head' bastions, showing the small number of guns needed for defence (compare Deal, ill. 113).

117 *Stokesay – 'builded like a castle five miles owt of Ludlo' (John Leland, 'Itineraries', 1538) – seen across the pool which once fed its moat. The early tower, with a later half-timbered gallery (left), adjoins Laurence of Ludlow's great-hall block, with his massive refuge tower or keep to the right, all built c.1300.*

11 'Builded like a castle': castles and fortified manors in England, c.1300–1520

In every shire with Jakkes and Salades clene
Myssereule doth ryse and maketh neyghbours werre.

JOHN HARDYING, c. 1457

Though a large number of the new fortresses of late medieval England were specifically designed for defence against Welsh, Scottish and European enemies, there were a great many more – especially away from the borders and the dangerous south-east coast – which remained simply the fortified residences of their owners. Depending on whether the emphasis was on the military or the residential side of their character, these can be roughly divided into castles and fortified manor houses, the first being primarily fortresses and the second essentially houses capable of being defended. As, in the later fourteenth and fifteenth centuries, 'castles' became more luxurious and 'defensible houses' became more defensible, the distinction between the two becomes increasingly blurred. Nor was the difference always clear to contemporaries: John Leland, surveying the fortresses of England in Henry VIII's time, was frequently forced to hedge his bets by referring to 'a castelett', 'a goodly manor place or castle' or 'a house builded castle-like'.

At first there can have been little difficulty in deciding which was which. Semi-fortified residences certainly predate the Norman Conquest, for the kings and nobles of Saxon England are known to have feasted their retainers in timber halls protected by ditches and wooden palisades. Defensible houses like these are clearly distinguished from motte-and-bailey castles in the Domesday Survey of 1086, but no surviving example can be securely dated much before about 1200, when Boothby Pagnell Manor in Lincolnshire was begun. Although its walls are of solid stone, it has doors and windows at ground level, and its only real defence is the moat which surrounds it. What it lacked as a fortress it made up in comfort and convenience, and its builders, the Pagnell family, 'had a great minde to lye at Bouthby' rather than at their motte-and-bailey castle of Newport Pagnell in Buckinghamshire.

Comfort and security, the two principal elements of a defensible house, are balanced rather better at 117 Stokesay 'Castle' in Shropshire. Laurence of Ludlow, a wealthy wool merchant, bought the place in about 1280, by which time it was already provided with a moat and a small stone tower. To these he added a luxurious house, with a private room or 'solar' and a great hall with huge windows to let in light and air. Such fine windows, however, were a dangerous indulgence in a place so close to the troubled Welsh border, and needed to be counterbalanced by

further defences. Obtaining a royal license to 'crenellate' (or fortify) his mansion in 1291, Laurence therefore surrounded its courtyard with a substantial curtain wall, heightened the old tower and gave it an overhanging gallery, and finally built a new tower, some 66 feet (20 metres) high, at the other end of the hall block. From its battlements archers could command the courtyard and the area round the house, but its primary function was to serve as a final refuge should an enemy break in. It could not be entered from any other part of the building, being reached only by means of a ladder leading from the courtyard to a door in the wall 6 feet (1.8 metres) above ground level. It was, in fact, a keep in the old tradition, as well as having obvious links with the tower-houses then rising along England's other, 97 northern, border.

With its moat, curtain wall and strong tower, Stokesay well deserves Leland's description 'builded like a castle', but less strongly fortified houses made do with no more than a refuge tower. One such is Longthorpe near Peterborough, whose tower was 118 added to an earlier undefended mansion in about 1300. It contained the owner's fine set of private rooms, still decorated with a famous set of wall 12 paintings and entered only from inside the old house. Outwardly it resembles nothing more than a contemporary border stronghold – complete with thick walls, a vaulted basement and loopholed battlements – built in a county far from the frontiers and the coast alike. Fear of foreign enemies cannot then have been the motive for its construction, which may indeed have been as much social as military. A rather more elegant tower at South Kyme near Sleaford in Lincolnshire was built by the Northumbrian Umfravilles of Chipchase (pp. 122–23), 92 but Longthorpe has no such border connections. Its builder, one Robert Thorpe, was the great-grandson of a local serf, and (though much risen in the world) was himself still technically the bondman of the Abbot of Peterborough. Like the merchant Laurence of Ludlow, he was therefore not quite out of the top drawer and his decision to build a tower – always the symbol of power and authority – may owe something to a desire to emphasize his family's new-found importance. Whether or not this was the case, we shall find that the determination to impress was almost as important an element of English late medieval houses and castles as the desire for comfort and the need for security.

118 *Longthorpe tower (c.1300), near Peterborough, with the gable-end of the earlier manor-house immediately adjoining. The tall lancet on the right face of the tower,* *lighting the painted room, is the one seen in pl. 12. (The wing to the right, like the rectangular window in the near face of the tower, dates from the seventeenth century.)*

Despite their value as refuges and marks of social distinction, semi-detached towers like those at Stokesay and Longthorpe left the remainder of the manor house an easy prey for the determined marauder. Some owners, therefore, preferred to make their mansions as compact as possible and to fortify the whole range of buildings. Bishop Burnell, Edward I's fashionable Chancellor, adopted this plan for his house at Acton Burnell in Salop, building a large rectangular block with four small corner turrets. These military frills, however, are belied by no less than three entrances on the ground floor, unprotected by even so much as a moat or ditch. Little Wenham Hall, Suffolk, is much better designed for defence, being essentially three towers of varying height, all topped with loopholed battlements, joined together in an L-shaped block. The longest and lowest arm contains the great hall, while the shorter and higher houses the chapel with a private chamber above it. At the angle of the two is a slender stair turret, overtopping and defending them both. The hall and chapel, being like the entrance on the first floor, can afford the con-

venience of fine large windows, but the ground floor wall is pierced only by narrow slits, thus partly making up for the lack of moat or curtain wall. These additional safeguards do, however, form part of the defences of Markenfield Hall in North Yorkshire, begun c.1310, which is otherwise similar in type. Little Wenham, built around the 1280s, is incidentally the earliest surviving English house constructed in brick, a material little used since Roman times. Though not so strong as great stone blocks, brick is easier to work with and – especially in the eastern counties where brick-clay is easier to come by than building stone – considerably cheaper. The lost town defences of Hull were entirely built in it, as were some of the most impressive fifteenth-century castles (pp. 149, 155).

The major castles of the fourteenth century were built exclusively in stone. Despite the example set by Edward I's concentric and keepless fortresses in Wales, the keep continued to flourish, and new ones were built at Knaresborough, North Yorkshire, in 1307–12 and at Dudley, Worcestershire, in about 1320. Both these were surrounded by the usual

124

119 The 'old soldier's dream' castle of Nunney in Somerset, begun in 1373, surrounded by its moat.

towered and curtain-walled baileys, but the keep at 119 Nunney in Somerset stands alone and guarded by a moat. Containing all the castle's living accommodation, it has been called a 'tower-house', and could indeed be viewed as a much-strengthened version of a mansion like Little Wenham. As there, the large windows of the lord's hall and chambers are placed high up, while the servants' quarters and store-rooms on the lower floors were originally lit only by narrow loopholes (their present square windows date from the seventeenth century). Nunney was begun in 1373 by Sir John de la Mare, a local knight who had allegedly done well for himself during Edward III's wars in France. His service there is certainly borne out by the appearance of his castle. With its four corner towers almost touching each other on the shorter faces of the rectangular central block, it resembles contemporary French strongholds like the notorious Paris Bastille more than anything elsewhere in England, and must have looked even more French when its towers had their original conical rooftops. Though this 'old soldier's dream' is machicolated throughout, it lacks the gunports for defensive artillery found in the south coast fortresses of the same decade. Far from the danger of foreign raiders as Nunney was, display was probably at least as important to its builder as defence.

John Leland found the interior of Nunney both cramped and dark, and its 'keep-house' style found little favour among the wealthier men who could afford to incorporate more space and luxury into their new castles. They chose instead to build in the 'quadrangular' manner which we have already noticed at Bodiam, with four wings of buildings 111 arranged round a central courtyard. The outer face of the quadrangle – which more often than not had substantial corner towers and sometimes subsidiary turrets as well – was to a greater or lesser degree defensible, while the inward-looking face could afford to be almost exclusively domestic. 'A fortress without, a palace within', the quadrangular castle combined display, comfort and security in almost perfect balance, and it is not surprising that it was the dominant form of major English fortified dwellings from about the middle of the fourteenth century until the time when they merged with the great undefended quadrangular houses of Queen Elizabeth's reign.

At first their development was gradual, beginning perhaps with 'Edwardian' fortresses like Harlech or 78 Beaumaris, which are rectangular in plan but have 83 curtain walls rather than ranges of buildings between their corner towers. Maxstoke Castle in Warwickshire, built in the 1340s, has wings of rooms on three sides of its courtyard, and Edward III erected a quadrangle of magnificent lodgings within the royal castle of Windsor during the 1350s and 1360s, but the first truly quadrangular castles belong to the last thirty years of the fourteenth century, when no less than ten of them were built.

One of the earliest of the series was Bolton Castle in 120 Wensleydale, North Yorkshire, begun by Richard 122 Lord Scrope in about 1377. It can only be described as spectacular, with four corner towers rising to almost 100 feet (nearly 30 metres), each as large in area as an average border hold, linked by ranges 40 feet (12 metres) high. Within this forbidding exterior is the central courtyard, with a door at each corner covered by a machicolation on the tower-head above. The doors gave access – albeit via twisting turnpike stairs designed for defence – to more than seventy rooms, arranged in five storeys in the towers and two or three in the connecting wings. Apart from the great hall, the chapel, and the private staterooms of the owner, there were seven suites of lodgings and twelve individual apartments for guests and gentlemen retainers, mostly on the upper floors. At a lower level were the 'offices' of the castle, including several kitchens and larders, a wine-cellar, a brewhouse, a bakehouse, a smithy, four stables, many storerooms, and even a horse-powered mill to grind corn into flour.

144

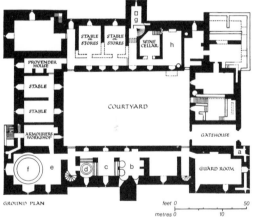

GROUND PLAN

feet 0   50
metres 0   10

PROVENDER HOUSE

STABLE STORES   STABLE STORES   WINE CELLAR   h

STABLE

STABLE

COURTYARD

ARMOURERS WORKSHOP

GATEHOUSE

f   e   d   c   b   a

GUARD ROOM

g

N

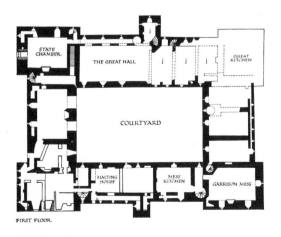

FIRST FLOOR.

STATE CHAMBER

THE GREAT HALL

GREAT KITCHEN

i

j   j   j

COURTYARD

MALTING HOUSE   MESS KITCHEN   GARRISON MESS

120–22 Bolton Castle, begun c.1377, in the lower reaches of Wensleydale. Top: a distant view from the south-west. Left: plans of the ground and first floors: (a) porter's lodge, (b) meal house with ovens, (c) bakehouse and brewhouse, (d) brewing vat, (e) threshing floor, (f) horse mill, (g) room above dungeon, (h) well chamber, (i) lobby, (j) butteries. Above: the destruction of the north-east tower after the Civil War (p. 183) reveals the great-hall range (right).

145

Scrope's fortress-palace clearly made an immense impression on his fellow northern magnates, and within five years of its inception John Lord Neville, who already possessed great strongholds at Raby in Durham and Middleham in North Yorkshire, had begun work on a quadrangular castle of his own at Sheriff Hutton. Built on an outcrop overlooking the plain of York, and 10 miles (16 kilometres) distant from that medieval metropolis of the north, it is now an awe-inspiring ruin. Yet enough of its 'cliff-like masonry' survives to show us that, though not so regular in plan, it was even bigger than Bolton, and by all accounts it was still more splendidly appointed. 'The stately staire up to the haul [hall]', says the ubiquitous Leland, 'is very magnificent, and so is the haul itself, and al the residew of the house: in so much that I saw no house in the north so like a princely logginges.'

Others quickly followed suit, among them Neville's son-in-law Sir Ralph Lumley. His castle at Lumley in Durham, begun in 1389 and still inhabited, very much resembles Bolton, but has four corner turrets set slantwise on each of its angle towers. Nor were the great house of Percy to be excluded from the race to keep up with the baron next door, for Sir Thomas Percy – younger brother of the Earl of Northumberland and twice closely connected by marriage to John Neville – weighed in with Wressle Castle, almost as conveniently close to York as Sheriff Hutton. Making no attempt to compete with the grandeur of Neville's fortress or the defensive strength of Scrope's, Percy's smaller castle relied for its effect on luxurious lodgings and an exceptionally high quality of finish. Built in 'very fair and great squarid stone' rather than the cheaper random masonry of its rivals, its white walls seemed 'as newly made' a hundred and fifty years later, and the one undemolished wing is still scarcely weathered. Its many fine exterior windows included a great protruding oriel, which once looked out over gardens and orchards full of topiary work. The 'exceedingly faire' garderobe impressed Leland, as did the ingenious folding desks in the tower-library called 'Paradise': he summed up the place as 'mynion' (dainty or pretty) and thought it, even by sixteenth-century standards, 'one of the properest houses beyond Trent'.

South of the Trent, too, quadrangular castles were much in vogue during the closing years of the fourteenth century. Based on the same all-inclusive principle as their northern counterparts, these southern castles are rather different in appearance, though they are just as clearly variants on a single pattern. Almost invariably moated, they have round or polygonal corner towers rather than rectangular ones, and are equipped with prominent gatehouses. Their prototype may well be Sir Warin de Lisle's castle of Shirburn in Oxfordshire, begun at about the same time as Bolton and constructed (exceptionally at this period) of brick. As in the north, others followed in rapid succession. Among them were Wingfield in Suffolk, built by Scrope's brother-in-law Michael de la Pole in 1384, and Bodiam (discussed above), begun twelve months later. As befits its special status of a bulwark of national defence, the latter is the most militarily effective of all fourteenth-century quadrangular castles, and apparently the only one to be equipped with gunports.

But if Bodiam Castle recalls foreign raids and English reverses in the Hundred Years' War, both it and its companions – as well as a number of splendid fifteenth-century fortresses – are to a great extent a reminder of the credit side of the struggle with France. We have already seen that the builders of quadrangular castles (and for that matter the other great men who took part in the building boom at the close of the fourteenth century) were often closely related by blood or marriage, and many of them had held important posts in the various governments of Richard II. Perhaps the most important fact about them, however, is that they were without exception successful soldiers. There was scarcely a campaign during the first half of the war, whether in France or Spain, on the Scottish marches or at sea, which did not see one or more of them involved. Nor did their victories (of which one of the most notable was Sir Thomas Percy's capture of twenty-two heavily laden enemy merchant ships in 1378) bring them only fame and glory. For, beneath the lip-service to the fashionable ideas of chivalry, war in the later Middle Ages was regarded, in the words of the great historian K. B. McFarlane, as 'a speculative, but at best hugely profitable trade'. Dallyngridge of Bodiam had ridden with one of the bandit 'Free Companies' whose sole aim was the accumulation of wealth, but the royal forces themselves were scarcely less devoted to profit. Every soldier from the Black Prince downwards received his wages (ranging from the average nobleman's 6s. 8d. a day to the archer's daily 4d. or 6d.), but the biggest sources of income were loot and, above all, ransoms. The trade in prisoners was highly organized; the nobler the captive, the larger the ransom. Really important men were handed over to the King in return for a handsome gratuity, but lesser prisoners were the 'property' of their lucky captors. Captains like

123 The only surviving wing of the quadrangular castle of Wressle, Humberside, housing the great hall between two corner towers. A more luxurious and less military version of Bolton (ills. 120–22), it was begun a few years later, c.1380.

Scrope of Bolton or Lisle of Shirburn also received a third or a half of the ransoms collected by the soldiers under their command, though they themselves had to pass on a third of their own profits to the King.

From time to time, of course, Englishmen were themselves captured and put to ransom by Frenchmen, but on balance the English came off very much the better, partly because the wars took place in enemy country, which they could and did plunder mercilessly. When we consider that the ransom of a French nobleman could be numbered in hundreds or even thousands of pounds, it is easy to see how an English captain with a modicum of luck and a deal of military sense could return from the wars much richer than he set out. A number of captains, among them the builders of our quadrangular castles, certainly did so return, and it is more than likely that their sumptuous and expensive new residences (Bolton is said to have cost £12,000, or over £2 million in modern terms, and Sheriff Hutton must have been still more pricy) were in whole or in part unwillingly paid for by their enemies.

The stream of loot and ransoms dried up during the long truce of 1396–1415, and it is notable that no major new castles were begun in these years. With the battle of Agincourt, when a marshal of France, two dukes, three counts and fourteen barons fell into English hands, not to mention hundreds of French knights and esquires, it began to flow again with redoubled vigour. The conquest of northern France, carried out mainly between 1417 and 1429, meant that successful soldiers could now add the revenues of confiscated enemy lands to the proceeds of a string of English victories, and by the 1430s the fortunes they made began to be reflected in a new spate of magnificent buildings. Like their forebears of forty years earlier, these great fortified palaces of the fifteenth century are a memorial to the late medieval passion for the public display of wealth, or, in the modern idiom, for conspicuous consumption. Along with fine clothes, great collections of plate and jewels, and troops of liveried retainers, they were indispensable to the self-esteem of the contemporary nobleman, and even more so to the social pretension of the newly rich.

Such a one was Sir John Fastolf, the offspring of a respectable but obscure Norfolk family, whose great wealth was almost entirely due to his prowess in the wars. No more than an esquire when he joined the

147

124 The great tower of Sir John Fastolf's fortified brick mansion or 'water-castle' at Caister in Norfolk, begun in 1431, with handgun loops at the top of its stair turret and ports for larger cannon near the level of the moat. The ruined great-hall range stands in the right foreground.

expedition to Harfleur in 1415, he was knighted three years later, and in 1422 became grand master of the household to John Duke of Bedford, Henry V's brother and commander of the English forces in France after his death. Fastolf himself was made Lieutenant of Normandy in 1423, and in the following year distinguished himself at the battle of Verneuil – known at the time as 'the second Agincourt' – where he captured the French commander. From this battle alone he claimed to have 'won by the fortune of war about 20,000 marks' (£13,333 6s. 8d.), and we can only guess at the total amount of French gold he had shipped home by the time he retired in 1439. He certainly became a very rich man indeed, and showed his wealth by accumulating vast quantities of land, by wearing a jewelled collar worth four hundred times the annual wage of an archer, and by spending over £6,000 on replacing the unassuming manor house where he had been born with a great new fortified palace.

124   This was Caister Castle, a mighty undertaking begun at the height of Fastolf's fame in 1431 and not completed until nearly twenty years later. Its outermost line of defence was the moat, which was linked by a specially cut canal to the river Bure, and so to the nearby port of Yarmouth. To prevent an enemy using this method of approach, incoming barges had to pass under an arch guarded by a tower before tying up at the dock within. The 'great mansion' itself, as Fastolf called it, was built almost entirely of locally produced bricks, and had two separate moated courtyards, the second reached only by a drawbridge from the first. This innermost court – a quadrangular castle in its own right – contained the great hall and state apartments, adorned with gold plate and hung with tapestries depicting, amongst other things, the siege of Falaise where Sir John had been knighted. Such a reminder of former glories no doubt heightened the old soldier's enjoyment of his separate parlours for winter or summer use, and of that almost unheard-of luxury, a bathroom with piped water. Both here and elsewhere, however, his carved and painted motto 'Me fault faire' ('I must be doing') kept him up to his hobby of persecuting his debtors and servants with the same ruthless zeal as he had displayed in the wars, causing one of them to remark 'Cruell and vengible he hath been ever, and for the most parte withoute pite and mercy.'

The splendours of Caister's interior are gone, but the crowning glory of its defences remains, the breathtakingly tall and slender tower at one corner of the inner courtyard. Apart from being yet another example of Fastolf's determination to impress, however, this tower 90 feet (27 metres) high serves much the same purpose as the more modest structure at Stokesay, that of a keep and final refuge. Twice as 117 thickly walled as the rest of the castle, it is topped by machicolations and equipped with gunports. Those near the ground were perhaps for the largest of Fastolf's eighteen cannon (two monsters which fired stones 9 inches, or 23 centimetres, in diameter), while the loops ringing the top were probably for his 'hand-gonnes'. Curiously un-British in appearance, Caister's great tower seems in fact to have been derived from the 'water-castles' of the Lower Rhine Valley. Just how strong the castle really was was soon to be apparent (pp. 154–55).

German influence is even more in evidence at Tattershall Castle in Lincolnshire, the ancestral home 127 of Fastolf's friend Ralph Lord Cromwell. He began to remodel the thirteenth-century stronghold in about 1434, adding a second moat outside the original one and reconstructing many of the residential buildings within the old towered curtain wall. Attached to the rebuilt hall, and constructed from over 300,000 bricks, was the centrepiece of the new works, the great tower-block 112 feet (34 metres) high. It was apparently the design of a mason named Baldwin Docheman (Deutsch Mann, or German), and it undoubtedly bears a close resemblance to the great tower of the Palace of the Order of Teutonic Knights at Marienburg in East Prussia (now Poland). Like its prototype, Cromwell's tower is an ambiguous mixture of defensive and domestic features. The machicolations on the faces of the building are most efficiently designed, but those on the turrets are mere shams; the walls are thick, but in many places weakened by internal rooms and corridors, and everywhere pierced with windows. Finally, on the outward face of the tower (which we might expect to be the strongest) defence is completely thrown out of the window – or, to be precise, out of eight huge windows, two on each floor from the ground upwards. This 'show-front' is admittedly protected from close attack by the double moat, but is horribly vulnerable to bombardment by even the most inefficient of cannons. The tower has no recognizable gunports, so the gun-stones found during excavations must have been fired either from its roof or from elsewhere in the castle's defences.

Lord Cromwell had enriched himself by service in France, but he was no career soldier, and his business was with finance rather than warfare. Treasurer of England for much of the time his castle was being built, he was well able to lend £4,000 to

the King himself, and was (principally by his own not always honest efforts) a multi-millionaire by the standards of his day. Nor was anyone allowed to forget it, for his badge of a bulging purse with the 126 motto 'Nay je droyt' ('Have I not the right') appears again and again in the decoration of his tower. Yet whatever his other faults, Cromwell was no niggard, and in fact suffered particularly badly from the contemporary passion for showy buildings. Quite apart from the works at Tattershall (which included the foundation of a large new church, complete with college and almshouses) he built or began houses and churches at Lambley in Nottinghamshire and Collyweston in Northamptonshire and raised a magnificent mansion at South Wingfield in Derbyshire.

At South Wingfield, with a characteristic desire to 15 go one better than anyone else, Cromwell ordered 125 one of the very earliest British examples of a double- 126 courtyard house, a vast palace arranged round a pair of quadrangles each fully as large in area as the whole ground plan of Bolton. Although undoubtedly a 121 'manor place' rather than a castle, South Wingfield occupies a very good defensive position at the tip of a narrow and steep-sided spur. It was entered via a fortified gateway into the 'base court', which contains barns, offices and servants' quarters and acts as a huge vestibule to the inner quadrangle of Cromwell's private apartments. Passing through a second gatehouse – and glancing up at the money 126 bags carved upon it – the visitor found himself facing the principal block of state apartments, including the banqueting hall with its high table lit by a great 15 oriel window. These were built on the very end of the ridge, a position which not only gave Cromwell's guests a good view but also afforded a measure of protection. The only specifically military part of the palace, however, is the refuge tower 72 feet (22 metres) high – itself containing a number of luxurious chambers – placed at the junction of the inner and outer courts and dominating them both: it also has a solitary gunport covering an outer wall.

If the tower of South Wingfield might perhaps have succeeded in beating off a casual attack, the contemporary keep of Raglan in Gwent was designed 128 to withstand a full-scale siege. It was the work of Sir William ap Thomas, yet another veteran of the French war, who by a combination of judicious marriages and political manoeuvring had by 1430 made himself the most powerful man in south-east Wales. Not afraid of using armed force to gain his own ends, he thought it prudent, at some time during the next fifteen years, to guard against retribution by building a virtually impregnable refuge on the

125, 126 South Wingfield Manor, Derbyshire, begun c.1440. Above: the fine vaulted undercroft beneath the great hall (see pl. 15), demonstrating the high quality masonry employed even in this obscure part of the fortified mansion. Below: panel above the inner gateway showing Lord Cromwell's badge of a bulging purse in the upper tier, flanking the central shield.

127 *Lord Cromwell's brick tower-house at Tattershall Castle (begun c. 1434), its machicolations belied by the eight huge windows of the show-front overlooking the moat.*

128 128 *The moated great tower at Raglan, Gwent, mutilated after the Civil War (p. 188), with its cross-slitted gunports near ground level and its low curtain wall. To the right is the main gatehouse of the castle proper (p. 154), with its own double tier of round gunports.*

moated mound of an old Norman castle. With its walls 10 feet (3 metres) thick, and its formidable height, originally topped by another storey and a ring of machicolations, the six-sided tower could only be entered by a cleverly designed drawbridge at the level of the first upper floor. Five of its faces were equipped with round gunports surmounted by cross-shaped aiming slits, and Sir William's son later added a low curtain wall with gun platforms covering each of its angles. All in all, said a seventeenth-century visitor, 'for strength, height and neatness it surpassed most, if not every other tower in England or Wales.' Fully self-sufficient though it was, containing a well and kitchen in addition to a hall, private chamber and bedrooms, Sir William's tower was not intended to stand alone, but as an adjunct to a larger and more luxurious residence which was in the event not completed until some years later (p. 154).

Others did not place quite such a high priority on defence, but their efforts – all products of the building craze of the 1430s and 1440s – deserve at least a mention. Sudeley Castle in Gloucestershire

follows the grandiose double-courtyard plan of South Wingfield. 'Partly buyldyd with spoyles goten in France', one of its towers was ironically named after the French lord whose ransom had helped to raise it. Herstmonceux in Sussex, brick-built and quadrangular, is almost as grand: surrounded by a moat, it has no less than four large and eleven small towers, as well as a great gateway equipped with gunports like those at Raglan. Hampton Court in Herefordshire (built with Sir Roland Lenthall's 'winnings' at Agincourt) is also quadrangular, but Faulkbourne Hall in Essex is somewhat more modest. An L-shaped brick manor house with a strong battlemented tower at its angle, it was the home of Sir John Montgomery, a comrade of Fastolf's who was instrumental in the capture of Joan of Arc.

Though so many of the places mentioned were built by old soldiers anxious to improve their social status, we must not imagine that their defences were the product either of pure nostalgia or of a desire to imitate the castles of a romantic bygone age. For, by the 1440s at least, England was becoming a more dangerous place to live in than it had been for a very long time, and propertied men did well to look to their own security. Perhaps the greatest single cause of the breakdown of public order was the weak and incompetent personality of King Henry VI, who allowed the reins of government to fall into the hands of a party of unscrupulous and self-seeking courtiers led at first by the Duke of Suffolk and later by the forceful Queen Margaret. These 'evil counsellors' were widely blamed for the successive English military defeats which ended the Hundred Years' War and (with more justice) for the impoverishment of the Crown and the utter corruption of the legal system. No longer able to trust to law or government to right their wrongs, men increasingly resorted to armed force to settle their disputes, and to the 'maintenance' of the most powerful local lords for their protection. Such lesser noblemen (who were themselves frequently at feud with each other) attached themselves in turn to the greater lords, either of the court party or of the 'opposition' headed by the King's cousin and heir presumptive, Richard Duke of York. Thus, in the words of the contemporary Chronicle of John Hardyng,

In every shire with jacks [armoured jackets] and sallets
  [helmets] clean
Misrule doth rise and maketh neighbours war;
The weaker goes beneath, as oft is seen,
The mightiest his quarrel will prefer,
That poor men's causes are put on back full far
Which through the peace and law well conserved
Might be amended, and thanks of God deserved.

Perhaps 'every shire' is something of an exaggeration, but East Anglia was certainly plagued by 'divers riottes, extorciouns, forsibil entreys and unlawfull disherytauns of gentilmen' incited by the agents of the Duke of Suffolk and his rival magnates. Suffolk also 'maintained' William Tailboys of Kyme Tower in Lincolnshire (p. 142). 'Named and noysed for a common murderer', Tailboys had feuds with almost everyone in the county, and even attempted to assassinate his neighbour Lord Cromwell on his way to a meeting of the royal council. Derbyshire, too, was disturbed, not only by two separate vendettas between groups of local gentry but also by the activities of a gang of bandits 'like as if it had been Robin Hood and his men'.

Such private wars often involved attacks on manor houses, as in the case of the Harcourt–Stafford feud. Meeting by chance at Coventry in 1448, the two parties fell to brawling and young Richard Stafford was stabbed in the back. Sir Robert Harcourt, who began the fight, was not even brought to trial, for he enjoyed the protection of the Duke of Suffolk. On 1 May 1450, however, Suffolk was himself assassinated by his political opponents, and that very same day the Staffords gathered two hundred of their friends and retainers and marched through the dark hours to the manor house of Stanton Harcourt in Oxfordshire. This was presumably unfortified, for Sir Robert had to barricade himself in the neighbouring church-tower while his enemies ransacked his home. His makeshift refuge served him well, deflecting showers of Stafford arrows and resisting an attempt to set it afire, and after six hours his assailants gave up and left. He was lucky to escape with his life, and soon afterwards guarded against a return visit by building a fortified tower – now called Pope's Tower – onto his house. It was not, however, to save him, as we shall see.

If revenge was the motive for the attack on Stanton Harcourt, there was no such excuse for the murder of Nicholas Radford, who had committed no worse offence than giving legal advice to Lord Bonville. But Bonville was at daggers drawn with the Earl of Devon, and at midnight on 23 October 1455 a hundred of the Earl's retainers besieged Radford's manor house of Upcott Barton near Tiverton in Devon. The old man, awakened by the flames of his burning outer gates, received a solemn promise from the Earl's son, Sir Thomas Courtenay, that no further harm would come to him and, powerless to resist, he admitted the attackers to the house. As he stood drinking a glass of wine with Courtenay, however, the Earl's thugs carried off every single movable piece of his property, even throwing his invalid wife out of bed in order to steal her sheets. This done, Radford was lured out of his house and hacked to death. Not content with all this, the murderers returned three days later to conduct an 'inquest' on the body, bringing in a 'verdict' of suicide. The naked corpse was then dropped into a grave, where it was battered beyond recognition with the stones prepared by Radford for his tomb. Courtenay and the other murderers were not even brought to trial.

Crimes like this give the lie to the view that castles and defensible houses were out of date by the latter half of the fifteenth century. The need for them, indeed, was to become still more acute, for six months before poor Radford's death the widespread feuds had escalated into open civil war. The first 'battle' of St Albans, fought on 22 May 1455, was really a faction fight between the Lancastrian court party, backed by the great northern family of Percy, and the Duke of York, who owed the support of the equally powerful Nevilles largely to their desire to settle scores with their Percy rivals. Thus the 'Wars of the Roses' began as they were to continue, with most men choosing sides for reasons of local politics or simple expediency rather than out of ideological conviction: personalities were what mattered, and the armies were made up of collections of private retinues who had orders to 'slay the lords and spare the commons'. Though most of the decisive battles of the struggle – often followed by the judicial murder of prisoners as 'traitors' to the winning side – were fought in the open field, in Wales and the far north castles still had an important part to play.

On Palm Sunday 1461 Edward IV, the son and crowned successor of Richard Duke of York, gained a crushing victory over the forces of the deposed King Henry VI, giving the Yorkists control over virtually the whole of England. Only Northumberland, with its three great castles of Bamburgh, Dunstanburgh and Alnwick, remained in Lancastrian hands, constituting a dangerous bridgehead for the Scottish and French invasion forces which Queen Margaret was doing her best to summon to her aid. Expedition after expedition was sent against them (Alnwick changed hands no less than seven times in three years), but no sooner had the Yorkist forces retired than the fortresses again fell into enemy hands. Finally, in 1464, Edward sent the royal train of siege artillery against these thorns in his side, and at this Alnwick and Dunstanburgh capitulated at once.

54 Bamburgh, the strongest of the three, cried defiance, though its garrison were warned that since the castle 'marcheth so nigh his ancient enemies of Scotland, he [King Edward IV] specially desireth to have it whole, unbroken with ordnance: if ye suffer any great gun to be laid to the wall and be shot . . . it shall cost you the chieftain's head, and so proceeding for every gun shot, to the least head of any person within the said place.' When this warning was contemptuously ignored, all the royal guns (named 'Newcastle', 'London', 'Dijon the brazen gun', 'Edward' and 'Richard the Bombard') fired at once, so that 'stones of the walls flew into the sea' and the castellan's chamber was 'smote through oftentimes'. Even so, the battered fortress had to be stormed by infantry before the wounded keeper could be dragged forth and sent to the block.

The only castle that now remained to the
77 opponents of Edward IV was Harlech, the strongest of Edward I's North Wales fortresses and indeed one of the most impregnable in the whole of Britain – as it had proved sixty years before, when it had been the last of Glendower's strongholds to fall to the English

(p. 110). It was commanded by one Dafydd ap Ieuan, who boasted that, just as he had held a fortress in France so long that all the old women of Wales talked about it, so he would hold Harlech so long that all the old women of France talked about it. And so he did, hanging on doggedly from 1461 until August 1468, when he at last capitulated to William Lord Herbert, who saved his life from a vengeful King by swearing to hand the castle back to him if he was not pardoned.

With the example of the 'Men of Harlech' before him, Herbert, who was the son of Sir William ap Thomas, the Raglan tower-builder, had little cause to believe that castles had outlived their usefulness. He himself, indeed, was responsible for building at Raglan one of the most castle-like of fifteenth-century palaces – or, rather, one of the most palatial of late castles. While its interior follows the fashionable double-quadrangle plan of South Wingfield, the exterior is immeasurably stronger, presenting a formidable array of high walls and machicolated towers and pierced with at least thirty-seven gunports. The greatest concentration of defences was around the main gate, which was swept 128 both by the fire of its own double tier of gunloops and by that of the cannon mounted in Sir William ap Thomas' tower, which now played its intended role as an independent keep to the 'bailey' formed by Herbert's new buildings. But it was all in vain, for in 1469 Herbert was defeated in battle in far-away Oxfordshire, and subsequently executed at the behest of his former fellow-Yorkist, Warwick 'the Kingmaker'. Hitherto the foremost supporters of Edward IV, Warwick and his Neville relations now tried to seize power for themselves: failing to do so, they turned Lancastrian, restoring Henry VI to the throne in 1470 and driving Edward into exile.

To those with private feuds of their own, the upheavals in the state between 1469 and 1471 were a golden opportunity to settle old scores: in Gloucestershire the rival Talbots and Berkeleys fought a pitched battle at Nibley Green, and Sir Robert Harcourt, despite his new tower at Stanton Harcourt, was murdered 'in his own place' by his old enemies the Staffords. At this time, too, occurred the famous siege of Caister Castle, which had been 124 inherited from Sir John Fastolf (albeit under somewhat suspicious circumstances) by the Paston family. It was also claimed by the mighty Duke of Norfolk, whose superior power and influence much outweighed the highly dubious nature of his title. At one time he brought no less than 3,000 of his tenants and retainers, together with a 'great multitude of

129 The patterned brick gatehouse at unfinished Kirby Muxloe, Leicestershire (begun in 1480), its round gunports surmounted by sighting slits.

guns', against the place, while the Pastons could only raise about 25 men to defend it. It says much for the strength of Fastolf's fortifications that this tiny garrison was able to hold out for five weeks, only surrendering ('for lack of victuals, gunpowder, men's hearts, lack of surety of rescue') when three sides of the walls had been virtually demolished by Norfolk's cannon. Their misfortune was that no other great lord was prepared to risk the Duke's wrath by relieving them, while the King himself relied too much on Norfolk's political support either to intervene or to punish his blatantly illegal action. 'The weakest goes beneath, as oft is seen, The mightiest his quarrel will prefer.'

It was a very different story when, a few months after the fall of Caister, Sir Thomas Burgh's manor house at Gainsborough in Lincolnshire was plundered and destroyed by his local rivals the Willoughbies and the Dymmocks. For Burgh was a personal friend of Edward IV, who immediately intervened with a royal army: frightened into open rebellion, the Lincolnshire men were easily defeated, and their leaders duly lost their heads. Together with the rest of Edward's friends, Burgh suffered an eclipse during the short-lived restoration of Henry VI, but in 1471 the exiled Yorkist King came home from exile, defeating Warwick and the Lancastrians and establishing himself on the throne more firmly than ever. More settled conditions now returned, yet even the most loyal supporters of the house of York could not feel themselves completely safe, and though Burgh built himself a new manor house (now called Gainsborough Old Hall) in domestic half-timbering, he took the precaution of adding to it a substantial brick refuge-tower.

King Edward's chief counsellor, William Lord Hastings, built on a much grander scale during this period of Yorkist prosperity, even rivalling Lord Cromwell's works of thirty years earlier. He, too, ensured that each of his new residences was defensible – as well he might, since much of his great wealth was founded on lands forfeited by banished or executed Lancastrians. Amongst these profits of civil war was Belvoir Castle: there Hastings met with some resistance to his takeover, so, 'upon a raging will', he completely unroofed it, carrying off the lead to Ashby-de-la-Zouch and incorporating it in his new great tower there. Raised on the site of another confiscated castle, Ashby tower (now badly decayed) was a more robust version of that at Tattershall, with all its accommodation – hall, kitchen and bedrooms – contained in one thick-walled block some 90 feet (27 metres) high.

Not content with this, or with his other 'Manor Place, like a Castelle building' at Bagworth, Hastings began in 1480 to build a third Leicestershire residence at Kirby Muxloe. Like so many fortified palaces of the fifteenth century, this was quadrangular and built in brick, with a moat, four corner towers and a robust gatehouse. It had, however, a more comprehensive system of gunports than any other house of its day, intended to guard against almost any eventuality. Each corner tower had six loops at ground level, and another near the top to sweep the rampart walk of the neighbouring walls: the gatehouse had a further half-dozen at ground level, and two more below the level of the moat – no doubt designed to fire on an attacker who had succeeded in draining away the water. They were never to be put to the test, for before the place was half finished Hastings met an end that was sudden and unexpected even by the violent standards of the fifteenth century. His loyalty to Edward IV was unwavering even after the King's death in 1483, and he would not fall in with Richard III's plans to depose Edward's sons (and Richard's nephews), 'the Princes in the Tower'. Under cover of their old friendship, Richard summoned Hastings to a council meeting, accused him of 'treason', and had him dragged outside, where 'his head was laid down upon a log of timber and there stricken off'.

Richard's defeat at Bosworth in 1485, which gave the throne to the Tudors and virtually concluded the

130 *The imposing but lightly-defended gatehouse in the entrance range of Oxburgh Hall, Norfolk, built* c.*1482, has cross-gunloops which are contradicted by the large windows above the entrance.*

Wars of the Roses, also marked the beginning of the end for the fortified private residence in the area south of the Scottish border zone. With the gradual re-establishment of law and order under Henry VII, the danger of armed attacks by local rivals receded, and Kirby Muxloe was one of the very last great English houses designed with defence as its first priority. Though defensible houses, of a sort, continued to be raised for nearly half a century after Bosworth, from now on security was to be increasingly subordinated to comfort and display.

The movement of domestic fortifications towards a purely symbolic role was signalled by a fashion for 130 imposing gatehouses, like that of Oxburgh Hall in Norfolk. Apart from a very shallow moat, it was the house's only defence, but just how effective it would have been is open to question. It could, admittedly, originally be reached only by a drawbridge, and is equipped with machicolation over its entrance as well as with cross-shaped loopholes at ground level; the series of apertures which light the stairway in one of the towers, too, could have doubled as ports for handguns. But the effect of these warlike features is softened by the many outward facing windows of

the rest of the house, and more so by the great mullioned windows of the state chambers in the gatehouse itself.

Oxburgh was begun during the last years of Yorkist rule, but the passion for grandiose gatehouses reached its height during the reign of Henry VIII (1509–47). No major new building in the southeast was then considered complete without one, and they appear not only at palaces like Hampton Court and St James's in London and mansions like Cowdray in Sussex or Leez Priory and Layer Marney in Essex, but also at Eton and the colleges of Cambridge. Many-windowed, ornately decorated, and lacking even the modest defensive arrangements of Oxburgh, these Tudor extravaganzas were meant purely and simply as symbols of power.

The power they proclaimed, however, was no longer the power of individual noble families, but that of Henry VIII himself. He it was that built the palaces, financed the colleges, and promoted the men who built the mansions. Wolsey of Hampton Court was his chief minister, Sir William Fitzwilliam of Cowdray his household treasurer, Henry Lord Marney of Layer Marney his chamberlain and close friend, and Richard Rich of Leez Priory (whose betrayal of Sir Thomas More was only the most notorious of his many dirty tricks on the King's behalf) his solicitor-general. Supreme in Church and State, the King would brook no rivals, still less allow them to build fortresses of their own.

131 The unfinished state of Thornbury 'Castle' in Gloucestershire, almost the last private palace with any pretensions to defensibility, is a further testimony to the triumph of monarchy over any other power in the land. Its builder, Edward Stafford, was Duke of Buckingham and Earl of Hereford, Stafford and Northampton, the most influential and perhaps the richest of the English hereditary peerage. But his descent from Edward III placed him too close to the throne for his own safety, and he was unwise to upset the upstart Wolsey by the heinous crime of deliberately spilling water on his shoes. His great house rising at Thornbury, too, was an uncomfortable reminder of his links with the mighty king-making aristocrats of the fifteenth century. Planned on a stupendous scale, its three defended outer courtyards surrounded a splendid inner quadrangle of state apartments, whose chief glory was to be its embattled and loopholed entrance front set with four great towers. Only one of these had reached its full machicolated height when, in 1521, Stafford was suddenly called to London, to be tried and executed on a charge of treason trumped up from a few chance remarks reported to Wolsey by an ambitious member of the Duke's own household. No one, least of all his fellow peers, dared lift a finger to save him.

Even if the Tudor monarchs had not been so jealous of any other strongholds than their own, it is doubtful whether the 'defensible house' would have survived much longer in the English interior. The need for protection against hostile neighbours had passed and, with the rapid developments in artillery, a full-scale siege could only be resisted by specialized defences which were expensive, complex and, above all, incompatible with the everyday life of a palace or manor house. It is difficult to imagine a Tudor nobleman living in something resembling one of Henry VIII's coastal forts: he had, in any case, no need to do so, for England in the sixteenth and early seventeenth century was a land at peace within itself. But conditions in Scotland and the borderlands were very different, and it is there we must travel to continue the story of the defensible house.

131 The truncated towers (left) of the entrance front at Thornbury 'Castle', Gloucestershire, left unfinished in 1521, are now balanced by a later house to the right of the gateway.

12   A house for thieves to knock at: Scotland and the Borders, *c*. 1400–1638

I will build me such a house as thieves will need to knock at ere they enter.

PATRICK FORBES, after the sack of his castle of Corse, Aberdeenshire, in about 1500

The Scots . . . spend all their time in wars, and when there is no war they fight with one another.

DON PEDRO DE AYALA, 1498

132 The fearsome array of wide-mouthed gunloops which faces unwanted visitors at the sixteenth-century gatehouse of Dunnottar Castle (p. 127 and pl. 11).

If the building of domestic fortifications bears a direct relationship to the prevailing level of violence and disorder, there was no better breeding ground for them than fifteenth- and sixteenth-century Scotland. Of the eight monarchs who ruled her during this period only three died in their beds – two of them allegedly of despair – and the disasters that dogged her royal house were reflected in a seemingly endless succession of murders, executions, feuds and civil wars.

The beginning of the fifteenth century found the throne of Bruce occupied by his great-grandson, the aged and crippled Robert III. His reign was to be remembered for 'the greatest discord, wrangles and strife between magnates and nobles, because the King, weak in body, nowhere exercised rigour'. Such government as existed was carried on by his brother, the Regent Albany, whose own designs on the throne led him to immure the elder of Robert's two sons in Falkland Palace, where the Prince is said to have gnawed at his hands in agony before dying of starvation. To save his younger son James from a like fate, the King secretly despatched him to France, but he was captured at sea by privateers and carried off to captivity in England. The news of this disaster killed the old King, who died declaring himself 'the worst of kings and the most wretched of men in the whole realm', and for the next eighteen years Albany and his son Murdoch ruled Scotland as monarchs in all but name. Not until 1424 did the exiled Prince finally return, 'an angry man in a hurry', to be crowned as King James I.

His long years in captivity had given him plenty of time for reflection on the troubled state of his nation, and he swore that 'If God grant me life and aid, even the life of a dog, throughout all the realm I will make the key keep the castle and the bracken bush [protect] the cow.' His methods of bringing about peace were not gentle. He rounded up and executed nearly every male member of the Albany family and, summoning fifty unruly Highland chieftains to a meeting at Inverness, imprisoned or hanged them all. He made laws to prohibit the 'bands' by which noblemen allied with each other for feuds and private wars and, in a vain effort to make his subjects practice their archery, 'the King forbiddis that na man play at the fut ball under the payne of 4*d*.'. (In later years 'the golf' was also ordered to be 'utterly criyt [cried] doune and nocht usyt'.) It was too good – and perhaps too totalitarian – to last, and one night in February 1437 a band of malcontents slipped into the Dominican priory of Perth where James was staying. Unarmed, he hid himself in the drain-shaft of a privy, but was discovered and stabbed to death, no less than twenty-eight wounds being found on his body.

The King's only son was but six years old when his father died. Child monarchs were a perennial curse to Scotland, and this second James was no exception: his long minority saw widespread private wars between warring factions of nobles, the greatest of whom were the mighty Douglases. When 'James of the Fiery Face' – so called from his flaming red birthmark – came of age, he set himself to put down these over-powerful subjects, not scrupling to murder a Douglas earl with his own hands. As in contemporary England, these upheavals in the state were reflected in an almost total collapse of law and order, and, according to Robert Lyndesay of Pitscottie, prudent men despairingly 'contained themselves and their friends within strong fortresses and left their goods that could not be kept within a stronghold to the thieves and reivers . . . thinking it sufficient to save their lives until better fortune came.'

The 'strong fortresses' where they 'contained themselves' were, virtually without exception, the tower-houses which had been the standard pattern of Scottish domestic fortifications since the days of Robert the Bruce (p. 120). Comlongon in Dumfries, probably built early in the reign of James II, is an example of the most common fifteenth-century type, a simple rectangular tower. Externally, it differs little in essence from Drum or Threave, or for that matter from Halton or Chipchase on the English side of the border; but, in addition to the main accommodation on its five interior floors, it has a series of small rooms contained within the 11-foot (3.5-metre) thickness of its walls. Amongst these is a two-storey prison, the upper cell being allowed the luxury of a slit-window and a privy, while the lower one is simply a lightless pit into which victims were dropped from above. Such pit-prisons, rare in England, are a fairly common feature of Scottish castles: perhaps the most horrifying of all is the one at St Andrews, where the bishops' prisoners were lowered – or thrown – 30 feet (9 metres) down a funnel-shaped shaft cut out of the solid rock. While a number of unfortunates are known to have 'fameischet with hunger' in such noisome holes, it is cheering to read that a seventeenth-century prisoner

133
134

101
93

136

in the pit of Cromarty Castle 'made ane passadge throw the prison wall being eleven feet [3.5 metres] thick and made his escap'.

The extra accommodation provided by Comlongon's mural chambers was minimal, and the more spacious and luxurious later towers tended to be L-shaped, following the pattern of fourteenth-century Craigmillar. Borthwick in Lothian, built in 1430, has (uniquely) not one but two extra wings attached to its main block, giving it a U-shaped ground plan. A still stronger and more impressive variation on the tower-house theme is the grim castle of Hermitage, which stands guard over Liddesdale in the Borders – 'the bloodiest valley in Britain'. Here, in about 1400, the Douglas family added four great corner towers (all of different sizes) to an earlier rectangular block, linking the tower-tops together in a lofty flying arch on each of its shorter sides. ¹³⁵

What resulted bears a passing resemblance to castles like Bolton, but Hermitage has little in common with the quadrangular fortress-palaces of contemporary England. Only one such palace was built in fifteenth-century Scotland: this was Linlithgow in Lothian, begun by King James I in the year of his return from England, where he must have seen – if not actually stayed at – houses like Bolton, Wressle and Sheriff Hutton. Like them, Linlithgow is built round a great central courtyard, and despite much later rebuilding of the interior it still bears a marked external resemblance to the fashionable English models on which it was based.

Though the Scottish monarchs are known to have possessed 'an instrument called a gun' in 1384, defensive gunports were slow to make their appearance in the fortifications of the northern kingdom. The earliest are said to be those in the turretted and machicolated curtain wall round Craigmillar tower, built perhaps in 1427: they are keyhole loops of the type noted in south-east England during the 1370s and 1380s. James II took a special interest in artillery and (through the good offices of his Flemish father-in-law) imported a formidable siege train from the Low Countries, including a 'great bombard' which is probably to be identified with 'Mons Meg'. This massive gun, still to be seen at Edinburgh Castle, weighs $8\frac{1}{2}$ tons (8 tonnes), and was capable of firing an iron ball weighing half a ton (500 kilograms) for a distance of half a mile (800 metres), or a lighter stone ball for over a mile and a half (2.5 kilometres). It was this siege train, laboriously hauled about the country, that finally gave James the victory over his Douglas enemies during the 1450s. One by one their castles were battered into

133, 134 *The mid-fifteenth-century tower-house of Comlongon, Dumfries, with its corbelled-out and partially enclosed battlements and iron-grilled windows (above), shows in its great hall a carved aumbry or sideboard, to the left, and a fireplace surmounted by the Scottish royal arms flanked by angels bearing the arms of the Murrays of Cockpool, who built the tower-house and still own it.*

135 Hermitage, perhaps the most forbidding castle in Britain, completed c.1400 in the border valley of Liddesdale: note the flying arch linking the two corner-towers on the left.

101 submission, though it is notable that the garrison of Threave – strongly sited and by now reinforced with a gun-looped curtain wall of its own – apparently held out against 'Mons' long enough to make it worthwhile bribing them into surrender.

Ironically enough, it was his beloved guns that killed King James in 1460, as Lyndesay of Pitscottie recorded: 'this prince, more curious nor became him or the majesty of a king did stand near hand by the gunners when the artillery was discharging, his thigh bone was dung in two by a piece of a misframed gun that broke in the shooting . . . and died hastily thereof.' Had he stood a little further off, the story of artillery fortifications in Scotland might have been rather different, for he had already begun 137 work on the first Scottish castle specifically designed for defence by and against firearms, Ravenscraig in Fife. Built across the neck of a promontory guarded on the seaward side by steep cliffs, it consists of two thick-walled round towers linked by a central block, all pierced with large keyhole ports designed to sweep the landward approaches to the fortress. It was, however, an experiment not to be repeated in

136 An incoming prisoner's eye-view down the bottle-dungeon at St Andrew's Castle, Fife (p. 159).

161

137 *Looking along the ditch of James II's artillery castle at Ravenscraig, Fife, with a large keyhole gunport (right) covering the approach and a later wide-mouthed loop commanding the drawbridge.*

medieval Scotland, where the traditional tower-house remained triumphant.

But the increasing power of offensive artillery was not to be gainsaid. James IV (1488–1513), perhaps the ablest Scottish king since Robert the Bruce, set up a gun-foundry in Edinburgh Castle and, mounting his guns on ships, proved to the rebellious chieftains of the Western Isles that their previously inaccessible island strongholds were no longer a safe refuge. Cairn-na-Buig, in the remote Treshnish Islands west of Mull, fell to the King's fleet in 1504, perhaps the first British castle to succumb to naval bombardment, and Stornoway on the Isle of Lewis was battered into submission two years later. Determined to uphold his authority amongst the Gaelic-speaking 'Wild Scots' of the north and west, James now set about commissioning fortresses of his own there. One such was Urquhart on the shore of Loch Ness; originally some 50 feet (15 metres) above the level of that monster-haunted lake, it was intended to control movement along the Great Glen, the natural routeway which stretches from Inverness to Fort William. The site (that of a prehistoric fort and a thirteenth-century stone castle) was granted to John Grant of Freuchie in 1509, on condition that he built there a strong tower 'for a defence against the attacks of robbers and malefactors'.

Successful within the bounds of his own kingdom, where, apart from 'dauntoning the Isles', he brought temporary peace to the southern border by summarily hanging the foremost reivers, James met his downfall when he tried conclusions with England. Urged on by the French, in 1513 he invaded Northumberland with a vast army and an impressive train of artillery, which he used to reduce Norham and a string of lesser strongholds. On 9 September, however, he was outmanœuvred and defeated by the veteran Earl of Surrey at Flodden Field: some 10,000 Scots were slain, including virtually a whole generation of the nobility, and James himself fell in the thickest press of the fighting.

The disaster of Flodden saddled Scotland with yet another child-King – James V was scarcely a year old when his father died – and with a succession of regents whose policies veered now towards a French alliance and now towards friendship with England. The attempts of the half-French Duke of Albany to stir up war against Henry VIII during 1522 and 1523 resulted only in a series of highly destructive border raids by the English, who boasted that they had left near the frontier 'neither house, fortress, village, tree, cattle, corn or other succour for man'.

But not all the Scottish border holds gave in without a fight. The massive L-shaped tower of Cessford, near Jedburgh in the Borders, had been surrounded by an earthen rampart or 'vawmewre' as a defence against artillery, and was reckoned to be 'the strongest place in Scotland after Dunbar and Fast Castle'. On 19 May 1523 a raiding force of over 2,000 Englishmen besieged it, beginning by battering the earth rampart with their eleven cannon: this, however, produced small effect, and the largest of their guns soon broke its axle and fell silent. Attempts were now made, 'right dangerfully', to storm the place with scaling ladders, but though the English managed to carry the outer barbican amidst a hail of stones and bullets from the defenders, they could not gain the tower itself. Then the fire of a pair of cannon was directed at an old blocked window, and when a breach had been made some artillerymen 'right hardily' began to shovel gunpowder into the ground floor. But the walls were 14 feet (4.3 metres) thick, and before enough explosive could be got in to do any damage the Scots set fire to the loose powder and badly burned three of the brave gunners. At this stage the owner of the tower, Sir Andrew Kerr, agreed to surrender it on condition that the garrison should be allowed to march out, and the English commander accepted with a sigh of relief. For, he later wrote to Henry VIII, 'I saw not how it wolde have been won if they within wold have contynued their deffending.'

The failure of Albany's pro-French policy led to a *coup d'état* whereby the Earl of Angus, the pro-

61

138

139

138 *The ruins of Cessford tower, the border stronghold of the Kerrs besieged by the English in 1523. In the foreground are the remnants of the outer earthen rampart or 'vawmewre'.*

139 *Below: the sixteenth-century tower-house (left) and thirteenth-century curtain walls of Urquhart Castle on the shore of Loch Ness, guarding the routeway along the Great Glen.*

English head of the perennially troublesome Douglas family, gained control of the young King. But in 1528 James threw off his tutelage, and besieged him in Tantallon Castle with a great gun named 'Crook-Mouth Meg' and eleven other pieces. The result proved, even more graphically than the siege of Cessford, that the thick walls of medieval castles could on occasion resist the still comparatively primitive artillery of the day. Despite the fact that 'there never was so mickle pain, travail, expense and diligence done and made for the winning of a house', it still remained untaken after twenty days of bombardment, and the siege was abandoned. To add insult to injury, Angus then sallied forth by moonlight and captured the royal artillery as it was being hauled away.

103

Tantallon's successful defence may well have been the inspiration for a remarkable fortress begun a few years later by James V's favourite, James Hamilton of Finnart, and finished by his half-brother, the Regent Arran. This was Craignethan Castle, Lanarkshire (Strathclyde Region), built on a spur of land easily approachable only from the west. All its defences were therefore designed to resist a bom-

140
141

140, 141 *Craignethan, Castle, Lanarkshire, mainly the work (in the 1530s) of the vicious but highly talented James Hamilton of Finnart. In the plan, notice (left to right) the many gunloops in the outer courtyard wall; the gunlooped 'traverse' added later to sweep the northern end of the ditch; the caponier; the thickness of the inner rampart; and the gunloops in the western wall of the tower-house. Above: a view across the ditch, showing the gunlooped caponier (foreground), the footings of the solid rampart which once protected the inner courtyard (centre left), and the western wall of the tower-house (background) with a wide-mouthed gunport near ground level.*

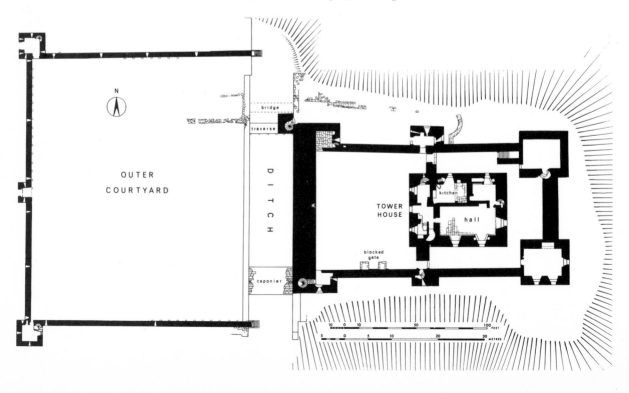

bardment from this direction. First came a large outer courtyard, every inch of whose exterior walls was covered by the fire of twenty-two wide-mouthed gunloops. Between this and the inner court was a 30-foot (900-metre) wide ditch, itself swept by guns mounted in a covered passage (or 'caponier') which cut across it at right angles: this caponier, incidentally, is by far the earliest example known in Britain. Beyond the ditch was a solid rampart 16 feet (5 metres) thick, protecting the western side of an inner court equipped with corner towers and with a further thirty or so carefully placed gunports. Within these defences, finally, was the hub of the fortress, a squat tower-house whose own western wall was immensely thick and virtually windowless. Craignethan, in short, was perhaps the most comprehensively defended private castle of its day, and one of the very few British fortified residences – as opposed to purpose-built and purely military forts like Henry VIII's Deal – raised with the specific intention of resisting heavy artillery. But, like Ravenscraig in the previous century, it proved to be a dead end, for its ingenious defences were soon made obsolete by advances in the range and power of siege guns, and by the consequent introduction of the bastion (pp. 139–40).

112
137

Scotland has no counterpart to the scheme of state-built forts undertaken by Henry VIII: James V relied for the defence of his border on the traditionally-designed strongholds of his subjects. In 1535 every border landowner having estates worth £100 or more was required by law to build a stone barmkin, or fortified enclosure, 'for the resett and defence of him, his tenants, and their goods in troublous time: with a tower in the same for himself if he thinks it expedient'.

The 'troublous times' were not long in coming. King James died in 1542 (allegedly from despair at the rout of his army by the English at the battle of Solway Moss) and the evil angel that dogged the Scottish monarchy now produced its masterpiece. For the heir to the throne was a week-old baby, and, what was infinitely worse, a week-old baby girl, Mary 'Queen of Scots'. Her future husband would presumably be the real power in Scotland, and both Protestant England and Catholic France were determined to gain control of her. To complicate matters still further, the Scots themselves were now divided in religion, the Protestants favouring England and the Catholics inclining towards France. It was the latter, led by the Regent Arran and Cardinal Beaton, who gained the ascendancy, repudiating an agreement to marry Mary to the eldest son of Henry VIII and renewing the 'Auld Alliance' with France.

The jilted English King was furious, and in 1544 and 1545 he launched his fleet and army against Scotland in a series of large-scale forays known as the 'Rough Wooing'. His commander, the Earl of Hertford, was ordered to

Put all to fyre and swoorde, burne Edinborough towne, so rased and defaced when you have sacked and gotten what ye can of it, as there may remayn forever a perpetuel memory of the vengeaunce of God lightened upon them for their faulsehode and disloyailty. Do what ye can out of hande . . . beate down and over throwe the castle, sack Holyrod house, and as many townes and villaiges about Edinborough as ye may conveniently, sack Lythe [Leith] and burne and subverte it and all the rest, putting man, woman and childe to fyre and swoorde without exception where any resistence shal be mayde agaynst you . . . not forgeting among all the rest so to spoyle and turne upset downe the Cardinalles [Beaton's] town of St. Andrews, as thupper stone may be the nether, and not one stick stande by an other, sparing no creature alyve within the same. . . .

Scotland's lack of up-to-date coastal defences allowed Hertford to sail up the Forth with impunity in May 1544, and the army sent to oppose his landing abandoned their artillery and fled. Leith, despite the 'great trenches and ditches' dug to protect it, was speedily taken and converted into a fortified base for the invaders, who then marched on Edinburgh. Smashing down the city gates with their cannon, the English stormed in, and spent the next two days sacking and destroying 'so that neither within the walls nor in the suburbs was left any one house unburnt'. Though the castle proved too strong for them, they pillaged Holyrood House and ravaged Craigmillar before loading their loot onto their ships and marching homeward by land, leaving a wide trail of blazing towns and villages along their path. During the fourteen days of his 'prosperous voyage', Hertford informed the King with chilling exactness, he had destroyed 192 'towns, towers, stedes, barnekyns, parische churches and bastell-houses', slain 403 Scots, and driven off 10,386 cattle, 12,492 sheep and 1,296 horses. A month later, in June, Lord Eure let all hell loose in the Borders, and in 1545 Hertford himself returned, destroying another 16 'castles, towers and piles', 5 market towns, 243 villages, 7 monasteries and 3 'spytells and hospitalls'.

90
102

Apparently unable to make any real resistance to the English incursions, the Catholic party which ruled Scotland struck instead at their Protestant countrymen, and on 1 March 1546 Cardinal Beaton had the famous preacher George Wishart strangled and burnt before St Andrews Castle. Three months later, however, a band of sixteen Protestant conspirators (including the formidable John Knox) strolled calmly through the fortress's open gates, heaved the porter into the moat and, having ushered the Cardinal's servants outside, took possession. Beaton himself barricaded his chamber door, but the conspirators gained an entrance by threatening to set it afire with a brazier of hot coals, and stabbed the Cardinal to death as an 'obstinate enemy to Christ Jesus'.

Calling on Henry VIII for aid, and reinforcing themselves with a number of friends and sympathizers, the Protestant desperadoes now proceeded to hold St Andrews Castle against all comers. It was not until half a year after the murder that the Regent Arran brought a force against them, and though his six cannon damaged the castle's roof and battlements with 'feathered bullets' – presumably a kind of artillery dart – its walls were 'never a hair the worse' when plague in the town forced the futile siege to be lifted three months later. It was a very different matter when, in the summer of 1547, the defenders found their stronghold surrounded by a force of professional soldiers sent by the King of France. Working with amazing speed and efficiency, the Frenchmen dug trenches round the castle, mounted guns on the college steeple and cathedral walls to command 'all the close and wallheads within the same castle that no man might work therein for fear of his life' and, to avoid endangering their own gunners, hauled their battering pieces close to the wall by an ingenious system of remote-controlled ropes and windlasses. Within six hours a breach large enough for a hundred men had been made, and the Protestants surrendered, to be carried off to France and condemned to slave-labour in the galleys.

The death of Henry VIII had delayed the English force that might have saved them, but in September 1547 Hertford, now Duke of Somerset and regent for the young King Edward VI, crossed the border and, aided by the guns of his accompanying fleet, routed a large Scottish army at Pinkie in Lothian. This was no mere raid, and the English proceeded to occupy much of southern Scotland, refortifying Roxburgh and establishing strong garrisons wherever else they could: it seemed almost as if the days of Edward I had come again. To prevent a complete takeover, the Scottish government had no choice but to link their fortunes inextricably with France. In return for sending Princess Mary there as a wife for the French King's son, they received the aid of an army of 7,000

mercenaries, and in 1549 the English made peace and withdrew. The last full-scale war between the two nations was over.

The French army, however, remained, a prop to the Catholic administration and an affront to the growing number of Scots Protestants. Neither could England afford to ignore the threat of such a highly professional force on her northern borders: in 1558 work was begun on providing the vital frontier town of Berwick with the most up-to-date of artillery defences, namely a system of mutually supporting bastions. The theory behind such systems has already been discussed (p. 139). That at Berwick was by far the largest of them, and indeed the greatest work of fortification of any kind, to be undertaken in sixteenth-century Britain. Some £129,000, and over ten years' labour, was devoted to protecting the two landward sides of the port with a defensive perimeter nearly three-quarters of a mile (1.2 kilometres) long, consisting of a 100-foot (30-metre) thick rampart of rammed earth faced with masonry. Carefully positioned along it were five huge bastions of similar construction. Capable of resisting any siege gun then known, and mounting long-range cannon of its own, the system was also comprehensively defended against close-quarter attack. A storming party which attacked the face of a bastion would come under the fire of the pair of guns in the recessed flank of its neighbour, while an attack on the rampart between two bastions would be caught in a murderous cross-fire from the flank guns of both of them.

The French were soon too busy to think of an invasion of England, for in 1559 the Protestant Scots, led by the piously named Lords of the Congregation of Jesus Christ, rose in open war against them, calling on Queen Elizabeth for military aid. In the spring of 1560 an English army crossed the border in the novel role of invited allies, and attacked the great French stronghold at Leith. Though their attempts to storm the place were bloodily repulsed, they eventually succeeded in starving it out, and both English and French agreed to withdraw from Scotland and leave her to manage her own affairs in peace.

It was a vain hope. Scarcely a year after the peace treaty that unlucky monarch, Mary Queen of Scots, returned from France an eighteen-year-old widow. For a few years she tried to reconcile her own Catholicism with the stern Calvinism now upheld by most of her subjects, but she made the mistake of first marrying the worthless Lord Darnley and then falling for the 'rash and glorious' Earl of Bothwell. One night in February 1567 Darnley was found

142
143
116

142, 143 *The finest set of artillery defences in England, the Elizabethan bastioned trace (see p. 140) protecting Berwick-on-Tweed against the Scots and their French allies. In the aerial view the Brass Bastion is at the bottom, and the river Tweed on the right; notice the raised earthen gun-platforms, or 'cavaliers', added to the bastions during the Civil War period.*

    Above: a stretch of the ramparts swept by the battery in the recessed flank of the Brass Bastion (compare the diagram, ill. 116).

strangled with his own belt, and Bothwell was universally accused: Mary's subsequent marriage to him was therefore her ultimate foolishness, and the scandalized Lords of the Congregation deposed her, defeated her supporters in battle, and drove her to take refuge in genteel imprisonment with her cousin Elizabeth of England.

In her stead they crowned James VI, her baby son by Darnley, but in 1570 Mary's supporters struck back, plunging Scotland into a three-year civil war of almost unprecedented savagery. 'At this time', lamented a contemporary, 'all the realm was at division, for no man that met another by the way durst show him his mind nor whose man he was, so that this realm stood in a miserable estate of hunger, the sword and civil war daily.' 'God sent the spirit of hatred among them', and neither side scrupled to slaughter prisoners out of hand. The 'Queen's Lords' held Edinburgh Castle for two long years, burning and harrying the country round about, until at last the King's party called in an English expeditionary force to reduce the stronghold with cannon and mortar fire. Despite the terms of their surrender, its chief defenders were then hanged, and their quartered bodies set on the city gates. Perhaps the worst atrocity of all this bitter war occurred in Aberdeenshire, where the Queen's man Adam

Gordon of Auchindoun fought it out with Lord Forbes. Defeating him in battle, Gordon then set about systematically destroying his strongholds, one of which – probably the small tower of Corgarff – was held by Lady Forbes with her three children and twenty-four servants. A traitor showed the attackers how to remove the 'ground-wall stone' that blocked the foot of a privy shaft and, thrusting in combustibles, Gordon burnt the interior of the castle, with all its occupants, to ashes.

It is scarcely surprising to find the upheavals of the 1560s and 1570s reflected in the construction of large numbers of new tower-houses, many of them, doubtless, built with the proceeds of lands confiscated from the despoiled Catholic Church. These decades, too, produced a new type of tower ingeniously designed for close-quarter defence by muskets and pistols. This was the so-called 'Z-plan', a rectangular central block with towers protruding at two diagonally opposite corners, so that their gunloops covered every part of the building's external walls. A classic example is Claypotts, near Dundee in Tayside, begun in 1569. Here ten gunports, wide-mouthed to give the maximum field of fire, defend the virtually windowless ground floor, and the awkward angle between main block and north-east tower is particularly cleverly dealt

144 Detail of the angle between the main block (left) and the north-east tower (right) at Claypotts, showing the ingenious channelled gunloops and the privy shaft in the main block (at ground level on the left).

145 *Claypotts, Tayside, begun in 1569: the classic Z-plan tower-house, with its oversailing and crow-stepped top storey and comprehensively loopholed ground floor. The gun-channel is on the right.*

144 with. A gun firing from a loop in the main block, and along a specially cut channel in the masonry, could be made to 'shoot round the corner' and sweep the exterior face of the tower, while another in the tower, aimed along the same channel but in the opposite direction, covered the adjacent wall of the main block and deterred the likes of Adam Gordon from using the privy shaft there to smoke out the defenders.

Ingenious though they are, the defences of Claypotts are greatly outnumbered by those of its
146 virtual contemporary, the Z-shaped castle of Noltland on the island of Westray in the Orkneys. Strongly positioned overlooking the island's only harbour, this was the lair of the notorious Gilbert Balfour, a shady character even by the standards of sixteenth-century Scotland. One of the murderers of

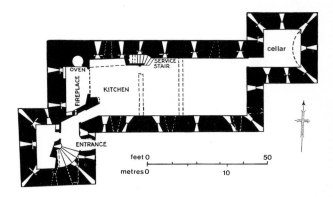

146 *Ground-floor plan of Noltland Castle, Orkney, showing 31 of its 60 wide-mouthed gunloops, including one set in the stair-well to fire at the door.*

169

Cardinal Beaton, he subsequently attached himself to Bothwell, and was widely believed to have led those who strangled Darnley in 1567. After Bothwell's downfall he prudently retired to the Orkneys (where he denied his erstwhile master refuge), but returned to fight with the Queen's Lords in the civil war. On their defeat he fled abroad, to be eventually executed for plotting against the King of Sweden. His stronghold, not unnaturally, displays an obsession with security. More than sixty gun-ports, arranged in three or four tiers like the broadside of a man-of-war, sweep every conceivable approach to the walls, and there are windows only on the best protected side. Even within the place loopholes cover the staircase and entrance corridor, and Balfour's own rooms are isolated from the rest of the interior by a thick first-floor-to-roof wall, thus forming a fortress within a fortress.

Even Balfour's precautions did not run to 'bugging devices' like the one found at Castle Fraser in Aberdeenshire, the largest of all Z-plan towers, built in 1576. This was a 'lug', or secret room within the thickness of the walls, containing a pipe whose almost undetectable end issued at a secluded window-seat in the hall below, the best place in the castle for a 'private' conversation. In the circumstances of the time it was perhaps as well to know what one's visitors and servants were talking about.

After the victory of the King's party in 1573 order gradually returned, and by the time James came of age in 1587 he was something like master in his own house; the more so because, in that same year, his mother was executed at Fotheringay after one plot too many against her 'host', Queen Elizabeth. Elizabeth herself was now getting on in years, and it was tacitly accepted that, as her nearest living relation, James would rule England as well as Scotland on her death.

The prospect of permanent peace between the two nations, however, did little to improve conditions in the Borders, where nearly three centuries of raid and counter-raid had bred the toughest and most unruly race of men anywhere in Britain. Accustomed to making their living by armed robbery and highly organized cattle-rustling, these borderers saw no reason to change their habits simply because the Anglo-Scottish wars had come to an end. Their loyalties, indeed, were not to the nation to which they nominally belonged – 'they are a people that will be Scottish when they will, and English at their pleasure' said Thomas Musgrave, an English border official – but to their own clan or 'surname', with its complex network of feuds and alliances. 'English'

borderers thought nothing of bringing in their 'Scottish' relations to assist in profitable ventures on their own side of the frontier, and the 'Scots' returned the compliment equally freely. Nor was it easy to bring offenders to book, for those whose own property was not in immediate danger would neither hinder passing raiders nor testify against them in court, for fear of beginning a deadly feud. 'Hardly dare any gentleman of the country', lamented the official, 'be of any jury of life or death if any of them be indicted . . . they are so grown to seek blood, for they will make a quarrel for the death of their grandfather, and they kill any of the name they are in feud with.'

This almost Sicilian situation (brilliantly described by G. M. Fraser in his book *The Steel Bonnets*) meant that fortifications of every variety flourished and abounded in the sixteenth-century borderlands. The most important of them were the strongholds of the hard-pressed government officials, the Wardens of the English and Scottish East, Middle and West Marches, and the Scottish Keeper of Liddesdale, who had the onerous responsibility for the peace and order of the frontier zone. The Scots Wardens, almost invariably local men, used their own family castles – Caerlaverock and Lochmaben in the West [10] March, Hermitage in Liddesdale, Cessford in the [135] Middle March and Home Castle in the East, amongst [138] others – as their headquarters. The English border officials had at their disposal a chain of government fortresses ranging from Berwick in the East March [143] via Wark, Norham, Harbottle and Chipchase in [61] Northumberland to Bewcastle and Carlisle in Cum- [55] bria. The latter were held by forces of semi-regular troops drawn from outside the Borders, who could thus operate without the fear of feuds. Chipchase [92] normally had a garrison of 50 horse and 20 foot, while Bewcastle – a thirteenth-century castle on the [147] site of a Roman fort – accommodated 50 horse and 50 foot, a pitifully inadequate force to police the raiders' road from nearby Liddesdale.

By the 1580s many of the English fortresses, no longer threatened by a major war with Scotland, had begun to fall into decay, though Berwick and Carlisle remained immensely strong. Even the mighty walls of Carlisle, however, proved on one occasion no match for the cross-frontier Mafia of the Borders, which sprang Kinmont Willie Armstrong from his prison there on the dark night of 13 April 1596. Kinmont, a prominent 'Scottish' bandit, had (while technically exempt from arrest under the terms of a truce) been kidnapped by the soldiers of the English West March Warden, an action which infuriated the

147 A Scottish raider's view across Bewcastle Waste to the thirteenth-century English border fortress of Bewcastle, Cumbria, set within the ramparts of a Roman fort. Its captaincy was perhaps the most dangerous post on the frontier.

'Bold Buccleuch' – Walter Scott, officially the Keeper of Liddesdale and unofficially a notable reiver in his own right. Failing to secure Kinmont's release by diplomatic pressure, Buccleuch tipped the wink to eighty of his kinsmen and allies, and had a quiet word with the prisoner's relations in England, many of whom happened to have a grudge against the English Warden, and some of whom also happened to have useful contacts amongst the garrison of Carlisle. When the time came, therefore, there was no one to report that Buccleuch had crossed the border, and the raiders met with no opposition when they forced a postern gate in the castle wall, which may indeed have been 'accidentally' left open for them. At any rate, Kinmont and his rescuers were clean away before the hue and cry was raised, and the English Warden was made a laughing stock without the loss of a man on either side.

The bloodless course of this exploit was altogether exceptional, and the undoubted romantic appeal of the daring border raiders (much canvassed by Buccleuch's descendant Sir Walter Scott) must not be allowed to hide the fact that contemporary life in the frontier zone was a frequently sordid and invariably dangerous affair. Every dwelling there had either to be completely expendable – like the makeshift thatched huts of the poor, 'about the burning of which they are nowise concerned' – or else capable of resisting attack, and the construction of 'defensible houses' extended much further down the social scale than anywhere else in Britain. A cheap but effective type, reported from the Scottish side, was the 'square tower' with immensely thick and fireproof clay walls supported by an internal framework of interwoven wattles. Such, most probably, was the 'strong pele' of a certain Ill Will Armstrong, which, the English complained in 1516, 'could not be burnt or destroyed until it was cut down with axes'. Seven years later the English commander charged with ravaging Teviotdale sent for three hundred 'sixpenny axes' to destroy 'roved [woven] houses which will not burn'. Other Scottish borderers (and no doubt English ones) built their houses of great oak logs tightly bound together, interlined with layers of earth to make them more resistant to fire, and 'so thickly mortressed [mortared?] that it will be very hard . . . to break or cast them down'.

Such clay and timber strongholds are known only from descriptions, but over seventy examples of the defensible stone farmsteads called 'bastles' (from the French *bastille*) still survive, all within 20 miles (30 kilometres) of the border line, and all apparently dating from the sixteenth or early seventeenth century. Unique in Britain, they were designed to defend both humans and their livestock (the principal quarry of the 'outriding men') under one roof. The beasts were kept in the windowless ground floor, whose entrance was secured from within by two heavy door-bars slotting into the stone lintel. The man who bolted it then reached the living quarters on the floor above by climbing through a small trapdoor. The upper storey itself had iron bars in its few small windows, and its narrow door was high above ground level and originally gained by a removable ladder: only when more peaceful times came were stone steps built up to it. Bastles tended to be built in clusters for mutual support, and the one illustrated, which stands in the hamlet of Gatehouse near Bellingham in Northumberland, has a neighbour only 50 yards (45 metres) away.

Pre-eminent amongst the defensible houses of the Borders, in the sixteenth century as for the past three

148 *A bastle at Gatehouse, Northumberland; access to the upper floor was originally by ladder.*

hundred years and more, was the stone tower. Some two hundred examples still survive on the English side alone, differing only in detail from their counterparts in Scotland or from the scattered refuge towers – like Stokesay and Longthorpe – of the southern and midland English counties. Many of them had originally been built during the dark days of Bruce's deep-penetrating forays in the early fourteenth century (p. 119), but since that time the advantage of war had generally lain with England, and her border shires had suffered little by comparison with the frequently and systematically ravaged marches of Scotland. By the time of Queen Elizabeth, therefore, many of these English towers, especially those distant enough from the frontier to escape the attentions of freelance reivers, had been adapted to make them more comfortable and convenient, often by the addition of a lower range of buildings containing a hall and kitchen. Such was the case at Yanwath Hall, near Penrith in Cumbria, where the tower is of the fourteenth century, the hall range with its protruding bay window of the fifteenth, and the dangerously low mullioned windows in the tower later still.

Nearer the frontier line, and especially in the West March, the stamping ground of the two toughest border clans, the nominally Scottish Armstrongs and their 'English' rivals the Grahams, uncompromisingly defensive towers continued to be built throughout the sixteenth century. Many of them were replacements for earlier strongholds destroyed in the course of feuds. In 1527, for instance, the Armstrongs demolished the Graham tower of Kirkandrews, just on the Cumbrian side of the frontier, and in the following spring the Grahams retaliated by burning Hollows Tower, an Armstrong hold not far away in Dumfries. Not to be over-matched, Black Jock Armstrong carried on the game a few weeks later by firing another Graham tower at Netherby. Both Kirkandrews and Hollows were duly rebuilt. Along with nearby Brackenhill, Cumbria, a Graham tower raised in 1586, they present a very similar appearance despite their notional difference in nationality. If anything the Scottish influence prevails, for all three have the steep 'crow-stepped' gables so characteristic of later Scots towers.

At Hollows one of these gables is topped by a stone beacon, designed to pass on warning of approaching enemies and prevent them from gaining the advantage of surprise. Constant vigilance was needed to avoid this, especially when the tower was under-manned, as the defenders of Lochwood in Dumfries discovered in February 1547. An English force crept stealthily up to the place by night, climbed the surrounding courtyard wall, and, silently overpowering a few women asleep in the outbuildings, hid themselves there till daybreak. A man who then looked out from the tower-top saw nothing amiss, and ordered the usual double doors – the outer of wood and the inner an iron-grilled yett – to be unlocked, whereupon the attackers rushed in and took possession. When the defenders were more wary or more obstinate, wooden doors could be burnt, and iron grilles were no protection against the tower being filled with stifling smoke from damp brushwood. But smoke from a besieged tower could summon aid as swiftly as a beacon, and raiders had always to be on their guard against being taken in the rear by a swarm of the defenders' relations. A less conspicuous method of attack, calling for both courage and superiority of numbers on the besiegers' part, was to scale the tower walls, prise a hole in the roof, and break in from above. Whatever the device chosen, to hit and run was the ideal, and, at any rate after the end of the Anglo-Scottish wars, formal sieges with heavy artillery played little part in border feuds.

Speed and surprise, indeed, were the reivers' chief weapons, and attempts were made to slow them down by building banks and ditches round villages or (by an order of the English government made in 1555 and repeated in 1584) planting thick thorn hedges across open land. Difficult to negotiate with herds of stolen cattle, these obstacles might impede homeward-bound raiders long enough for the pursuit (or 'hot trod') to catch up with them. The most ambitious of all sixteenth-century border defences, however, never got beyond the planning stage. Inspired by the remains of Hadrian's Wall, an English writer of the 1580s proposed the building of an 'inskonce', an earthwork ditch and rampart, stretching the whole length of the frontier from sea to sea and interspersed every mile or so with bastioned and fortified villages.

The end of border lawlessness came quite suddenly. On 24 March 1603 James VI of Scotland was finally proclaimed James I of England, and the frontier zone between the two old enemies became – in name at least – simply the 'Middle Shires' of the united kingdom of Great Britain. Determined to reduce 'the very heart of his realm' to the same peaceful condition as the rest of it, James cracked down on the reivers at once. English and Scottish officials at last acted in unison, the special Borders laws were repealed, and cross-frontier thieving, even of so little as a shilling, was made punishable by

149 Hollows, Dumfries, with its crow-stepped gables, was an Armstrong tower built in the late sixteenth century after its predecessor had been burnt by the 'fractious and naughty' Grahams and then demolished by an English border Warden. The gable in front held a beacon.

death. Borderers were forbidden to carry weapons or possess fast horses, towers had their yetts removed and symbolically beaten into ploughshares, and armed feuds were ruthlessly suppressed: the new order, moreover, was backed up by wholesale hangings and transportations, the Grahams being exiled *en masse* as 'a fractious and naughty people'. Within a few years the old border way of life had been swept away and, after three centuries and more, the tower-houses which had originated on the troubled frontier at last ceased to be built there.

In Scotland proper, however, they continued to be raised well into the 1600s. There the tower had long since been the standard form for great houses as well as strongholds, and many seventeenth-century examples are far more domestic than military in character. Lacking the ingenious defences of Z-plan towers like Claypotts and Noltland or the stern strength of Threave and Comlongon, some of these late towers nevertheless achieve unparalleled heights of aesthetic perfection. Most delightful of all, perhaps, is Craigievar in Aberdeenshire, which gains much of its striking effect from the contrast between its plain lower walls and the riot of fairy-tale turrets,

145
146
133

19

domes and gables at its summit. Despite all this, some regard is still paid to security, evidenced by the comparatively few windows near ground level and the sturdy iron yett which guards the door. Completed in 1626, Craigievar is one of the last major Scottish towers, and as such one the very last of the long line of British defensible houses.

At the time of its building, the second year of the reign of Charles I, it must have seemed that – outside the Highlands at least – the need for strongholds was quickly becoming a thing of the past. Yet, within scarcely more than a decade the whole of Britain was to be shaken by a civil war which tested her fortresses to the utmost.

*150, 151 Craigievar Castle, Aberdeenshire (see pl. **19**). Left: detail of the turretted upper storeys, with their imitation cannons and carved grotesques. Below: the ornate strapwork ceiling of the great hall and the Scottish royal arms above the fireplace, original plasterwork of 1626.*

13 'Dangerous and unprofitable to this State': the Civil Wars, 1642–1660

152 A contemporary plan of the siege of Newark by Richard Clampe, 'Ingenier'. At the top is a piece of siege money, and at the bottom are the commanders of the besieging armies, with the Scots General Leven on the right and General Poyntz behind him. (For the key see p. 186; and see also pp. 179, 180 and ill. 154.)

I cannot forebear . . . to acquaint your Lordships with what I conceive may be both dangerous and unprofitable to this State, which is to keep up forts and garrisons, which may rather foment than finish a war.

SIR JOHN MELDRUM to the Committee of Both Kingdoms, November 1644

The previous chapters have shown how Britain's fortresses developed over the centuries, until the time came when a long period of peace made them seem little more than relics of past unhappy times. This one will trace what happened when an all-pervading civil war suddenly recalled them to action, producing a need for defences unparalleled since the anarchic days of Stephen and Matilda. The causes and issues of the struggle between King and Parliament are still very much a matter for debate, and fortunately do not concern us here. What is certain is that fortifications, hurriedly adapted or improvised to meet the crisis, played a vital part in the fighting, and at times dictated the whole strategy of the war. Never before, and certainly never since, did the defensible places of Britain see so much action in such a short time.

When open hostilities between Charles I and his Parliament became inevitable during the summer of 1642, England was profoundly unprepared for war. She had suffered no internal upheavals for over a century and a half, and had stood aloof from European conflicts since the time of Queen Elizabeth. She had, therefore, not even the beginnings of a regular army, and her strongholds were by and large in a state of decay, only the fortified ports of Hull and Portsmouth being able to boast really up-to-date defences. As these places also contained stocks of much needed arms and equipment, they were of immediate and vital importance to both sides, and it was over their control that – even before a formal declaration of war – fighting first broke out.

With London and the arsenal of the Tower securely in the hands of his enemies, the King counted on Hull to supply the army he was gathering at nearby York. The Governor, appointed by Parliament, had other ideas, and not only refused to admit Charles to the town but afterwards opened the sea-sluices to flood the low-lying country outside his bastioned defences. As the King's half-hearted levies attempted to set up a blockade, the small but efficient regular navy declared for Parliament, giving them a command of the seas which was again and again to prove a crucial factor in the war. Reinforcements could now be shipped to stiffen Hull's resistance, and while the garrison sallied out against their attackers the port's store of arms was borne safely off to London.

Things went no better at Portsmouth, for though the Governor there declared for the King, he almost immediately found himself blockaded to seaward by five Parliamentary ships, and before long he was also closely besieged by land. According to a contemporary account, the Parliament men wisely avoided an attack on the strongly bastioned defences, and instead pelted the town at a range of half a mile (800 metres) from a battery across the harbour at Gosport. Their guns demolished a church tower used as a look-out post and forced the defenders to work all night on a slit trench, 'that at the sight of the firing of our ordnance, they might leap down into it'. Royalist return fire was less successful, for though they 'shot incessantly for fourteen days and nights, in which they shot at least three hundred bullets', they killed only one man and failed to dislodge the enemy guns, whose position was protected by a thick barricade of faggots. Next, learning that its commander 'had more drinke in his head than was befitting', the Parliamentarians surprised Henry VIII's old artillery fort at Southsea, scaling its walls by night and turning its heavy guns on Portsmouth. Thus bombarded from two directions, the port soon surrendered, the Governor obtaining generous terms by threatening to fire the 1,200 barrels of powder in the main magazine and blow the place to blazes.

In August, while the shot was still flying at Portsmouth, the first ordinary English town came under attack when the King (having moved his base to Nottingham) made an attempt on Coventry. Though the place had neither modern defences nor a garrison, the townsmen cried defiance from their medieval walls, and when the gates were blown open with gunfire the charging cavaliers found their passage blocked by 'Harrowes, Carts and pieces of Timber laid crosse waies on heaps'. After a stiff fight the attackers 'retired at more than their ordinarie pace', leaving two of their cannon in the hands of the jubilant citizens. Northampton, meanwhile, 'expecting their turne to be next', had 500 men and 100 women working day and night to reinforce its ancient walls with thick earthen ramparts.

The King consoled himself for his reverses by raising his royal standard at Nottingham in a formal declaration of war, but by this time the fighting had already spread, and 'every county had more or less the civill warre within it selfe'. The struggle for the major arsenals was echoed in attempts by the local supporters of either side to seize county magazines, attempts which often ended in bloodshed and sometimes in minor sieges. As early as July the first victim of the war had fallen in a confused skirmish at Manchester, where Lord Strange's efforts to gain the town's arsenal for the King had been repulsed by the fiercely Parliamentarian inhabitants. Under the direction of a refugee German engineer, one 'Captaine Roseworme', the Mancunians then set about securing their unwalled town against a return visit. Earthworks were thrown up to cover the main roads and bridges leading into it, and chains stretched across the principal streets to halt cavalry charges.

These meagre defences had scarcely been completed when, in September, Lord Strange advanced on the town with seven cannon and a sizeable force of Lancashire and Cheshire Royalists. Early on Sunday morning the cavaliers occupied Salford, separated from Manchester only by the river Irwell, and the following day their guns began to batter Deansgate with 6-pound (2.7-kilogram) shot. For three days the bombardment alternated with attacks on the barricades and attempts to storm Salford bridge, but the psalm-singing defenders stood firm behind their earthen defences, and Strange's demands grew less and less exacting, until on Wednesday he offered to depart if the townsmen would give up only a part of their magazine. They replied that 'they would not give him a yard of Match' (the least of their possessions, used to fire a matchlock musket) 'but would maintain their cause and Armes to the utmost drop of their blood'. Faced with this resolution, and appalled by their mounting losses, Strange's soldiers now began to desert in droves: though he built works at Deansgate end as if to mount a formal siege, his bolt – and probably all his powder – was shot, and on Saturday he disconsolately marched away.

Both sides had also begun to seize the private stores of arms in the country houses of their opponents, usually without much opposition. Caldecote Hall in Warwickshire, however, put up a heroic resistance to a raid by Prince Rupert, the King's German nephew and his foremost cavalry leader. Though the 'garrison' consisted only of the family and servants of the absent owner, four men and six women in all, they armed themselves with a dozen muskets and refused to admit him. The women acted as loaders while the men shot down three of Rupert's officers and some fifteen of his men, and 'when their bullets began to faile, they fell to melting all their household pewter, and having bullet moulds in the house speedily made more'. Not until the house was filled with smoke from its burning outbuildings did they surrender: whereupon Rupert, amazed by their small number, chivalrously marked his respect for them by marching off without doing further damage.

Though the supporters of Parliament had so far defended themselves well, they had been unable to prevent the rapid growth of the King's army, and at the beginning of October he set out to march on London and finish the war at a stroke. The Earl of Essex blundered into him at Edgehill in Warwickshire, but though the amateur armies fought each other to a standstill, the long-feared battle – the first on English soil since the Wars of the Roses – ended in a draw. It did, however, delay the Royalist advance for nearly a fortnight, and it was not until 11 November that they reached Colnbrook, near the present London airport of Heathrow.

During this crucial interval City and Parliament desperately prepared to defend themselves. The Londoners, boarding up their shops and taking down their muskets and breastplates from the wall, went off to drill with the Trained Bands, and the ancient walls of the City were put in repair, with cannon planted at each of the gates. Meanwhile thousands of volunteers, men and women alike, laboured at the outer defences, a great system of earthworks encircling London, Westminster and Southwark. Some 18 miles (30 kilometres) long, the rampart and ditch linked twenty-one forts and strongpoints, each of which either blocked or guarded one of the roads leading into the capital. All have long since been destroyed by urban expansion. Beginning in the region of modern Millbank, the trenches moved northwards via a battery in Tothill Fields (19, near the present Vauxhall Bridge Road), a redoubt blocking the east end of King's Road, and another battery on Constitution Hill, to the great bastioned fort at Hyde Park Corner. This covered the road from the west, the King's most likely direction of approach. From here the defences continued up Piccadilly (where there was a bulwark) to a fort in Wardour Street and a pair of redoubts at modern St Giles's Circus: these flanked Tottenham Court Road, the access from the north-west. Next came a breastwork near the site of the British Museum, and another blocking Gray's Inn Road; north of this point a pair of detached works guarded the City's water supply, the reservoir near the 'Angel' in Islington. The line then extended through two batteries in Finsbury to a pair of strong forts covering Kingsland Road, Shoreditch, the way in from the north. It next turned southwards, linking a redoubt near the present site of Shoreditch tube station, a fort guarding Whitechapel Road (the entrance from the east) and another in the docks,

155

before reaching the river at Wapping. South of the Thames, the line protecting Southwark had four major forts. One covered Old Kent Road (the access from the south), another stood at the Elephant and Castle, a third at St George's Circus and the last, near modern Vauxhall station, looked across to Millbank where we began our description.

On 12 November Rupert (nicknamed 'Prince Robber' by the Londoners) sacked Brentford, and it seemed that the hastily built defences were about to be tested. But the tales of plunder and atrocity served to stiffen the capital's resolution, and when the King advanced on Chiswick the next day he was faced with 24,000 men – Essex's army combined with the Trained Bands and contingents from the Home Counties – drawn up behind the hedges and garden walls around Turnham Green. All day long the armies faced each other, but while the Londoners

153 One of the few Civil War earthworks to survive nearly complete, the fine pentagonal sconce at Horsey Hill, Cambridgeshire.

154 Artist's impression of the Queen's Sconce at Newark in April 1646, showing from left to right the pitfalls and

palisade beyond the ditch; the horizontal 'storm-poles' to impede an assault on the ramparts; the bastions; the wood-revetted breastwork for musketeers; the semi-subterranean powder store; and the drawbridge. In the distance is General Poyntz's headquarters, from which the besiegers have thrown forward a small redoubt (p. 186 and ill. 152).

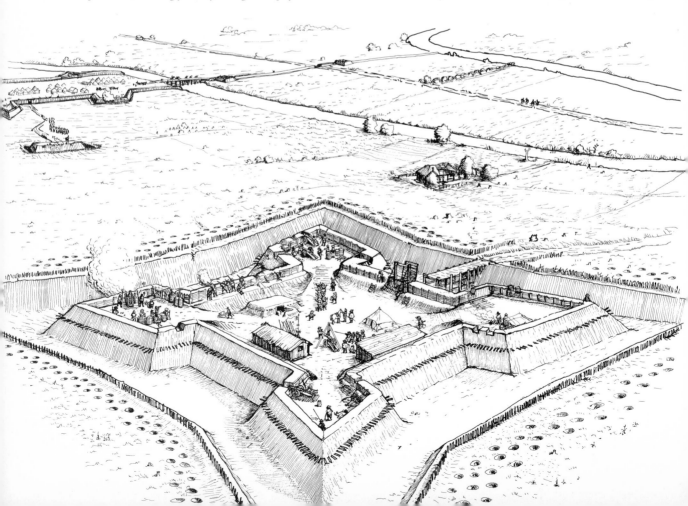

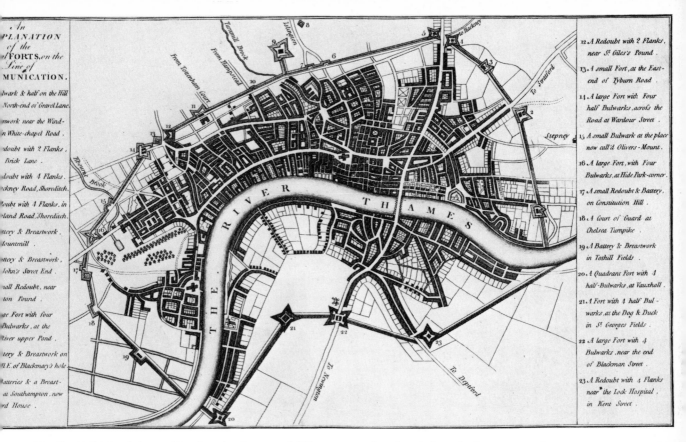

An
PLANATION
of the
FORTS, on the
Line of
MUNICATION.

...wark & half on the Hill
...North-end of Gravel Lane.
...rework near the Wind-
...in White-chapel Road.
...doubt with 2 Flanks
...Brick Lane.
...doubt with 4 Flanks
...ckney Road, Shoreditch.
...oubt with 4 Flanks, in
...land Road, Shoreditch.
...tery & Breastwork.
...ountmill.
...tery & Breastwork,
...John's Street End.
...all Redoubt, near
...ton Pound.
...ge Fort with four
...Bulwarks, at the
...River upper Pond.
...tery & Breastwork on
...E. of Blackmary's hole
...atteries & a Breast-
...at Southampton, now
...rd House.

12 A Redoubt with 2 Flanks,
near St Giles's Pound.

13 A small Fort, at the East-
end of Tyburn Road.

14 A large Fort with Four
half Bulwarks, across the
Road at Wardour Street.

15 A small Bulwark at the place
now call'd Olivers-Mount.

16 A large Fort, with Four
Bulwarks at Hide Park-corner.

17 A small Redoubt & Battery,
on Constitution Hill.

18 A Court of Guard at
Chelsea Turnpike.

19 A Battery & Breastwork
in Tothill Fields.

20 A Quadrant Fort with 4
half-Bulwarks, at Vauxhall.

21 A Fort with 4 half Bulwarks, at the Dog & Duck
in St Georges Fields.

22 A large Fort with 4
Bulwarks, near the end
of Blackman Street.

23 A Redoubt with 4 Flanks
near the Lock Hospital,
in Kent Street.

155 The Civil War defences of London, showing several different types of earthwork fort. The description in the text (pp. 177–78) proceeds clockwise from no. 19 at the lower left.

sent their own Sunday dinners by the cartload to keep up the morale of their defenders, the King's men were tired, hungry and outnumbered two to one, and it became increasingly clear that they would not advance. That night, indeed, they pulled back to Hounslow on the first leg of a retreat to Oxford. The war, which many had thought would be 'over by Christmas', was plainly going to be a long-drawn-out affair.

With such a prospect in view, the urgent need for new fortifications was clear to both sides. During the long years of peace military engineering had been a largely neglected art in England, whereas in Europe it had flourished and developed during the protracted fighting of the Thirty Years' War (1618–48). Their own experience being limited to militia drills and sham-fights, amateur soldiers therefore turned for advice either to Britons who had served abroad or to foreign experts like Captain Roseworme of Manchester and the Dutchman Bernard de Gomme, who became the King's principal designer of fortresses. Failing that, would-be engineers could work from textbooks like Robert Ward's *Animadversions of Warre*, and many of the strongpoints round London and elsewhere resembled examples illustrated in such manuals.

The simplest type were open-backed breastworks and batteries, defended by earth ramparts, ditches and palisades so as to give frontal protection to artillery and musketeers. Self-contained forts were built in a variety of geometric forms so as to give the maximum field of fire for all-round defence. In the swastika-shaped 'redoubt with flankers' (nos. 9, 14, 20 and 21 on the London plan) every face was swept from one side, but where time and resources allowed the star-shaped 'sconce' was the ideal. Either rectangular or polygonal, this had a bastion at each corner, so that the faces between were covered by fire from both flanks. The one at Hyde Park Corner (no. 16) has left no traces, but such sconces survive in a fair state of repair at Horsey Hill and Earith in 153 Cambridgeshire, both Parliamentarian works. The first covers the crossing of the river Nene near Peterborough, while the second guards the approaches to Ely via the Ouse and a causeway over the fens. Still more impressive is the Queen's Sconce at 154 Newark, an advanced outwork of the Royalist 152 fortress-town. Covering more than 3 acres (1.2 hectares), it is surrounded by a ditch up to 70 feet (21 metres) wide and 15 feet (4.6 metres) deep: originally, no doubt, there was a palisade either at the bottom of the ditch or round its outer edge.

179

155 The defences of London, as we have seen, were thrown up hurriedly and on an *ad hoc* basis. Intended mainly to control access roads, they left whole areas of the capital's perimeter (especially in the north and south) defended only by sections of bank and ditch too long to be covered by flanking fire from the widely dispersed strongpoints. Bristol and Plymouth, also fortified for Parliament during the early stages of the war, were similarly defended by a line of linked forts, those at Plymouth stretching across the neck of the peninsula on which the port is built. This style of defence, however, did not compare in efficiency with carefully planned
143 Elizabethan fortresses like Berwick, where the entire perimeter was treated as a single defensive unit, every part of it being covered by a series of mutually supporting bastions.

Such complete bastioned traces, even in the form of earthworks without reinforcing stone walls, required large supplies of money, labour and time to build. They were, nevertheless, attempted around a
152 few places of paramount importance to the King,
159 notably Oxford and Newark. Oxford, Charles's wartime capital and principal military base, was fortified at an eventual cost of £30,000, every male inhabitant being required to work on the defences under pain of fine. A recently rediscovered painting, apparently executed for the son of a Royalist governor, shows how the double line of bastions was strongest and most complex on the northern side, the only one where the town is not naturally protected by streams and rivers.

The Line about the city [remarked a Parliamentary writer at the end of the war] was very high, having many strong Bulworks so regularly flanking one another, that nothing could be more exactly done: round about the Line, both upon the Bulworks and the Curtin, was strongly set with storm-poles; upon the out-side of the Ditch round the Line, it was strongly Palisadoed, and without that againe were digged severall pits in the ground, that a single Foote-man could not without difficulty approach the brink of the Ditch.

As a further precaution – and an advance warning of possible attacks – strategically placed towns in an outer ring covering the distant approaches to Oxford were also garrisoned and fortified. They included Banbury, Woodstock, Enstone and Islip to the north, Brill (where remains of earthwork defences can still be seen near the church) to the east, Wallingford and Abingdon to the south, and Burford and Faringdon to the west.

152 Newark, where both the Great North Road and the ancient Fosse Way crossed the Trent at its lowest bridging point, was only marginally less important to the King's war effort. A vital link in the communications between Oxford and Charles's powerful supporters in the north, it also served as a forward base from which the latter could, given the opportunity, mount an invasion of the heartland of Parliamentarian support in East Anglia. One of the very few places where Civil War earthworks still survive, this 'nest of base and bloody cormorants' (as the Parliamentarians called it) was first garrisoned late in 1642, and was unsuccessfully attacked in 1643 and 1644. After each siege its defences were strengthened, until one of the besieged could report with satisfaction that it had 'such deep graffs [ditches], bastions, horns, half-moons, counter-scarps, redoubts, pitfalls, and an impregnable line of sodd and turf palisadoed and stockaded, and every fort so furnishd with great guns and cannons that this bulky bulwark of Newark represented to the besiegers but one entire sconce'. Little remains of the main bastioned trace, but several of the outworks are still to be seen, including the Queen's Sconce, one of 154 a pair of strong detached forts built in 1644.

In addition to their outer line of earthworks, all the places so far mentioned had an inner circuit of ancient stone walls, which could (at a pinch) be employed as a second line of defence. Many more towns, notably York and Gloucester, adapted their medieval walls as the mainstay of their defences. Dilapidated stonework was given a thick lining of earth as a reinforcement against cannon fire, gates were blocked, ditches were cleared of rubbish, and bastions or detached forts thrown up to cover especially vulnerable areas. Here and there, too, even more antiquated structures were pressed into service. At Wareham in Dorset the rampart of the 43 Saxon burh, already seven hundred years old, resumed its active life, and at Dorchester in the same county Maumbury Rings, successively a Neolithic henge and a Roman amphitheatre, became a fort for the defence of the town.

In smaller towns and villages the only substantial stone building was often the parish church, and this frequently found itself converted into the hub of a system of breastworks and barricades, with snipers firing from the tower to command the surrounding streets. Their eyrie, however, presented an easy target for enemy cannoneers, and the little Parliamentarian cloth-town of Bradford in Yorkshire hit on the novel idea of padding their church-tower with 'large sheets of wool . . . so close to each other and so nigh the roof of the church, that it would be with difficulty for a ball to penetrate the steeple'.

Whether towns were defended by the latest thing in bastioned fortifications or simply by barricades of carts and woolsacks, it was their will to hang on against seemingly overwhelming odds that really counted. This was especially true in the crucial period between the summer of 1643 and the spring of 1644, when the desperate resistance of a handful of places was instrumental in preventing a combined attack on London by three powerful Royalist armies. The crisis began at the end of June 1643, when the Earl of Newcastle routed the Yorkshire Parliamentarians and proceeded to overrun the whole of the north, leaving only Hull holding out against him. During the next few weeks the steadily advancing western Royalists twice defeated Sir William Waller, and on 26 July Prince Rupert stormed the outworks of Bristol in three places. Two of his columns were bloodily repulsed but a third, hurling explosive 'hand-grenadoes' like anarchist bombs, broke through at a weak point between two forts, and pressed on to the inner line of city walls. Here they were long checked before a barricaded gate, but when reinforcements arrived from another column the defenders capitulated, leaving England's second seaport in Royalist hands. With its fall most of the neighbouring Parliamentary garrisons lost heart, and 'came tumbling in to the obedience of the King'.

Parliament's prospects now seemed black indeed, for London (already troubled by a rising of Kentish royalists) stood in danger of a three-pronged attack delivered by Newcastle from the north, the King himself from Oxford, and the western army from Bristol. Charles, too, was confident of imminent victory, but instead of moving directly on the capital he decided to reduce first the few places still holding out in his rear. Prince Maurice, Rupert's younger brother, was therefore sent to conquer Exeter, Plymouth, and Lyme Regis with the western army, while the King's force headed for the strategically placed city of Gloucester.

Held by only 1,400 men, and defended by an unimpressive combination of reinforced medieval walls, fortified barns and low earth breastworks, Gloucester was expected to surrender immediately when faced with the 8,000 soldiers and heavy guns of Charles's army. But it declined to do so, and on 10 August a full-dress siege was begun by the cutting of the town's fresh water supply. Soon the great guns were hammering at the defences, and mortars were lobbing in 60-pound (27-kilogram) grenadoes, hollow iron shells filled with gunpowder which, if their fuse was not speedily extinguished, exploded with the effect of shrapnel. Yet the earth-lined walls stood firm, the one breach being made good with absorbent woolsacks, while a pig which was one of the few victims of the bombardment was consumed with relish by the garrison who 'afterwards well jeered the enemy therewith'. The besieged, indeed, utterly refused to be daunted by the 'terrible engines of warre', and sallied out almost daily to spike the Royalist guns and destroy their entrenchments.

The news of Gloucester's resolution at such a dark hour cut through the cloud of gloom over London like a shaft of sunlight. Parliament and City combined to send a relief force – five regiments of the Trained Bands and the bulk of Essex's army – hastening to her aid, and on the night of 24 August a beacon on a distant hill told the watchers in the town that help was on its way. But Essex had hardly begun his march, and the news of his setting-out caused the enemy to redouble their efforts: all the next day their guns and mortars rumbled continuously, and at night red-hot shot came 'flying in the ayre like a starre shooting'. Again the results were disappointing, and the Royalists began to prepare for a grand assault with more traditional methods of siegecraft. Attempts were made to drain and fill in the moat, a mine wormed its way towards the city gate, and the King's classically minded chaplain directed the construction of wheeled bridges 'after the manner of the Romaynes' to span the breastworks. The garrison delayed them at every turn, meanwhile throwing up a second line of defence inside the gates and forging 'great borers' to penetrate the mine and flood it with boiling water. Bows and arrows – perhaps for the last time in English history – were used to supplement muskets and conserve powder, but by 5 September the defenders had only three or four barrels-full to resist the expected storm. That morning, however, the incredulous soldiers on the wall saw the King's men marching away horse, foot and guns: Essex had come at last.

'Great was the failing of the King's hopes in this defeat', said a contemporary, and some saw the relief of Gloucester, with Charles's subsequent failure to cut off Essex's retreat, as the turning point of the war. One obstinate town had blunted the central spearhead of the threefold attack on London, and another was soon to deflect its northern prong. When the siege of Gloucester opened Newcastle had already overrun Lincolnshire, but while his back was turned the garrison of Hull created so much alarm by their wide-ranging raids that, ignoring a royal order to continue his advance, he was forced to return northwards and besiege the place. He was soon hopelessly bogged down before it, for it was impregnably fortified and (as before) supplied by the Parliamentary navy. After a month's futile investment, a strong force of soldiers, sailors and townsmen sallied forth and overran the Royalist entrenchments, and the same night the demoralized besiegers retired to York.

The western spearhead was at first more successful, for Exeter surrendered to Prince Maurice at about the time of Gloucester's relief. Shortly afterwards, however, he too was tied down in an unsuccessful siege of Plymouth, which he abandoned on Christmas Day 1643. Despite this failure, he was ordered to advance on London through the southern counties during the spring of 1644. In his path lay the 'little vile fishing town' of Lyme Regis in Dorset, defended against his 6,000 men only by a line of turf and boulder forts and a dry ditch, and garrisoned by 1,100 men under Robert Blake, later a famous admiral. The Royalists declared that it would be 'but a breakfast-work' to take it, and some swore not to dine until they had done so. Any that kept their vow must have grown very hungry, for the siege, begun on 20 April, lasted nearly two months.

During this time Maurice bombarded Lyme with grenadoes and 32-pounder (14.5-kilogram) shot, attempted to fire it with flaming arrows and red-hot iron bars hooked to catch on roof-tops, and even (it was said) hired a witch to set it ablaze by 'devilish artes'. His men stormed the breastworks five times, sustaining such heavy losses that they had to be driven on by the swords and whips of the cavalry: each time they were ferociously repulsed, leaving the Prince's captured standard to wave only over the town's public lavatory. Once again Parliament's navy proved crucial, coming to the rescue with food, powder and a party of armed seamen at the height of the fighting, and the garrison held out until Maurice, his army reduced by half, retired westwards before an oncoming relief force. The 'little vile fishing town' had turned the last prong of the King's triple attack.

Little has so far been said of castles and fortified houses during the Civil War. On occasion they too played their part in the grand strategy of King and Parliament, but more often their importance was purely local, part of the backdrop of little wars against which the principal armies marched and fought. In the most hotly disputed areas, indeed – Yorkshire, the Midlands, the Welsh Marches and the south-west – there was scarcely a defensible place that was not at some time garrisoned by one side or the other, and often by both in succession. Apart

from a handful of coastal forts modernized under Queen Elizabeth (p. 140), most of these places were well over a century old, for no proper castles had been built in England since the fifteenth century, and fortified houses had petered out there during the first half of the sixteenth.

By far the most effective of these strongholds were the small group of Royalist-held castles which were given a completely new set of up-to-date outer defences, most notably Basing House in Hampshire, Donnington Castle in Berkshire, Raglan in Gwent, Belvoir in Nottinghamshire and Pontefract in Yorkshire. Basing, the residence of the wealthy, loyal and Catholic Marquis of Winchester, was a towered and fortified Tudor palace built within the encircling ditches and ramparts of a mighty Norman ring-motte and its two baileys. Its walls were thus protected from artillery fire, and on its roof were mounted small cannon 'wherewith they are able to play upon our Army though we discern them not'. To these already formidable defences the Marquis (under the direction of 'Humphrey Vanderblin . . . the ingenious and valiant German') added an outer circuit of low bastions, and outside these again were yet another line of bastion-shaped trenches. The Parliament soldiers who vainly besieged and blockaded it for over two years declared it 'absolutely the strongest place in England', and its garrison played merry hell with traffic between London and the south-west until October 1645, when Cromwell himself attacked it with over 6,000 men and an exceptionally powerful train of artillery. His 60-pound (27-kilogram) shot eventually battered a breach in the walls, and after a horrific four-hour storm the place was ransacked and demolished.

The extent and complexity of Basing's new defences was unusual, and most fortresses re-used in the Civil War were content with a few makeshift additions to their ancient walls. At South Wingfield Manor in Derbyshire, for instance, a large bastion can be seen at the northern end of the building, and a series of breastworks and batteries cover the approaches to the outer gatehouse. Ideally situated to command an important road, the manor was held first for Parliament and then for the King, falling to Parliament again only after a bombardment by heavy artillery. But powerful siege guns were rarely available to local forces, and were in any case notoriously difficult to transport: where possible they were moved by boat. Unless and until they could be brought into play, a strongly positioned or remote castle, even one without any 'modern' defences whatever, could prove just as formidable as

A. THE OLDE HOVSE. B. THE NEW. C. THE TOVER THAT IS HALFE BATTERED DOVNE. D. THE KINGES BREAST WORKS. E. THE PARLIAMENTS BREAST WORKS

156, 157 Basing House, Hampshire: the house during the siege of 1645, in a contemporary engraving by the famous Bohemian artist Wenceslas Hollar, who served as a soldier in the Royalist garrison; and an aerial view of all that now remains. The 'Old House' was built within the Norman

motte (centre) and the 'New House' stood beside it (bottom). One of the Civil War bastions attached to the motte appears on the left, pointing towards the viewpoint of Hollar's engraving.

it had been in the Middle Ages, and many an antiquated but thick-walled fortress enjoyed a new lease of effective life. Bolton, Skipton and Scarborough castles held on long after the rest of Yorkshire had fallen to the Parliamentarians, and Corfe played a similar role in Dorset, while little Brampton Bryan – defended by the determined Lady Brilliana Harley with her family doctor and a few servants – survived for two years as the only Parliamentarian stronghold in Royalist Herefordshire.

In areas where castles were few, or where they were too dilapidated to be tenable, garrisons were frequently established in far less obviously defensible places. Lightly fortified manor houses, some with only a moat and courtyard wall, were eagerly seized on as outposts, and Elizabethan or Jacobean mansions, defended by sketchily constructed earthworks, were also pressed into service. Nor were church buildings exempt. Lichfield Cathedral, whose close had the misfortune to be surrounded by a fortified wall, was garrisoned by Staffordshire

158 The battered and bullet-scarred door of Alton Church, Hampshire, its roughly cut loopholes long since repaired.

others attempting to enter the Church being led on by Sergeant-Major Shambrooke . . . who in the entrance received a shot in the thigh.' When the door was forced the Royalists continued the fight from behind barricades of dead horses piled across the aisles, and it was not until their colonel was shot down in the pulpit that they finally surrendered.

As the war continued, minor garrisons proliferated like a cancerous growth. When one side strengthened and manned a place, the other set up another garrison to blockade it, whereupon a third outpost might be established to blockade the blockaders, and so on: only by the destruction of any tenable strongholds could the vicious circle be broken. Such activities had little real effect on the course of the war, and indeed served to perpetuate it by diverting troops from the marching armies, the only forces capable of striking a decisive blow to the enemy. The financial problems of both sides, moreover, drove them deeper into the mire, for while marching armies had to be paid, garrisons were left to maintain themselves by levying 'contributions' (in reality little better than protection money) on the surrounding countryside. Rival outposts plundered each other's territory continually, and the whole pernicious system bid fair to reduce parts of England to the same miserable condition as the Germany of the Thirty Years' War.

The deadlock had to be broken, and in attempting to do so both sides widened the scope of the war by calling in aid from other parts of Britain. The King made peace with the Catholic Irish rebels, freeing the English soldiers who had been fighting them to join the army by the end of 1643. But their numbers were comparatively small, and their reputation for brutality – exacerbated by their massacre of the garrison of Barthomley Church in Cheshire and furiously magnified by Parliamentary propagandists – meant that their presence probably did Charles's cause more harm than good. The news of his truce with the 'idolatrous Romish butchers' in Ireland certainly had the effect of cementing a far more momentous alliance, that between Parliament and the Presbyterian Scots. Fearing that a victorious monarch might shortly turn his attention to them, and on the vague understanding that Presbyterianism would one day be established in England, the Covenanters agreed to send a well-equipped army to Parliament's assistance.

The 'blue bonnets', over 20,000 of them, came over the border one snowy day in January 1644, utterly transforming the war in the north. Though the Royalist Marquis of Newcastle did his best to

Royalists near the beginning of the war, and besieged by their opponents in March 1643. Though a sniper in the spire shot their commander dead, the Parliamentarians took the place, only to be turned out a month later by Prince Rupert who – for the first time in England – packed a mine with gunpowder to breach the defences. When the Royalists finally departed (after yet another siege) the cathedral was so badly damaged as to require substantial rebuilding.

A number of village churches, too, served as garrison posts, with breastworks against their graveyard walls and firing-steps built up to their windows. Alton Church, in Hampshire, still bears the marks – loopholes cut in a door and bullet-scars on the interior walls – of the hard fighting which took place there in December 1643, when Sir William Waller surprised the Royalist garrison and drove them back on their strongpoint. 'By this time', wrote a Parliamentary lieutenant, 'the Church-yard was full of our men laying about them stoutly, with Halberts, Swords and Musquet-stocks, while some threw hand-granadoes in the Church windowes,

158

impede their progress, by the end of April he was cooped up behind the medieval walls of York, with the Scots and the local Parliamentary army of Lord Fairfax blockading him on three sides. A month later an East Anglian contingent under the Earl of Manchester and Lieutenant-General Cromwell marched in to complete the encirclement, and the siege of the northern capital began in earnest. In terms of numbers involved, it was to be the greatest siege of the Civil War, for the combined forces of the attackers totalled something like 30,000, and the Scots alone had more than 60 cannon.

Against them York could muster scarcely 5,000 regular defenders and a score of guns, but her situation was perhaps not as desperate as it appeared. The city had long been prepared and provisioned against a siege, and her 3½-mile (5.6-kilometre) circuit of stone walls was in good repair: Clifford's Tower had been lately refurbished, and a number of detached sconces covered her most vulnerable approaches. Cannon were mounted on the city gates, on the ancient motte called the Old Baile, and on a floating barricade of boats across the river Ouse. Her citizens, too, were in good heart, buoyed up by rumours that the invincible Prince Rupert was marching to their aid.

The besiegers, meanwhile, were scarcely distinguishing themselves, and their divided command led to the ignominious failure of their most determined attempt at a storm. Major-General Crawford, one of Manchester's subordinates, tunnelled under the corner tower of St Mary's Abbey wall, which provided an outer line of defence on the northern side of the city. Filling his mine with gunpowder, he fired it at noon on Trinity Sunday (16 June), when many of the garrison were at church, and charged in over the rubble with 600 picked men. Anxious to reserve all the glory for himself, however, he had informed neither Fairfax nor the Scots of his intention. No diversionary attacks were therefore made elsewhere, and the Royalists surrounded Crawford like a swarm of disturbed hornets, driving him off with the loss of over half his force. Some of them had been trapped in the wreckage of the fallen tower, and all the next day the besiegers heard their 'very dolefull cry, some calling Help help; others Water water'. But they could not be rescued, and their lingering death added further to the discouragement of their comrades, who 'could not be brought to storme any more'; a Scots chaplain, indeed, wrote that 'Crawford's foolish rashness . . . will force us to look on these walls till hunger make them fall, whereof as yet we hear not much'.

What they did hear, after another fortnight's virtual inactivity, was the news of Rupert's rapid approach, and they raised the siege to face him. Spurred on by Charles's message that 'If York be lost, I shall esteem my crown little less', the Prince outmanoeuvred them to slip into the city with 14,000 seasoned men, and for a few brief hours it seemed that the northern capital might yet be saved for the King. But the next morning Rupert marched out to fight the ill-advised battle of Marston Moor, and that night the remnants of his shattered army were being chased almost up to the walls in the moonlight. With its garrison reduced to a mere 500, York finally capitulated two weeks later: its gallant three months' resistance had done no more than delay the collapse of the Royalist cause in the north.

Elsewhere, however, things were going badly for Parliament. A few days before Marston Moor the King had beaten Sir William Waller at Cropredy Bridge in Oxfordshire, and at the end of August he virtually destroyed Essex's army in Cornwall. The Scots, too, were beginning to look nervously over their shoulders, for the Earl of Montrose had raised the Royal standard in their homeland and, with a small guerrilla force of Irish veterans and wild Highland clansmen, was routing every Covenanting army sent against him. In the closing months of the year Charles relieved Basing House and Donnington Castle under the very noses of three large but demoralized Parliamentary armies plagued by another divided command, and by December 1644 the end of the war seemed as far off as ever. 'Our victories', complained a disconsolate Member of Parliament, 'seem to have been put in a bag with holes; what we won one time, we lost another.'

The answer, as Cromwell and others clearly saw, was the formation of a well-paid and well-disciplined 'New Model Army', controlled directly by Parliament through a single commander – Sir Thomas Fairfax, the hero of many a hard fight in the north. It took the field in the spring of 1645, and on 14 June encountered the King's main army at Naseby in Northamptonshire. The Cavaliers who had derided the raw 'New Noddle' were utterly routed, their entire force of infantry being destroyed and their cavalry badly cut up. Here, at last, was the decisive blow needed to turn the tide of war, and from now on the flood of Parliamentary victories swept all before it.

Marching into the Royalist south-west, the New Model took fortress after fortress, preferring a short bombardment and a devastating attack to more cautious methods of siegecraft. At two o'clock on the morning of 21 July they stormed the bastioned outer defences of Bridgwater in Somerset, and within an hour they had 'mounted the enemy's works, beat them from their ordnance, turned them upon their enemy and let down the drawbridge . . .' to allow the waiting cavalry to charge in and 'scour the streets'. Fired by red-hot shot, the town's inner defences capitulated the following day. Bath and Sherborne Castle in Dorset were next to fall, and a few cannon shots were sufficient to breach the walls of Nunney and make its eight-man garrison lay down their arms. Bristol, held by Prince Rupert with 2,000 men and 140 cannon and much strengthened in its defences since its last capture, was a tougher nut to crack, and some of Fairfax's officers were in favour of a formal siege. Taking advantage of the triumphant enthusiasm of his men, the General resolved instead on a well-organized storm, and just before dawn on 10 September a hill-top beacon triggered simultaneous attacks in four places. Scaling ladders, carried by men rewarded with five shillings apiece, led on the cheering columns, and by five in the morning they had taken one of the strongest forts and put its defenders to the sword. With his outer line breached, Rupert withdrew to the castle, but his situation was hopeless and at eight he asked for a truce. Though the New Model soldiers were all for a fight to the finish, Fairfax allowed the Royalists to march away to Oxford, leaving behind all their cannon and firearms.

At Berkeley Castle in Gloucestershire, taken a fortnight later, the Royalist Governor grumbled that 'God had turned Roundhead, the King's forces prospered so ill', and by the end of 1645 only a mixture of ill-founded optimism and obstinacy prevented Charles from suing for peace. In the midlands, however, the two great fortress-towns of Newark and Oxford continued to hold out behind their formidable bastioned defences. Too strong to be stormed or bombarded into submission without careful preparation, they were to be reduced by methods which made the previous sieges of the war look haphazard and amateur.

As 1646 began Newark was blockaded by a large force of Scots and Parliamentarians under Lord Leven and General Poyntz, but the garrison, nothing daunted, sallied out against their quarters almost daily, and on one occasion came within a hair's breadth of kidnapping Poyntz in his own bedroom. The veteran of many a long-drawn-out siege in Holland and Germany, the General thereupon resolved to conduct the attack in the cautious and scientific manner he had learnt there. His first step

was to raise bastioned earthworks round each of the four villages where his men were quartered (A on the plan). Next he sealed off the town from relief, and at the same time cooped up its garrison, with a 5-mile (8-kilometre) long semi-circle of trenches, broken only where impassable rivers made it unnecessary (B). Just near enough to Newark to allow the besiegers to use their cannon, this 'line of circumvallation' was thoroughly swept by the flanking musket fire of thirty mutually supporting forts and sconces placed at regular intervals along it. The Scots, meanwhile, were manœuvring closer to the western side of the town, where they threw up a massive star-shaped fort named 'Edinburgh' to defend their quarters (C).

Begun in February 1646, these works were complete at the end of March, by which time the besiegers numbered 16,000 to the garrison's 2,000 or so. Poyntz, however, continued his methodical textbook approach, diverting the rivers that powered the garrison's water-mills, raising a fortified field headquarters (D) within close battering range of the Royalist-held Queen's Sconce (E), and drawing a new line of circumvallation only a few hundred yards from the defences (F). From here he began his final preparations for a storm, sapping a deep zigzag trench (G) to shelter his men as they moved up to the assault. The ideal of Poyntz's whole scheme, however, was to reduce Newark's chances of successful resistance to the point where it would capitulate without the bloodshed of an all-out attack, and on 27 April his men's long and hard labour was crowned with success. With plague raging in the town, and no hope whatsoever of relief, the Royalists at long last agreed to treat for a surrender.

A week later, while negotiations were still going on, King Charles suddenly arrived in the Scots camp: unwilling to fall into the hands of the Parliamentary forces approaching Oxford, he had travelled disguised across the country in a vain and desperate bid to rally the Covenanters to his aid. Instead they treated him as a prisoner, and marched rapidly away with him to Newcastle. Meanwhile the New Model Army, having stamped out the last embers of Royalist resistance, arrived before Oxford on 1 May. Hardened stormers though they were, even they could see that 'this was no place to be taken at a running pull, but likely rather to prove a businesse of time, hazard and industry'. Fairfax settled down to a formal siege, even taking the unprecedented step of ordering tents for his soldiers, who had hitherto slept in the open when no billets were available. He also allowed his men overtime rates for digging

119

152
159

152

154

159

159 *Oxford under Parliamentarian siege, in May–June 1646, looking from the north towards the town's formidable bastioned trace designed by Sir Bernard de Gomme (see p. 180). The figure on the white horse may be intended for Fairfax, whose tented encampment and*

headquarters on Headington Hill can be seen to the left, protected by bastions and linked to the line of circumvallation. This remarkably accurate view was painted by Jan de Wyck for the first Earl of Dartmouth soon after the Restoration. (By courtesy of the Earl of Dartmouth)

siege-works, and within three or four days they had fortified his main quarters on Headington Hill and started on a bastioned line of circumvallation. It had scarcely been completed when, in June 1646, the King despaired of a military alliance with the Scots and ordered his last remaining fortresses – among them Oxford, Worcester, Lichfield and Wallingford – to surrender. The First Civil War was effectively over.

Even now a few remote strongholds, not receiving or not choosing to believe the King's message, 'like winter Fruit, hung long on'. Pendennis in Cornwall, the last to fly the flag of Royalist resistance in England, held out behind its formidable Elizabethan defences until supplies completely failed on 17 August, and Raglan in Gwent survived two days longer. Strengthened with an outer line of bastioned earthworks (still faintly visible) at the very beginning of the war, the great medieval palace of the Herberts easily beat off 1,500 besiegers during June and July, only surrendering when Fairfax came in

with 2,000 more men and the New Model's 'Engineere Extraordinary' sapped his way to within 50 yards (45 metres) of the walls. Too far from the mainstream of events to warrant such specialist attention, the Edwardian castles of north Wales remained defiant longest of all. Denbigh survived until October, Conwy until November, and Harlech resisted until March 1647, for the third time in its history the final refuge of a lost cause.

There were many, however, who would not admit that the King's cause was lost. Foremost among them was Charles himself, now back in England and held in polite captivity while ostensibly negotiating a peace settlement with Parliament. At the same time he was busily fomenting a new war, playing on the dissension between those of the victors who (like the Scots) favoured Presbyterianism and those 'Independents' (like Cromwell and most of the New Model) who wanted a much less rigid form of Church government. At Christmas 1647 he concluded a secret deal with the Scots, undertaking to enforce

187

Presbyterianism throughout Britain if they and their allies south of the border would restore him to power.

The Second Civil War began where the first had ended, in Wales, when the formerly Parliamentary garrison of Pembroke Castle declared for the King late in March 1648. Soon afterwards Royalist/Presbyterian revolts, backed by a mutinous section of the fleet, broke out in various parts of England, and early in July a large but ill-organized Scottish army entered Carlisle. At this juncture the resistance of two strongholds, tying down the best part of the New Model in the south, nearly tipped the scales for the King: Fairfax was fully occupied in a regular siege of Colchester, where the Royalists of Kent and Essex were holding out stoutly, while Cromwell had so far failed to reduce Pembroke. 'This place', he wrote of the great medieval castle, '[is] not to be had without fit instruments for battering'; and the ship on which his siege-guns were being brought down the Severn had first gone aground at Berkeley and then been delayed by contrary winds. The guns arrived in the nick of time, and by 11 July, while the Scots delayed in Carlisle, Cromwell had bombarded Pembroke into submission and begun his rapid northward march, picking up reinforcements as he went. He attacked the invaders at Preston in Lancashire five weeks later, and the victory he won there virtually ended the war.

The fate of King Charles – 'that man of blood', as the more extreme elements in the army were calling him – was now sealed: rightly charged with levying war against his people, he was tried and executed in January 1649. His death left all Britain in a state of shock, but while England was hurriedly declared a 'Commonwealth and Free State', the outraged Scots – after all, he had been their King too – at once proclaimed his eighteen-year old son as Charles II. In such a situation more fighting was inevitable, and in the summer of 1650 Cromwell led his veteran army northwards across the border. Though heavily outnumbered, they routed the Scots forces in a dawn attack at Dunbar on 3 September and pursued them to Stirling, the ancient and well-nigh impregnable 'Key of Scotland'. Behind its formidable defences the Scots, encouraged by the presence of young Charles, regrouped and recruited for ten months, until at last Cromwell outflanked them to threaten their position from the rear. The road south was thus left open, and Charles took it at once, confident that his father's old friends in England would flock to his banner as he marched triumphantly on London. He could not have been more wrong, for Englishmen were sick of

war and sicker still of Scots armies, and they either ignored him or went off to swell the ranks of Cromwell's closely pursuing forces. These caught up with him at Worcester, where the very last real battle of the Civil Wars was fought on 3 September 1651, the anniversary of Dunbar: by the end of the day Charles's army had been destroyed, and he himself was in flight – via the famous oak-tree – to exile in Europe.

Only a few fortresses in Scotland now held out for the Stuarts. The last of them, the sea-girt castle of Dunnottar, was blasted into surrender by mortar shells in May 1652, after the Scottish crown jewels left there for safekeeping had been lowered down the cliff and smuggled away to concealment in a nearby church. There they would remain for eight years, while General George Monck exercised a firm but beneficent rule over Scotland, bringing peace even to the wild Highlands with two dozen vigilant garrisons strung out in forts from Leith to Stornoway. His five largest bases were stone-built and bastioned in the latest style, and two of them, at Ayr and Inverness, still survive in part.

While these new fortresses were being built, hundreds of older ones were being deliberately destroyed. As the endless round of costly sieges and the little wasting wars between garrison and garrison had shown, Britain possessed far too many defensible places for her own good at such an unstable period, and from 1645 onwards Parliament frequently ordered that unnecessary strongholds should be 'slighted' by the demolition of crucial parts of their fortifications. Where medieval masonry proved too obdurate for picks and hammers, it was – like the great tower at Raglan – undermined, or even blown up with gunpowder. Local people joined in the destruction with a good will, at once gaining free building materials and insuring themselves against the re-establishment of demanding garrisons on their doorsteps. Sentimental modern writers have condemned such proceedings as 'malicious Puritan vandalism', but to contemporaries they seemed the most elementary common sense.

By 1660, when General Monck cut through the tangled skein of English politics after Cromwell's death and restored Charles II, men were anxious to return to normality and forget the 'unnaturall warres' as quickly as possible. Even the new Scottish bases were now swept away, and most of the improvised earthworks of the struggle would soon disappear, leaving little besides ruined castles to commemorate the last great trial of Britain's defensible places.

160 *The deadliest of all enemies of fortification, a rifled muzzle-loading gun firing a 64-pound (29-kilogram) shell, mounted on a swivelling carriage within a Haxo casemate at Fort Brockhurst (pp. 198–99). Named after their inventor, such gun emplacements were built in masonry and covered with a thick layer of earth; their open backs allowed the smoke of a discharge to clear quickly.*

14 'They cannot come by sea': the fortresses of Britain from 1660 to the Nuclear Age

I do not say they cannot come, I only say they cannot come by sea.

ADMIRAL LORD KEITH, speaking in Parliament at the time of the Napoleonic invasion threat, 1803

Though defensible places were never again to play so vital a part in British history as they did during the Civil Wars, the building of them by no means ceased with the Restoration. The day of the private fortified residence was over, and the new fortresses were all purely military works, erected by successive governments in response to a series of threats to the nation as a whole. With a sixty-year interlude for the Jacobite troubles, the majority of them were therefore coastal defences, closely linked with the Royal Navy and counterpointing in their development its fluctuations of strength or weakness. The perfect balance of ships to sweep the seas of invaders and forts to protect naval bases was rarely achieved, but on the whole the partnership worked, and only when shore defences had to bear the burden alone did disaster ensue.

In 1667 Britain had been at war with her Dutch trade rivals for two years, and her navy had more than held its own, crowning the 1666 campaigning season by burning some 150 enemy merchantmen in the harbour of Terschelling. Then funds, always in short supply, failed altogether, and Charles II had no choice but to lay up his fleet at Chatham, relying on coastal fortifications for defence while he arranged a peace. Sir Bernard de Gomme, the designer of the Civil War defences of Oxford, had already begun work on a bastioned 'citadel' at Plymouth and on the modernization of the Portsmouth defences, and as far afield as the Shetlands Fort Charlotte was raised to guard the Sound of Bressay. The fleet itself, meantime, seemed safe enough behind a great iron chain stretched across the Medway, while further downriver a line of artillery forts and blockhouses extended as far as Sheerness on the Isle of Sheppey.

No one expected the Dutch to attack while peace negotiations were in progress; but the enemy were intent on avenging the Terschelling raid, and early in June 1667 a force of 51 men-of-war and 14 fireships was sighted off the Thames Estuary. The defence system of the Medway now proceeded to collapse like a pack of cards. First the fort at Sheerness was abandoned by its scratch garrison and burnt by a Dutch landing party, over half its badly-mounted guns having buried themselves in the ground at their first discharge. The blockhouses further upriver did not manage even a single shot, for 'some wanted guns, some platforms . . . and carriages, others bullets, others had bullets too big for their guns'. The much-vaunted chain, finally,

was snapped by a fireship sailed at it full tilt, while more fireships set its guard vessels ablaze and concentrated gunfire knocked out the neighbouring shore batteries.

The British fleet, stripped of crews and cannon, now lay at the enemy's mercy. That same day the Dutch took the abandoned flagship, the 'Royal Charles', with a mere nine men in a longboat, and when the tide turned the next afternoon they continued upriver to burn three more great ships which had been sunk in shallow water to prevent their capture. Only at this stage did they meet with any real opposition from the shore defences, namely from the guns of the Elizabethan Upnor Castle and a battery of heavy cannon, rushed down from the Tower, on the opposite bank. Even so the enemy lost not a single ship, and no more than fifty men, before returning homeward with the captured 'Royal Charles', on whose decks a trumpeter was heard playing a mocking song called 'Joan's placket is torn'.

The feelings of national shame and outrage which followed the Chatham disaster were, if possible, heightened by the realization that the enemy could almost as easily have sailed up the Thames and bombarded London. In 1670, therefore, de Gomme was commissioned to guard the river approach to the capital with an impregnable fort at Tilbury, which remains, largely unaltered, as the best surviving example of seventeenth-century fortification in Britain. Its main offensive strength obviously lay towards the river, which was swept by more than fifty heavy guns arranged in protected emplacements along the shore (A). An attacker from the landward side, meanwhile, was faced with up to six successive lines of defence, each covered by the guns of the next. First he must take the redoubt (B) which blocked the outermost entrance to the system, and negotiate a narrow causeway (C) over the outer moat (D), all the while under fire from the defenders on the bastioned 'covered way' (E). Having got thus far, he found himself pounded by the guns of the ravelin (F) – an island in the inner moat which shielded the entrance to the fort from direct bombardment – and by those of the main fort itself. In these uncomfortable circumstances he then had to cross the inner moat (G) via a timber bridge (H) to the ravelin and another much longer span (J), broken by two drawbridges, from the ravelin to the fort. Finally, if he survived, he had to storm the ramparts under an enfilading hail of grapeshot and canister (tins packed

161, 162 Sir Bernard de Gomme's artillery fort guarding the Thames at Tilbury, begun in 1670. Top: from the air, with the river at the left; for the key see the text. Notice the eighteenth-century magazines and officers' barracks (bottom) within the ramparts, and the circular platforms for Victorian rifled guns (p. 197) on the bastion in the foreground. Above: the bastioned entrance front, looking across the inner moat (G, in the air view) from the covered way (E).

with musket balls which exploded with the effect of a huge shotgun) fired at point-blank range by the massed guns in the bastions (K).

When William of Orange's Dutch army landed at Torbay in Devon in 1688, however, not an English gun was fired against them, for they came as the invited saviours of the nation from the militant Catholicism and absolutist rule of James II. But the 'Glorious Revolution' did not pass off so quietly in Scotland, and in 1689 John Graham of Claverhouse – known as 'Bonnie Dundee' or 'Bloody Claver's' according to one's political standpoint – raised the Highland clans for James and cut a Williamite army to pieces in the pass of Killiecrankie.

Only the little cathedral town of Dunkeld now stood between the clans and the Perthshire lowlands, but the single regiment of Williamites which garrisoned it were Cameronians, fanatical Presbyterians whose memories of recent persecution by the Stuarts stiffened their resolve to defend the new order to the death. Holding the cathedral and a nearby walled mansion as strongpoints, they beat off attack after attack, the musketeers cutting bullet-lead from roofs and the pikemen using their long weapons to thrust burning faggots through the windows of houses taken by the enemy. Unused to street fighting, the Highlanders suffered crippling casualties, and after three hours the Cameronians sallied forth to drive them from the blazing town at point of pike.

Though Dunkeld broke the back of the 1689 revolt, the remote and conservative Highlands remained loyal to James's exiled descendants for another sixty years, providing an indispensable reservoir of support for Jacobite risings in 1715, 1719 and 1745. Each was planned as part of a grander scheme, involving powerful foreign aid and a coordinated outbreak in England, and each failed when neither of these factors materialized. Ill-luck, ill weather and the vigilance of the Royal Navy foiled French and Spanish attempts to use Scotland as a second front in their European wars with Britain, while the majority of British people demonstrably preferred the Protestant and constitutional Hanoverians to the Catholic and absolutist Stuarts. But neither Stuarts nor Highlanders were easily discouraged, and their joint efforts provide the background to the last chapter in the active life of British fortifications.

When the Jacobite banner was first raised at Braemar in September 1715, the dangerous weakness of the government forces in Scotland was counterbalanced by their possession of the two great castles of Edinburgh and Stirling. The strategic importance of Edinburgh was enhanced by its arsenal and treasury, and at the very beginning of the revolt the Jacobites – in a ludicrous parody of Thomas Randolph's fourteenth-century exploit (pp. 117–18) – attempted to take it by surprise. A hundred conspirators were to gather beneath the walls by night, whereupon three bribed members of the garrison would pull up their scaling ladders and admit them to the castle. Both secrecy and exact timing were clearly vital, but a number of plotters spent the evening boasting of their exploits while 'powdering their hair' in a tavern, and when they arrived on the scene the appointed hour had already

passed. Half the scaling ladders were then found to be missing, and the remainder proved far too short to reach the battlements. Soon afterwards the appearance of a garrison patrol put the crestfallen Jacobites to ignominious flight.

Stirling proved more crucial to the outcome of the 'Fifteen'. Commanding the bridges over the Forth, the castle deterred the main force of Jacobite Highlanders gathered at Perth from marching southward until the government army was strong enough to meet them in the field at Sheriffmuir. The battle was inconclusive:

> There's some say that we wan
> Some say that they wan
> And some say that nane wan at a', man . . .

But the Jacobites retired once more to Perth, and on the same day the rebel forces of Northumberland and the Borders were forced to surrender at Preston in Lancashire. These two events combined to take the heart out of the rising, and by February 1716 it had collapsed altogether.

Yet the clans had yet to be decisively defeated in battle, and the government realized (like General Monck and others before him) that the only way to ensure the peace of Scotland was to exercise some measure of control over the Highlands. After Dundee's revolt Monck's old base at Inverlochy had been repaired and renamed Fort William, and in the years immediately following the 'Fifteen' four new fortified barrack blocks were built among the hills and glens, the best preserved being at Ruthven near Kingussie. Like its companions, its walls are loopholed for muskets and swept by the fire of two turrets at diagonally opposite corners, in the manner of a Z-plan tower-house. These few forts were totally inadequate for the task that faced them, and in 1719 there was a further Jacobite rising in the Highlands, supported by a few hundred Spanish troops who set up their headquarters at Eilean Donan Castle on the west coast. Though their stronghold was reduced to rubble by the guns of three British warships, and the clansmen who turned out to aid them were scattered after a single skirmish, the incident served to emphasize the fact that Highland disaffection could well open the door to a full-scale foreign invasion.

A far more comprehensive programme of 'pacification' was clearly necessary, and in 1724 General George Wade was sent north to undertake it. The roots of his problem lay centuries back in time, for neither the Romans nor later road-builders had ever penetrated the Highlands, and the trackless mountains remained largely inaccessible to the cavalry

163 *The gaunt remains of the fortified barracks at Ruthven in Badenoch, abandoned since its destruction by Jacobite Highlanders in 1746, stands on what was probably a Norman motte: notice the loopholed wall, and the remnant of a corner tower to the right.*

and artillery of government armies. During the next fifteen years, therefore, Wade's soldiers worked for an extra sixpence a day on their wages to construct 259 miles (some 420 kilometres) of road and 40 bridges, linking fort with fort and opening up the whole system to reinforcement from the Lowlands. The most important of these great 'military roads' runs down the Great Glen, the vital strategic routeway cutting across the mountains from sea to sea. Beginning at Inverness in the north-east (where Wade modernized the castle and renamed it Fort George) it passed along the south shore of Loch Ness to a new bastioned outpost called Fort Augustus, ending at Fort William on the south-west coast.

Admirable though Wade's achievements were, they failed to prevent the last and most dangerous of the Jacobite risings. The landing of Prince Charles Edward Stuart in July 1745 found most of the guardian forts undermanned or even empty, and the Prince used the new roads for his triumphant advance on Edinburgh. Though unable to take the castle there, he destroyed the only government army in Scotland at nearby Prestonpans and – against the advice of his supporters – determined to march on London.

Early in November 1745 his army arrived at Carlisle, where the ancient and dilapidated castle was held by an equally ramshackle garrison of 'Royal Invalids' (men too aged or infirm for field service) and a number of raw Cumbrian militia. These stalwarts needed little persuasion that their case was hopeless, and after the place capitulated the Jacobites continued their southward advance as far as Derby. Just over a month later, retiring before three government armies, they again passed through Carlisle on their way back to Scotland, and as they did so Charles inexplicably re-garrisoned the castle, though 'it was not in a condition to resist a cannonade of four hours, being utterly untenable'. In fact it stood just two days' battering before surrendering to the Duke of Cumberland on 30 December, the last English fortress ever to suffer a siege.

Stirling Castle, invested by the Jacobites a week afterwards, put up a much more successful resistance. The garrison, admittedly, were more amused than threatened by the efforts of Monsieur Mirabelle, the French officer in charge of siege operations, who showed himself 'totally destitute of judgment, discernment and common sense' by digging his approach trenches in a place where scarcely a foot of soil covered the solid rock. Ignoring the opportunity for a new advance presented by the rout of a government relieving force at Falkirk, the Prince allowed Mirabelle to continue operations, and the defenders complacently allowed him to spend a fortnight building a misplaced battery for the castle guns to demolish in half an hour. By now several hundred Jacobites had been 'sacrificed to his folly', and with morale plummeting and Cumberland approaching Charles had no choice but to abandon the siege and seek safety in the Highlands.

Back in their element, detachments of clansmen now set about the hated Highland forts. Ruthven was first to fall, followed by Fort George at Inverness, whose drunken Governor would scarcely allow his men to fire before he surrendered. Next

193

was Fort Augustus, where a lucky shot blew up the powder magazine, and with an accumulation of captured artillery the Macdonalds and Camerons descended on Fort William. Here they met with determined resistance from Captain Caroline Scott's men, who sent back fragments of their shells as grapeshot, sallied out to spike their guns, and carried off their cattle under their very noses. After a fortnight of such treatment the Highlanders marched away, abandoning the last siege ever conducted in Britain to rejoin the Prince's army for the final contest with Cumberland on Culloden Moor.

The horrors of that battle, and of the brutal 'pacification' that followed, are fortunately no concern of ours. Determined to break the fighting power of the clans for ever, the government determined to extirpate the whole Highland way of

life, backing up their new race-laws with more roads and forts. Easily the most impressive of these last is Fort George at Ardersier in Inverness-shire, begun in **20** 1748 as a stronger replacement for its namesake 164 destroyed during the rising: a more advanced descendant of bastioned works like Berwick and 143 Tilbury, it survives unchanged as one of the most 161 complete artillery fortifications in Europe. The ultimate in promontory forts, it protrudes like a great stone ship into the Moray Firth, with its strongest defences – ditch, ravelin and two great bastions – covering the only landward approach. Eighty cannon once lined its walls, including a twenty-gun battery commanding a narrow neck of the Firth. Within are two alternative sets of accommodation for a small army of 1,600 red-coated infantry: elegant Georgian barracks for peacetime 165

164 *Plan of Fort George (see pl.* **20***). The glacis (1) is a long smooth slope up to the outer edge of the works, allowing an attacker no cover from the defenders' fire; places of arms (3, 14) are sheltered assembly points for defending troops preparing a sally or counter-attack; lunettes (4) are minor works strengthening the ravelin (6); traverses (5) break up the line of the parapet and prevent it from being swept by flanking fire should part of the covered way (2) be taken; and batardeaux (8) block the ditch at*

strategic points. Other defensive features are the ravelin itself (6) linked to the gate (9) by a bridge over the ditch (7); bastions (10, 11, 15, 16) and demibastions (17, 18); casemated curtains (12) pierced by sallyports (13); and the point battery (19). Inside are the parade ground (20), artillery block with the governor's house (21, 22), staff block (23, 24), barracks (25), magazine (26), workshops (27), ordnance stores (28), provisioning building (29) and chapel (30).

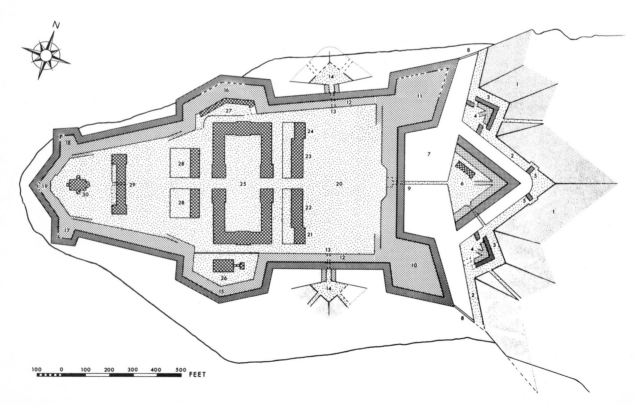

100 0 100 200 300 400 500 FEET

165 *Looking across the parade ground of Fort George at the artillery block and staff quarters (22 and 23 on the plan).*

use, and shell-proof rooms within the 70-foot (21-metre) thickness of the ramparts for employment during a siege. The fort took twenty-one years to build and cost over £175,000.

While Fort George was being erected, a new military road was constructed to connect it with Blairgowrie on the northern fringe of the Lowlands. Two old tower-houses along its route, Braemar and Corgarff, were adapted as fortified barracks by the addition of a star-shaped loopholed wall, and they continued to be garrisoned until the end of the eighteenth century. By this time, however, the fear

16

of Highland risings had long since evaporated, and the chief threat to Britain emanated not from the supporters of an exiled king but from the avowed enemy of all monarchs – Revolutionary France.

On 22 February 1797 some 1,400 convicts and galley slaves, dressed in cast-off uniforms and led by an American adventurer, landed on a lonely stretch of Pembrokeshire coastline at Carregwasted Point. Under the entirely false impression that the peasantry of Wales were eager to embrace the cause of Liberty, Equality and Fraternity, the French Directory had despatched these unlikely ambassadors of Revolution to raise the Welsh *sans-culottes* and lead them to the sack of Liverpool and Chester. The half-starved invaders, however, discovered an abandoned wedding feast in the first farmhouse they came to, and the advance guard promptly drank themselves into a state of happy oblivion. All remaining discipline now went by the board, and the bands of tipsy plunderers became an easy prey for the enraged locals they had come to 'liberate': Big Jemima, a gargantuan female cobbler from Fishguard, is said to have rounded up a dozen of them with a pitchfork. Before forty-eight hours had passed they were only too pleased to surrender to a scratch force of militia, and the British administration, half suspecting that the operation had been mounted to dispose of a collection of unwanted nuisances, took its revenge by politely sending them back to France with the next exchange of prisoners.

This comic opera episode was, in fact, the last time that enemy troops were to set foot on the soil of Britain, and from now on her defences would be built to counter threats which never actually materialized. But the threats were real enough, and few appeared more dangerous than that presented by Napoleon Bonaparte, the formidable successor of the Directory. By the end of 1803 his 90,000-strong invasion force was poised in all the major ports between Holland and Le Havre, with some 2,300 transports – mostly flat-bottomed rowing barges – ready to carry them across to the Isle of Thanet in the course of a single calm and moonless night. Supremely confident that his plan would succeed (he even had a medal struck in advance to commemorate the fall of London), Napoleon could not or would not recognize that invasion was impossible while the Royal Navy maintained its absolute control of the Narrow Seas. 'I do not say they cannot come', declared a British admiral, 'I only say they cannot come by sea.' Constantly patrolling British warships bombarded the landing craft if they so much as ventured trials, and when in October 1805 the

166 *Cross-section of a Martello Tower, showing the gun on its rotating platform; the solid 'bomb-proof' roof; the living quarters; the ladder to the entrance; the storerooms; and the thicker wall to seaward (right).*

French and Spanish battle fleets finally emerged to clear a passage by force, they were utterly defeated at Trafalgar. Their sacrifice was in vain, for Napoleon's 'Army of England' was already marching eastward to fight Britain's Russian and Austrian allies; and the great invasion crisis was effectively over.

In the time-honoured tradition of locking stable doors after bolted horses, it was not until now that work actually began on new coastal defences, though they had been planned when the crisis was at its height. The inspiration for their design came from the Torre di Mortella in Corsica, which had impressed British opinion by its resistance to naval bombardments in 1793 and 1794, setting fire to one frigate and damaging another before its eventual capture by a landing party: 103 'Martello Towers' were therefore built in England, the first 74, guarding vulnerable points along the 50-mile (80-kilometre) stretch of cliffless coast between Eastbourne in Sussex and Folkestone in Kent, with a western outlier at Seaford, being completed by 1808. Then, with Napoleon threatening to revive his invasion schemes, the system was extended to the East Anglian salt-marshes, and by 1812 29 more towers had been raised between Clacton in Essex and Aldeburgh in Suffolk. Of the total number 43 survive, and the example at Dymchurch, Kent, has been restored to its original form.

Echoing in their appearance the sand-pies made by children with upturned buckets, Martello Towers were essentially small keeps adapted to the age of artillery. Each of them mounted a 24-pounder cannon on its roof, capable of traversing

166

167 *Spitbank, one of four seabed forts between Portsmouth and the Isle of Wight guarding the Spithead naval anchorage. Begun in the 1860s, the concrete fort is partially armoured with iron plates on the (distant) seaward side.*

through a full circle on a rotating platform and equipped to fire the red-hot shot so dreaded by wooden-hulled ships. To minimize the effect of counter bombardment, the towers were built oval rather than perfectly round, with their narrowest face towards the sea and their interior accommodation so arranged that its strongest wall – 13 feet (4 metres) thick and more – fronted in the same direction, while 10 feet (3 metres) of solid roof protected the occupants from the plunging fire of mortars. For defence against landing parties the entrance was at the level of the upper floor, reached either by a ladder or, where the tower had a surrounding ditch, by a drawbridge. Within were living quarters for the garrison (up to 24 men) and their officers, with storerooms for enough ammunition and provisions to allow the tower to stand a siege of some duration.

Differing only in scale and detail from Henry VIII's artillery forts, Martello Towers were the last of a long line of British shore defences raised during the era of wooden sailing ships and smooth-bored cannon. Within fifty years of Napoleon's final defeat at Waterloo, however, all such fortifications, along with the bastioned trace and its derivatives, had been rendered hopelessly out of date by radical changes in both land and sea warfare. Just how much things were changing became clear during Britain's first post-Napoleonic encounter with a major European power, the Crimean War of 1854–56. Her hitherto invincible fleet (now fitted with auxiliary steam engines) was bloodily repulsed by the Russian coastal forts at Sebastopol, modern

structures mounting up to a hundred guns enclosed in long rows of massively protective masonry embrasures or 'casemates'. Her French allies, on the other hand, astonished everyone by producing three floating batteries armoured with iron plates 4 inches (10 centimetres) thick which emerged unscathed after demolishing the enemy forts at the Black Sea port of Kinburn. The age of the 'ironclad' had begun, and France was first in the field, launching her first sea-going armoured battleships in 1858 and thus achieving an instant – if temporary – naval superiority in the Channel. After the war, with Anglo–French relations at a low ebb, something like a panic resulted in Britain, and in the following year a Royal Commission was set up 'to Consider the Defences of the United Kingdom'.

Worried though they were by ironclads, these gentlemen were only too aware of a far more dangerous threat to Britain's security. For over three centuries the development of artillery had remained virtually static, but now the advanced nations were experimenting with a revolutionary new weapon, the rifled gun. Firing pointed shells spin-stabilized by a spirally grooved barrel, these could achieve vastly greater range, accuracy and hitting power than any smooth-bored cannon, and they have been rightly called 'the deadliest of all enemies of fortification'. Used in combination with armoured ships, such guns would render the existing defences of Britain useless overnight.

Realizing that the re-fortification of the entire coastline was scarcely feasible, the Commissioners concentrated on protecting the Navy's principal

197

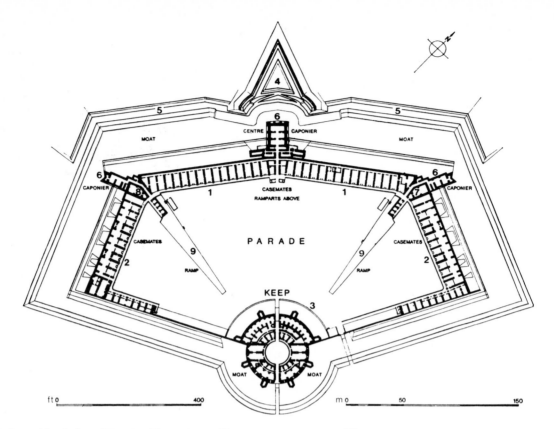

168 Ground-level plan of Fort Brockhurst, Hampshire, 1858–62. It is a polygon of casemates at this level, serving for barracks and, in the flanks (2), for 18 guns. A further 35 guns were mounted at rampart level, some in Haxo casemates (ills. 160, 169). Note the ravelin (4) and covered way (5) guarding the main approach; caponiers (6) defending the dry moat; ramps (9) for hauling guns to the ramparts; magazines (7, 8); and the gun-mounting keep (3).

Channel bases against bombardment with the new artillery. The results of their recommendations were 76 new forts around Chatham in Kent, Portsmouth in Hampshire, Plymouth in Devon and Milford Haven in Dyfed, built during the 1860s at a total cost of over £10 million. The vast majority were shore batteries, curved arms of casemated embrasures derived from the troublesome works at Sebastopol, designed to block the seaward approaches to the vital ports with zones of overwhelming fire. The best remaining examples are Hubberstone Fort at Milford Haven, Fort Bovisand near Plymouth, and Hurst Castle in Hampshire, the last flanking one of Henry VIII's coastal forts and guarding the entrance to the Solent.

Where harbour approaches were too wide to be swept by land batteries, circular towers with tiers of casemated guns were built at immense trouble and expense on the seabed itself. All these mid-channel forts survive, four of them – St Helens, No Man's Land, Horse Sand and Spitbank – rising from the Spithead anchorage outside Portsmouth, and one each outside Plymouth and the subsidiary harbour of Portland in Dorset.

In addition to keeping enemy ironclads at a distance, it was necessary to prevent a French invasion force getting close enough to the bases to bombard them from the rear. To this end Portsmouth and Plymouth were ringed with a series of mutually supporting forts, the least altered of the 19 survivors being Fort Brockhurst at Portsmouth and Crown Hill Fort at Plymouth. These works, the last major land fortifications to be built in Britain, were in their day among the most advanced anywhere in the world. They resemble nothing seen in previous centuries, for the rifled gun had finally ended the long reign of the bastioned stronghold, enabling attackers to pound its intricate defences to rubble at long range. The defenders' best reply was to direct as many guns as possible on the enemy batteries from a simple polygon of casemates. For close range defence they trusted to galleries or caponiers projecting into (and protected by) the surrounding ditch; but in fact if the attacking artillery got this close the fort was as good as lost, and caponiers, like the inner 'keeps' attached to some early polygonal fortresses, were soon abandoned as relics of old-fashioned thinking.

167

168
169

160

169 The interior of Fort Brockhurst seen across the left-hand gun-ramp on the plan, showing the open-backed Haxo casemates for heavy guns (ill. 160) on the parapet of the near rampart and the long rows of arched casemates below. Designed to mount over seventy guns, Brockhurst was never fully equipped.

The rapid developments in rifled artillery, indeed, turned the age-old contest between attack and defence into a desperate race, and the 'Commission forts', originally conceived in granite and brick, needed to be strengthened even before they were completed. Armoured shields, made of alternate layers of wrought iron and teak up to 2 feet (60 centimetres) thick, were fitted to protect the casemates of shore batteries, while most of the seabed forts, which might expect to face bombardment at closer range, were eventually constructed entirely in iron and concrete. These attempts to counter ironclad ships with ironclad forts, however, were soon checkmated by the increasing accuracy of the new guns, which threatened to turn such large and obvious targets into veritable deathtraps. The defence then retorted by minimizing the visibility of their coastal batteries, one of the most ingenious methods of doing so being the 'Moncrieff Disappearing Gun Carriage', which allowed shore guns to reveal themselves only when actually firing, whereafter their own recoil would swing them down into a concealed loading pit. Costly devices like these

were in some measure an admission of defeat by the fortifiers, and after the 1890s coastal guns were usually in cheap and unobtrusive open embrasures.

By now the emphasis of national defence had in any case shifted to the building of 'the greatest navy the world has ever seen'. Behind such a shield Britain was never in real danger of invasion during the 1914–18 War – fortunately so, since the bulk of her coastal defences still faced south towards France rather than north and east towards Germany. The hit-and-run enemy cruisers which shelled Hartlepool in Cleveland and Scarborough in North Yorkshire in December 1914 underlined this deficiency, and thereafter whole stretches of the east coast, especially those near London, were entrenched against landing parties.

Ships and forts, however, could do nothing to stop the raids of Zeppelins and Gotha bombers. Though casualties were relatively light, these terrifying manifestations of a wholly new type of warfare made a deep impression on the British public. From now on bomber attack was, with much justification, regarded as the main threat to national security, and

199

170, 171 *A coastal pillbox disguised as a permanently closed beach kiosk, and another brilliantly camouflaged as a pile of logs, guarding a railway line.*

between the wars the government concentrated on the establishment of air defences and the maintenance of naval superiority, while fortifications, coastal or otherwise, were virtually ignored.

The Fall of France in May 1940 therefore found the land defences of Britain completely unprepared to repel the German army which had so suddenly appeared on the Channel coast. Invasion seemed imminent, and while the service chiefs believed it would be delayed until Hitler had gained air superiority, they urged that the whole nation should at once be 'organized as a fortress'. Churchill backed them with his famous promise to fight on the beaches and in the fields, and Britain embarked on perhaps the most makeshift and certainly the most rapidly executed programme of defence-building in all her history.

The first priority was obviously the coastline. Within a fortnight of Dunkirk 'emergency batteries' of long-range guns in quick-setting concrete casemates had been positioned round Dover and other major ports, and before long the system extended from Lincolnshire to Cornwall. Likely landing-beaches sprouted obstacles made from builders' scaffolding, barbed wire and concrete-block 'tank traps', while the Petroleum Warfare Department experimented with setting the sea on fire and prepared primitive but effective devices for spraying roads leading inland with sheets of flame. Martello Towers, Henrician forts, medieval castles and even prehistoric earthworks found themselves back in harness as artillery emplacements or machine-gun posts, and the strategically-placed relics of nineteen centuries of threatened invasions were now joined by the last-built and most numerous of all British fortifications, tens of thousands of concrete 'pillboxes'. These infantry strongpoints, though hurriedly built and sometimes badly sited, were frequently camouflaged in a manner little short of brilliance. Common disguises included beach kiosks, summer-houses, haystacks and piles of logs, while one at least masqueraded as part of a fairground roundabout and others as ruined sections of Pevensey Castle. Some clearly visible pillboxes, conversely, were actually mock-ups of wood and canvas, and many 'heavy guns' turned out on close inspection to be painted telegraph poles.

Such expedients could not hide the probability that the coastal defences would no more than delay the Germans, whose first wave alone – aimed, as we now know, at the area between Brighton and Folkestone – was planned to consist of 250,000 infantry, 650 tanks, 35,000 vehicles and over 500

172 *Three periods of defence at Pevensey, Sussex: disguised machine-gun posts of 1940 among the ruins of the Roman Saxon Shore fort (p. 38) and (rising in the background) the Norman keep.*

field guns. To prevent a *Blitzkrieg* breakthrough from 'tearing the guts out of the country', 'stop-lines' of pillboxes and anti-tank obstacles were established further inland, culminating in a 'General Headquarters Line' protecting London and the industrial midlands. Taking advantage of rivers and other natural defences where possible, this line ran east and south from Middlesbrough on the Tees through Yorkshire and Lincolnshire to the Wash, and thence through Cambridge to the Thames, continuing south of the capital via Maidstone and Basingstoke to Bristol.

The desperate and dangerous reliance on 'fixed defences', necessitated by the virtual immobilization of the British army after its losses at Dunkirk, was soon superseded by the determination to engage the invaders before they gained a foothold, and in August 1940 reserves were brought forward to cover the most vulnerable beachheads. But by now the fate of the nation was being decided in the skies, as the Luftwaffe strove to destroy the RAF and gain the air superiority Hitler needed to cross the Channel. They

failed – just – and with the postponement of 'Operation Sealion' in October 1940 the invasion threat to Britain faded, to recede still further with the German attack on Russia and disappear altogether with the D-Day landings of June 1944.

As the allied armies fought their way into Europe, however, the first V2 guided rockets fell on London, and in 1945 the atomic bomb devastated Hiroshima. The offspring of these two horrors, the intercontinental nuclear missile, changed the nature of the defence problem beyond all recognition, subordinating the age-old threat of invasion to the danger of total annihilation launched by an enemy half the world away. In this situation fortresses seemed scarcely relevant, and on the last day of 1956 the coastal defences of Britain officially ceased to exist. Whether future threats will be purely nuclear ones now appears questionable, but towers and walls have today been replaced by early warning 173 stations and fallout shelters and – for the time being at least – the long story of British defensible places seems to have come to an END.

173 *Waiting for doomsday, the great white globes of Fylingdales early warning station stand on the Yorkshire moors near Whitby, less than ten miles from a Roman signal station which once kept watch for Picts and Saxons.*

Bibliography

1 From the earliest times until 55 BC

J. Forde-Johnston, *Pre-historic Britain and Ireland* (London 1976), and *Hillforts of the Iron Age in England and Wales* (Liverpool 1976)—D. W. Harding, *The Iron Age in Lowland Britain* (London 1974)—A. H. A. Hogg, *Hill Forts of Britain* (London 1975)—Sir I. Richmond, *Hod Hill* (London 1968)—A. L. F. Rivett, *The Iron Age in Northern Britain* (Edinburgh 1966)—S. C. Stanford, *Croft Ambrey* (privately printed 1974).

2, 3 The Romans in Britain

E. Birley, *Research on Hadrian's Wall* (Kendal 1961)—R. Birley, *Vindolanda* (Newcastle-upon-Tyne 1973)—P. Hunter Blair, *Roman Britain and Early England, 55 B.C.–871 A.D.* (London 1975)—J. C. Bruce, ed. Sir I. Richmond, *Handbook to The Roman Wall* (Newcastle-upon-Tyne, latest ed. 1966)—Julius Caesar, *The Conquest of Gaul*, trans. A. Handsford (Harmondsworth 1951)—R. G. Collingwood and R. P. Wright, *Roman Inscriptions in Britain*, vol. I (Oxford 1965)—P. Connolly, *The Roman Army* (London 1975)—B. Dobson and D. Breeze, *The Army of Hadrian's Wall* (Newcastle-upon-Tyne 1972)—S. S. Frere, *Britannia* (London 1967)—S. Johnson, *The Roman Forts of the Saxon Shore* (London 1976)—E. W. Marsden, *Greek and Roman Artillery*, vol. I (Oxford 1969)—Suetonius, *The Twelve Caesars*, trans. R. Graves (Harmondsworth 1957)—Tacitus, *On Britain and Germany*, trans. H. Mattingly (Harmondsworth 1948)—J. Wacher, *The Towns of Roman Britain* (London 1974)—G. Webster, *The Roman Imperial Army* (London 1969)—G. Webster and D. R. Dudley, *The Rebellion of Boudicca* (London 1962), and *The Roman Conquest of Britain* (London 1965)—Sir M. Wheeler, *The Stanwick Fortifications* (Oxford 1954)—R. J. A. Wilson, *Roman Remains in Britain* (London 1975).

4, 5 From c. 410 until 1066

Aethelweard, *The Chronicle of Aethelweard*, ed. A. Campbell (London 1962)—L. Alcock, *Arthur's Britain* (Harmondsworth 1973), and *By South Cadbury is that Camelot* (London 1972)—Aneirin, *The Gododdin*, ed. K. H. Jackson (Edinburgh 1969)—G. Ashe, *The Quest for Arthur's Britain* (London 1968)—Bede, *History of the English Church and People*, trans. L. Sherley-Price (Harmondsworth 1968)—J. Brønsted, *The Vikings* (Harmondsworth 1960)—R. A. Brown et al., *The History of the King's Works*, vols. I and II, The Middle Ages (London 1963)—P. Foote and D. M. Wilson, *The Viking Achievement* (London 1970)—Sir C. Fox, *Offa's Dyke* (London 1955)—G. Garmondsway, ed., *The Anglo-Saxon Chronicle* (London 1953)—J. A. Giles, ed., *Six Old English Chronicles* (London 1947)—C. W. Hollister, *Anglo-Saxon Military Institutions* (Oxford 1962)—G. Jones, ed., *The Oxford Book of Welsh Verse in English* (Oxford 1977)—J. Morris, *The Age of Arthur* (London 1973)—F. M. Stenton, *Anglo-Saxon England* (Oxford 1971)—Snorre Sturlason, *Heimskringla—Lives of the Norse Kings*, ed. Monsen, trans. Smith (Cambridge 1932)—H. Turner, *Town Defences in England and Wales* (London 1971).

6, 7 The Normans and Angevins, 1066–1272

Gesta Stephani, trans. K. R. Potter (London 1955)—*Histoire des Ducs de Normandie et des Rois d'Angleterre*, ed. F. Michel (Paris 1940)—E. Armitage, *The Early Norman Castles of the British Isles* (London 1912)—J. Beeler, *Warfare in England 1066–1189* (Cornell, New York 1966)—R. Allen Brown, *The Normans and the Norman Conquest* (London 1969), and *English Castles* (London 1976)—Jordan Fantosme, *Chronique de la Guerre entre les Anglois et les Ecossois* (in *Chronicles of the Reigns of Stephen, Henry II and Richard I*, ed. R. Howlett, Rolls Series, 1886)—C. W. Hollister, *The Military Organisation of Norman England* (Oxford 1965)—Ordericus Vitalis, *Ecclesiastical History of England and Normandy*, trans. T. Forester (London 1853)—A. L. Poole, *From Domesday Book to Magna Carta* (Oxford 1955)—D. F. Renn, *Norman Castles in Britain* (London, 2nd ed. 1973)—Roger of Wendover, *Flores Historiarum*, ed. H. G. Hewlett (Rolls Series, 1886–89)—Walter of Coventry, *Memoriale*, ed. W. Stubbs (Rolls Series, 1872–73)—William of Newburgh, *Historia Rerum Anglicarum* (Rolls Series: see Jordan Fantosme, above).

8 The conquest of Wales

The Mabinogion, trans. G. Jones and T. Jones (London 1974)—Giraldus Cambrensis, *The Journey Through Wales and The Description of Wales*, trans. L. Thorpe (Harmondsworth 1978)—Sir J. Lloyd, *History of Wales from the earliest times to the Edwardian Conquest* (London 1911), and *Owen Glendower* (Oxford 1931)—J. E. Morris, *The Welsh Wars of Edward I* (Oxford 1901)—A. J. Roderick, ed., *Wales through the Ages*, vol. I (Llandybie, Carmarthenshire 1959)—A. J. Taylor, *The King's Works in Wales, 1277–1330* (London 1974)—Rev. J. Williams ab Ithel, ed., *Brut y Tywysogion* (Rolls Series 1860).

9 Scotland and the Borders, 1066–1400

The Chronicle of Lanercost, ed. J. Stephenson (Edinburgh 1839)—J. Barbour, *The Bruce*, ed. W. W. Skeat (Scottish Text Society 1894)—G. W. S. Barrow, *Robert Bruce* (London 1965)—J. S. Cruden, *The Scottish Castle* (London 1960)—G. Macdonald Fraser, *The Steel Bonnets* (London 1971)—Thomas Gray of Heton, *Scalachronica*, trans. Sir H. Maxwell—J. MacLehose (Glasgow 1907)—D. MacGibbon and T. Ross, *The Castellated and Domestic Architecture of Scotland* (Edinburgh 1971)—W. Mackay Mackenzie, *The Mediaeval Castle in Scotland* (London 1927)—R. Nicholson, *Edward III and the Scots* (Oxford 1965) and *Scotland: The Later Middle Ages* (Edinburgh 1974)—J. Prebble, *The Lion in the North* (London 1971)—Walter of Exeter, *The Siege of Caerlaverock*, ed. N. H. Nicholas (1828)—Walter of Guisborough, *Chronica*, ed. H. Rothwell (Camden Soc. 1957)—'Good King Robert's Testament' can be found in P. F. Tytler, *History of Scotland*, vol. I, p. 376. See also J. Scammell, 'Robert I and the North of England', in *English Historical Review*, 1958.

10 Coastal defences and artillery, 1335–1600

L. Boynton, *The Elizabethan Militia* (Newton Abbot 1971)—Jean Froissart, *Chronicles* (various eds. and trans.)—Gutierre Diaz de Gómez, *The Unconquered Knight: Chronicle of Don Pero Niño*, trans. J. Evans (London 1928)—Geoffrey le Baker, *Chronicon*, ed. E. M. Thompson (Oxford 1889)—H. J. Hewitt, *The Organisation of War under Edward III* (Manchester 1966)—Ranulph Higden, *Polychronicon*, vol. VIII, trans. J. Trevisa, ed. J. R. Lumby (Rolls Series 1882)—E. F. Jacob, *The Fifteenth Century* (Oxford 1961)—Henry Knighton, *Chronicon*, ed. J. R. Lumby (Rolls Series 1895)—John Leland, *Itineraries*, ed. L. Toulmin Smith (Arundel, Sussex 1964)—G. Mattingly, *The Defeat of the Spanish Armada* (Harmondsworth 1962)—M. McKisack, *The Fourteenth Century* (Oxford 1959)—B. St. J. O'Neil, *Castles and Cannon* (Oxford 1960)—J. J. N. Palmer, *England, France and Christendom 1377–99* (London 1972)—*The Paston Letters*, ed. N. Davies (Oxford 1976)—C. Platt, *Medieval Southampton* (London 1973)—P. E. Russell, *The English Intervention in Spain and Portugal in the time of Edward III and Richard II* (Oxford 1955)—Thomas Walsingham, *Historica Anglicana*, ed. H. T. Riley (Rolls Series 1863).

11 Castles and fortified manors in England, c. 1300–1520

The Building Accounts of Tattershall Castle 1434–72, ed. W. D. Simpson (Lincoln Record Society 1960)—John Leland, *Itineraries*, ed. L. Toulmin Smith (Arundel, Sussex 1964)—K. B. McFarlane, *The Nobility of Later Medieval England* (Oxford 1973), and 'The Investment of Sir John Fastolf's Profits of War', in *Trans. of the Royal Historical Society*, 5th series, VII (1957)—C. Ross, *Edward IV* (London 1975), and *The Wars of the Roses* (London 1976)—R. L. Storey, *The End of the House of Lancaster* (London 1966)—C. A. Tipping, *English Homes*, pts. 1–3 (London 1924 etc.)—J. A. Wight, *Brick Building in England to 1550* (London 1972)—William Worcestre, *Itineraries*, ed. J. H. Harvey (Oxford 1969).

12 Scotland and the Borders, c.1400–1638

'The Late Expedition in Scotland, 1544', in *An English Garner* (London 1903)—J. Bain, ed., *The Border Papers* (Edinburgh 1894)—J. S. Brewer, ed., *Letters and Papers . . . of the Reign of Henry VIII* (London 1867 etc.)—W. C. Dickinson et al., *A Source Book of Scottish History* (Edinburgh 1963)—G. Macdonald Fraser, *The Steel Bonnets* (London 1971)—R. Hugill, *Northumberland and Border Castles and Peles* (Newcastle-on-Tyne 1976), and *Castles and Peles of Cumberland and Westmorland* (Newcastle-on-Tyne 1977)—Robert Lyndesay of Pitscottie, *His-*

torie and Chronicles of Scotland (Edinburgh 1899)—B. Long, Castles of Northumberland (Newcastle-on-Tyne 1967)—R. L. Mackie, King James IV (Edinburgh 1958)—I. McIvor, articles on Craignethan Castle in Ancient Monuments and their Interpretation (Chichester, Sussex 1977)—William Patten, 'The Expedition into Scotland 1547–48', in An English Garner (London 1903)—H. G. Ramm, Shielings and Bastles (London 1970)—G. Ridpath, The Border History of England and Scotland (London 1776).

13 The Civil Wars

Memoirs of Sir Henry Slingsby and Captain Hodgson (Edinburgh 1806)—A. R. Bayley, The Civil War in Dorset (Taunton 1910)—C. H. Firth, Cromwell's Army (London 1967)—L. Hutchinson, Memoirs of Colonel Hutchinson (various eds.)—Edward Hyde, Earl of Clarendon, History of the Rebellion and Civil Wars (various eds.)—R. Ollard, This War Without An Enemy (London 1976)—Joshua Sprigge, Anglia Rediviva (London 1647)—John Vicars, England's Parliamentary Chronicle (London 1644–46)—J. Washbourne, Bibliotheca Gloucestrensis (Gloucester 1825)—C. V. Wedgwood, The King's War (London 1958)—L. P. Wenham, The Great and Close Siege of York (Kineton, Warw., 1970)—A. C. Wood, Nottinghamshire in the Civil War (Oxford 1937)—P. Young, The Civil War Siegeworks of Newark (London 1964)—P. Young and R. Holmes, The English Civil War (London 1974).

14 From 1660 to the Nuclear Age

J. Baynes, The Jacobite Rising of 1715 (London 1970)—B. Collier, The Defences of the United Kingdom (London 1957)—C. Duffy, Fire and Stone: The Science of Fortress Warfare 1660–1860 (Newton Abbot 1975)—I. V. Hogg, Coast Defences of England and Wales, 1856–1958 (Newton Abbot 1974)—Q. Hughes, Military Architecture (London 1974)—C. L. Kingsford, 'The Highland Forts in the Forty-Five', in English Historical Review, XXXVII—The Chevalier de Johnstone, Memoirs of the Forty-Five (London 1958)—K. Mallory, The Architecture of Aggression (London 1973)—I. McIvor, Fort George (Edinburgh 1970)—D. Ogg, England in the Reign of Charles II (Oxford 1961)—Samuel Pepys, Diaries (various eds.)—P. G. Rogers, The Dutch in the Medway (Oxford 1970)—A. D. Saunders, 'Hampshire Coastal Defences since the Introduction of Artillery', in Archaeological Journal, CXXIII—C. Sinclair-Stevenson, Inglorious Rebellion: The Jacobite Risings of 1708, 1715 and 1719 (St Albans 1971)—E. H. Stuart Jones, The Last Invasion of Britain (Cardiff 1947)—S. Sutcliffe, Martello Towers (Newton Abbot 1972).

Index